THE HOUSE OF MITSUI

THE
HOUSE OF
MITSUI

OLAND D. RUSSELL

ILLUSTRATED

GREENWOOD PRESS, PUBLISHERS
WESTPORT, CONNECTICUT

Originally published in 1939
by Little, Brown and Company, Boston

First Greenwood Reprinting 1970

Library of Congress Catalogue Card Number 70-109836

SBN 8371-4327-6

Printed in the United States of America

TO

MARGARET, JOAN AND JOHN RUSSELL

ACKNOWLEDGMENT

Acknowledgment of appreciation and gratitude is hereby expressed to Ian Mutsu, Tokyo journalist who served as interpreter and translator in assembling material for this book.

PREFACE

America has her sixty families; Japan has her five — and the greatest of these is the Mitsui.

In Europe there were the Rothschilds, the Fuggers, the Siemenses who formed financial oligarchies, and in America the Vanderbilts, Astors, Morgans and du Ponts, but with all these Western families there has been an accidental continuity, their great wealth dispersed in varying degrees by international marriages. Mitsui wealth has remained Mitsui's — and Japan's.

The main islands of Japan form a crescent inclining toward the mainland of Asia. For the most part, they are little more than one hundred miles from China, but only the culture of the Chinese ever bridged the gap in the prehistoric days of the two countries. Historians fond of comparing the similar positions of Japan and England with respect to their adjacent continents overlook the relative distances of the two countries from the mainlands. Only the Mongols have ever threatened Japan, and they were beaten off. To England came the Romans, the Angles, the Saxons, Danes and Normans, each invasion bringing new waves of thought and influence, but Japan remained homogeneous.

Isolated on their islands of great natural beauty, the people of ancient Japan contrived to feel a close relationship with the deified forces of the visible world and in the absence of written records, as well as the usual contacts from the outside world, they traced their descent from the gods that they believed created the islands. Thus the family became the basis of Japanese life, the unit of civilization, and a corporation, the most characteristic mark of which was its perpetuity.

That, in brief, was the natural historical endowment of the Mitsui Family. Except for the safeguards of a family Constitution now three hundred years old, the genealogical course of the Mitsuis has differed little from the general aspects of hundreds of other family dynasties in Japan. In the field of commerce the Mitsuis became pre-eminent only because they were at the forefront of those energetic forces standing at the breach when Japan was "opened" to the world less than a century ago.

To set forth how the Mitsuis achieved that position is the purpose of this book. It has been said, frequently, that the economic history of Japan is the history of the Mitsuis. It is true, insomuch as these facts are borne in mind: that there was only the beginning of a crude commerce in Japan when the Mitsuis entered trade and that from early in the Seventeenth Century the Mitsuis have been in the vanguard of nearly every important commercial and financial development of the Island Empire until the present day. The Mitsuis had opened their bank in Tokyo before the Bank of England was founded, and the Mitsuis had a profit-sharing scheme for their employees when industrialism was at its worst in England.

The story of the Mitsuis is not only the story of the family but the story of some of the remarkable men of Japan who have made Mitsui. In all the eleven generations of Mitsuis since the business house was founded, there have been few great Mitsuis, but some of the great men of Japan have had a hand in expanding the fortunes of the family. Mitsui history is so inextricably interwoven with the economic development of Japan that a broad canvas is necessary to depict it in full. Certain business innovations of the Mitsuis, familiar enough in form to Western conception, cannot be fully appreciated unless the contemporary Eastern disparity is shown. With that in mind, the author has drawn somewhat fully upon the commercial history of the empire.

CONTENTS

CONTENTS

ILLUSTRATIONS

THE HOUSE OF MITSUI

Chapter *I*

THE GATHERING OF THE CLAN

HE RICHEST MAN IN Japan today is Baron Takakimi Mitsui. He is head of the House of Mitsui by virtue of being head of the main family of the eleven Mitsui branches. He is the eleventh descendant in direct line of the main dynasty from Sokubei, the sake-brewer who was the first Mitsui to enter trade.

The size of Baron Mitsui's private fortune is more difficult to compute than that of any American millionaire, because of the ramifications of the Mitsui holdings.

When the Baron came into the estate of his father, Hachiroemon Mitsui, who retired in 1933, his taxable inheritance was assessed at 166,400,000 yen,* about $55,000,000. A crew of specially assigned accountants and tax experts of the Saiwaibashi Tax Office in Tokyo worked more than a year delving through the billion-yen Mitsui interests to determine the approximate amount that went to the account of the young Baron, then thirty-three.

The total tax was finally fixed at 21,500,000 yen on the assessment. This was more than twice the highest inheritance tax ever levied in Japan, partly because the rate had been in-

* The average value of the Japanese yen in terms of American dollars has been as follows during the past decade: 1929, $0.46; 1930, $0.50; 1931, $0.49; 1932, $0.28; 1933, $0.25; 1934, $0.30; 1935, $0.30; 1936, $0.28; 1937, $0.28¾; 1938, $0.27½.
For the past four years the yen has been unofficially linked with sterling at the rate of one shilling two pence per yen. Generally, until the current war started, the purchasing power in Japan of the yen was approximately equal to that of the dollar in the United States.

creased only the year before as one of the innumerable methods of replenishing the nation's war chest. By special arrangement, the Baron was permitted to pay the tax in seven annual installments of about 3,000,000 yen. This meant 8,400 yen a day — or a little less daily than the yearly salary of Japan's Premier.

For seven years Baron Mitsui's inheritance tax will just about halve his income. In 1934 the *Hinode*, a popular and generally reliable Tokyo magazine, put his income at about 6,000,000 yen a year. In 1937, Shumpei Kanda, writing in another magazine, the *Shufunotomo*, estimated the head Mitsui's private wealth at 450,000,000 yen, or about $130,000,000. Archivists of the Mitsui Library could supply no concrete figures, but called attention to Mr. Kanda's article and acknowledged that his estimates were "probably pretty accurate."

The same writer lists the personal fortunes of the ten other Family Heads as follows: Takahisa, 170,000,000 yen; Geneyemon, 200,000,000 yen; Baron Takakiyo, 230,000,000 yen; Baron Toshitaro, 150,000,000 yen; Takanaga, 140,000,-000 yen; Takamoto, 60,000,000 yen; Morinosuke, 80,000,000 yen; Takaakira, 60,000,000 yen; Benzo, 60,000,000 yen and Takateru, 35,000,000 yen. This totals to 1,635,000,000 yen, or around $450,000,000 in the hands of the eleven Mitsui Family Heads of today. Still another tax assessment may serve as a guide. In 1938 the inheritance tax of Takanaru Mitsui, who became head of his branch of the family in December, 1936, was fixed at 12,000,000 yen, to be spread over seven years; or about 5,000 yen a day.

I had the pleasure of seeing a good part of the Mitsui clan gathered at a formal tea in May, 1938. Five of the eleven heads of the family were present.

THE HON. TAKAMINE MITSUI

(EX-BARON HACHIROEMON MITSUI)

Former President of Mitsui Gomei Kaisha, Retired 1933

The assembly was at the palatial old-style Japanese mansion of Hachiroemon Mitsui, eighty-two-year-old patriarch of the House and father of Baron Takakimi. Hachiroemon relinquished his title to his son when he retired in 1933. Although still in good health and with his faculties unimpaired, he lives a life of close retirement, never appearing in public and only rarely at family gatherings. He spends most of his time in the traditional Mitsui pastime of composing Sensai pictures. (See page 13.)

Baron Takakimi lives in a fairly modest two-story stone mansion, resembling a French château, at the rear of his father's Japanese-style house. But the main house was the scene of this formal tea.

The Mitsui mansion is in Imaicho, Tokyo. Imaicho is the designation of a general area in the vicinity of a car stop on the dusty taxi- and bicycle-thronged street of Tansumachi in the center of the capital. It is within a mile of the Diet Building and Premier's residence. The grounds occupy the entire top of a ten-acre hill which overlooks a good part of Tokyo. To reach the entrance of the Mitsui family home, a car must thread its way up a winding street so narrow that two cars cannot pass without stopping. On both sides of the street are typical Japanese shops selling sake, rice, hardware, cotton goods and knickknacks.

A gravel road leading off the street, up still another gradient, enters the imposing steel gates. It is noticeable that the customary nameplate is missing from the entrance. The Mitsuis have not advertised their several residences since the 1932 disorders in Tokyo. On the right-hand side of the gate is a box for guards and policemen. Two policemen were on duty at the gate, in addition to the chunky, alert-eyed plainclothes guards, the day I went to the Mitsui home.

Passing through the gate, the gravel roadway leads to a Japanese-style vestibule with a heavy tiled roof extending over the roadway.

Strict Mitsui protocol ruled. Alighting from the car I was greeted by the English-speaking secretary of the chief managing director of the Mitsui interests. He was in formal morning coat and striped trousers, as were all others present that day. Up three steps and just inside the reception hall, where an unnoticed corps of servants took charge of silk hats, sticks and gloves, were two more acquaintances of the Mitsui business staff. I was escorted down an incredibly long corridor, carpeted in red. Carpeting over the Japanese-style floors made it unnecessary to remove our shoes. Halfway down the corridor was the dignified Dr. Oka, sixty-six-year-old chief archivist of the Mitsui family and guardian of the family secrets. Rank was rising as more Mitsui attachés put in their appearance.

The two double doors opened off the corridor into the formal dining room of the mansion, foreign-style except for the classic panel decorations of the ceiling. The great banquet hall, capable of seating five hundred persons, had been rushed to completion for the state visit to Japan of the Prince of Wales in 1924.

Around two more corners and we emerged on a sunny passageway giving out onto the famous Mitsui gardens. This passageway led directly to the Chrysanthemum Room where the clan Mitsui was gathered.

The first to come forward for an introduction was Baron Takakimi, the host. Then in proper family rank the other family heads diffidently presented themselves and gravely shook hands. Next in rank came the business heads of the House, beginning with Kaneo Nanjo, keen-eyed, elderly Chief Managing Director of Mitsui Gomei Kaisha, the family's central holding company. There were two other managing directors and several ordinary directors. After all the men had been introduced, it was the ladies' turn; and the first of these, again reverting to Mitsui protocol, was the thirty-six year-old Baroness Takakimi, continuing on down to the non-Mitsui wives. Apologizing for his "poor English," Baron Takakimi spoke with obvious delight of a trip he had taken across America in 1929, returning from England. He inquired about current conditions in America and was particularly interested in America's views of the war in China. He skillfully withheld his own ideas on the subject.

Baron Takakimi is forty-four years old. He is five feet, seven inches tall — taller than the average Japanese — and has a sturdy, almost chunky frame. His eyes are quick and restless, his nose aquiline. He radiates nervous energy. It seems difficult for him to remain standing long in one place. After a proper interval, he suggested a walk in the garden. All the other Mitsuis gave way with unobtrusive deference, and he led the procession on a long ramble across the carpetlike lawn under ancient spreading trees, past treasured stones, miniature shrines, tea-ceremony houses and rest-rooms dotting the grounds.

Pulling a miniature camera from his hip-pocket, the Baron occasionally stepped ahead a few feet and snapped quick pictures of his guests He apologized, explaining that photography was one of his few hobbies. The pictures did not turn out very well. Walking, he confessed, wasn't even a pastime. The Baron did not seem to be one who could relax by walking among greenery.

The Baron was born in Tokyo and was graduated from Kyoto Imperial University in July, 1920. He had specialized in law and politics, but immediately forsook both and became an ordinary clerk in the Bank of Japan — not the Mitsui Bank

— where he was trained in the rudiments of accounting and bookkeeping. After a few years in the Bank of Japan, he went abroad with his bride and spent most of his time in London. The Baroness was presented at the Court of St. James's. Returning to Japan in 1929 by way of America, the Baron spent some time in New York and Washington. He is very proud of the fact that he was received at the White House by President Coolidge. Back in Japan, he became secretary to his father, then head of the House of Mitsui, and led a rather uneventful life, enjoying golf, baseball and motoring in American cars, until he succeeded to his father's title and position. He is commonly credited with taking more of a personal hand in Mitsui affairs than did his father; and his business judgment is respected by the high-priced managers who direct the many Mitsui organizations. Despite his comparative youth, he rules the Family Council with a strong hand.

During the garden stroll the two youngest of the Baron's four children, a boy of six and a girl of four years, made their appearance and were gravely introduced. The young Mitsui boy is a fine-looking lad, with closely cropped hair in Japanese schoolboy style. He wore an ample white satin blouse and black velvet pants. His sister was in kimono. She proudly said, "How do you do?" in precise English, and added almost immediately in Japanese that her new geta (wooden clogs) were too big. The boy remarked that his black patent leather pumps were too tight. An unobtrusive guard hovered within a few feet of the children.

The presence of a number of guards, gardeners and other menservants was noticeable, although they habitually eased themselves out of sight behind shrubbery as the party moved their way. A tuxedo-clad butler followed the party the whole route carrying a tray with silver boxes of cigarettes, Japanese and English, Corona Corona cigars, Japanese cigars and an alcohol lighter. Most of the Mitsui servants are from families that have served the Mitsuis for generations. It is said that before the Mitsuis hire even a gardener, they spend six months in an examination of his past.

There was an easy air of informality among the Mitsuis and their business chiefs as they wandered about the garden. Once the party was under way there was no kowtowing by lower-ranking firm aides to the members of the family. The Chief of the entire Mitsui Secretariat stepped up and flicked a garden worm off the Baron's back when it fell from a tree. From the topmost lookout spot, the Baron pointed out the landmarks of Tokyo, but apparently took chief delight in finding the small red-roofed house where the writer lived. He required each of the other members of the family to step up and observe the place, and each responded with varying degrees of wonderment and interest.

Benzo Mitsui, head of one branch of the family and acknowledged to be the best of the golfing Mitsuis, arrived late in gray tweeds. He apologized for his informal dress as he made the rounds greeting his relatives and their guests. His wife, also a golfer and reputed to be one of the best in Japan, was in kimono — a handsome, strong-muscled woman who spoke perfect English.

Three of the eleven Mitsui Family Heads are graduates of Dartmouth, in America. Most of them have been in America or Europe for postgraduate business training, or travel. When the Mitsuis travel, they go without ostentation, and make a great effort not to be known as members of the wealthiest family in Japan.

In contrast to Western millionaires, none of the Mitsuis

owns a private railway car, airplane or yacht. Their only extravagances are their art objects, perhaps a few more cars than necessary, and numerous country or seaside villas.

Takahisa Mitsui is head of the "second family." His age is the same as that of Baron Takakimi. He is a graduate of the Peers' School in Tokyo, and of Dartmouth. Since his return from America he has spent most of his business career in the Mitsui Bank.

Takanaru Mitsui, third in family rank, is sometimes referred to by his kinsmen as the "scholar" of the family. He was born in 1896 and at Tohoku Imperial University he specialized in botany. His principal business interest has been the agriculture products of the extensive Mitsui land holdings. Poultry farming is a personal hobby. Takanaru incidentally pays 5,000 yen a day inheritance tax on the estate of his father, Geneyemon Mitsui.

The eight other Family Heads, listed in order of the strict family rank, are: —

BARON TAKAKIYO MITSUI — one of the older members of the family. He was born in 1881 and became a baron in 1915 in recognition of his important contributions to Japan's rising place in the world of commerce during the early World War boom. He studied at the Peers' School in Tokyo and at Birmingham University in England. He started in the trading end of Mitsui, the *Mitsui Bussan Kaisha*, in London. Returning to Japan in 1913, he saw service in several Mitsui enterprises until he became manager of *Mitsui Bussan* in 1920. Thereafter, he was successively a director of the Mitsui Bank and chief director of the Mitsui Trust Company.

BARON TAKAHARU MITSUI — the transportation specialist of the family. He was graduated from Keio University's School of Economics in 1921. Thereafter he spent four years in Germany studying the history of transportation. He has traveled widely and has written a book on railway history of Japan. For his services in introducing Japanese culture in Eastern European countries, he holds decorations from seven European states.

BARON TAKANAGA MITSUI — another Dartmouth graduate. He was born in 1892. His father, Saburosuke Mitsui, was president of the Mitsui Mining Company. The son's interest turned to mining and his business career has closely followed his father's. His wife is from the old Choshu clan which formerly furnished Japan's army with most of its officers.

TAKAMOTO MITSUI — youngest Family Head, born in 1920 and still a student of the Seikei Middle School in Tokyo. He is a descendant of what is known as the Matsuzaka branch of the Mitsuis. While all the Mitsuis stem from the founder who originally settled in Matsuzaka, one particular branch remained in closer contact with the old home town and accordingly became known as the Matsuzaka branch. Takamoto is a nephew of Takanaga, the Family Head who immediately precedes him in rank.

MORINOSUKE MITSUI — the oldest Family Head. He was born in 1875, and married into the wealthy Sumitomo family, one of Mitsui's chief banking rivals. He was educated at the Yokohama Commercial School and upon graduation joined *Mitsui Bussan* in 1897. He worked a year in London and on his return became an auditor of *Mitsukoshi*, the big department store in Tokyo then owned by the Mitsuis. He is now a managing director of the Mitsui Mining Company and chairman of the board of Shibaura Engineering Works.

TAKAAKIRA MITSUI — a comparative newcomer in the business ranks of the family. He was born in 1911. After graduating from the Peers' School, he attended Kyoto Imperial University, where he specialized in the French language.

BENZO MITSUI — the golfing enthusiast, the only son of Yonosuke Mitsui, one of the kimono-clad Mitsuis who made the long journey to America in 1872 to learn Western business methods. Benzo was born in 1886. Upon graduating from the Peers' School he went to America in 1907 and was graduated from Dartmouth four years later. Returning to Japan, he entered *Mitsui Bussan* for preliminary training in foreign trade. Afterward, he returned to America on two tours of duty, first as head of the *Bussan* branch in Portland, Oregon, and later as executive of the *Bussan* branch in New York. He arrived back in Japan in 1922; and after fourteen years of energetic work with the *Bussan*, he gave up most of his executive responsibilities to find more time for golf. Benzo's wife is a younger sister of Viscount Okabe, a member of the House of Peers and director of the Society for International Cultural Relations, Japan's greatest and most heavily endowed international propaganda organization. Despite their long and variously appraised connections with the Seiyukai, the Mitsuis, through Benzo, were married into the Minseito Party, chief political rivals of the Seiyukai. Viscountess Okabe was the eldest sister of Count Kato, for years head of the Minseito and once Premier in the most liberal ministry Japan ever had. It was Count Kato who said, in 1925, that "the old militaristic ideas of political dominance of China by Japan seem largely to have disappeared."

TAKATERU MITSUI — born in 1898, and like so many other Mitsuis a graduate of the Peers' School before going to America to matriculate at Dartmouth. He returned to Japan in 1921 and worked with *Mitsui Bussan* until 1928, when he became managing director of Taisho Marine and Fire Insurance Company, one of the big Mitsui subsidiaries.

After the garden tour the party returned to the house, where an elaborate tea, with foreign-style sandwiches and ceremonial Japanese food, was served. There were silver-and-ivory chopsticks for the latter. Each piece of silver plate and china bore the familiar Mitsui personal crest, the old Sasaki design the Mitsuis adopted when they took in the Sasaki family three hundred years ago. (A few months later some of the crested Mitsui silver was sold for the benefit of families of soldiers killed in China.)

During tea, the ladies of the party and a few guests sat at tables; the Mitsui men stood in groups near the buffet table, each with a handful of sandwiches in one hand and a Scotch-and-soda in the other.

I sat beside Baroness Takakimi, a daughter of Marquis Matsudaira, head of an old and well-known family that once ruled the fief of Fukui. The Baroness talked easily and un-affectedly of her two hobbies, painting and her children. Each child has his own governess, but the Baroness looks after their lives in minute detail. She orders their food, sews their clothes, and questions them daily about their school work. She shuns public functions. The only near-public position she ever ac-cepted was the vice-chairmanship of the committee supervis-ing the Izumibashi Hospital, one of the Mitsui family philan-thropies. When she goes out, she takes one of the half-dozen American cars belonging to the family. The car is without crest or other designation. Occasionally she presides at meet-ings of other Mitsui wives, where frequently there are private showings of movies.

In her second hobby, the painting of *Sensai* pictures, she approaches professional standards. The pseudonym on her finished products is *Sekko*, which means "Fragrant Snow." Such *Sensai* pictures (pictures in relief made of pieces of silk) have been a specialty of the art-loving Mitsuis since 1772. They are difficult and tedious to compose, but some striking results may be obtained. In the early years of the Meiji Era, Kofuku Mitsui, grandfather of Baron Takakimi, made a de-tailed study of the art and considerably improved the method of producing the pictures. Kyoto artists went to the Mitsuis for instruction and the art became so popular that a professor-ship of *Sensai* was installed in a girl's school at Kyoto, with Kofuku Mitsui giving lectures on the art. The Mitsuis claim a further distinction for their private art — that the Emperor Meiji once consented to visit a Kyoto exhibition of *Sensai* pictures.

The Mitsuis trace their lineage back to the Fujiwaras, and the Fujiwaras claim descent from the gods that created Japan.

The Fujiwaras are to Japan a genealogical *Mayflower*. When the divine ancestor of the first Emperor descended by the Floating Bridge of Heaven to a successful landing on a mountain peak in Kyushu, a host of attendant gods came with him. Among them was Amatsu-Koyane, according to Japanese mythology, and the Fujiwaras with airy confidence name him as their godly progenitor.

Until that time Heaven and Earth were not far apart, and communication over the Floating Bridge was frequent. Immediately after that particular group arrived on Earth with the first Fujiwara, — or first Mitsui, if you please, — the Bridge appears to have evaporated, or to have been drawn up by godly hands. Thereupon Heaven itself, like a vast back-drop, moved slowly upward to its present approximate position, being forever parted from the Earth. That was the last party ashore.

Amatsu-Koyane received one important assignment before he left Heaven — which dates the Fujiwara-Mitsui relationship to start of the Empire, and the Empire's Divine Rulers back to the Beginning of Time. For Amaterasu-Omikami, the Sun Goddess, when she was preparing the earthly expedition of her Heavenly Grandchild to take over Japan, called that Deity into her presence and gave him a Divine Mirror: —

"My child," she said, "when thou lookest upon this mirror, let it be as if thou wert looking on me. Let it be with thee on thy couch and in thy hall, and let it be to thee a Holy Mirror. "The Luxuriant Land of Reed Plains [a translation of the archaic name for Japan] is a land over which our descendants shall rule. Do thou, Imperial Grandson, go and rule over it. And the Imperial Succession shall continue unbroken and prosperous, co-eternal with Heaven and Earth."

Then the Sun Goddess signaled Amatsu-Koyane, who stepped forward and received the Mirror in his hands. He was commanded to bear the Mirror, and attend upon it. Two other Divine Treasures were handed to lesser gods. They were the Kusanagi Sword, and the Yasakani Curved Jewels. Therewith the party was dispatched; and that is the mythological account of the beginning of the Empire of Japan.

The Mirror, Sword and Jewels, visible sign and seal of the right to rule over Japan, have been passed from Emperor to Emperor since the first accession. They (or their replicas) have been used at the coronation of each ruler down to the present day, and modern Imperial Household Law reads specifically: "Upon the demise of the Emperor the Imperial Heir shall ascend the Throne and shall acquire the Divine Treasures of the Imperial Ancestors."

Whether you care to believe the story of the divine origin of the Fujiwaras is of little consequence. The Mitsuis are no more inclined to accept it than any modern pragmatist. But all of it is in the Kojiki ("Chronicles of Old Matters of Former Ages") and the Nihongi ("Chronicles from the Earliest Times"). These are the oldest Japanese writings extant. The Kojiki was written in 711 A.D., and the Nihongi a few years later. Both are compilations of documents written several centuries earlier and thereafter lost. W. G. Aston, who laboriously translated the *Nihongi*, subsequently asserted that there could be no reliance on Japanese histories before 400 A.D. After carefully weighing other material, he found the first absolutely authentic date in Japanese history to be 461 A.D., because that is one confirmed by outside sources. But Aston and other scholars agree a "core of the truth" is in the quasi-historical tales of the *Kojiki* and the *Nihongi*, particularly if the miraculous and supernatural element is thrown out.

The Mitsuis prefer to trace their family back to Kamatari Fujiwara* in the Seventh Century, and let it go at that. Certainly they are on solid ground there. It should have been only moderately difficult for their genealogists to follow the thread back through a labyrinth of name-changing to the statesman who was Japan's first dictator.

Kamatari started a precedent in Japan that lasted for twelve hundred years. In the name of reform, he became the first usurper of Imperial prerogatives and installed the Fujiwara family in a monopoly of high governmental office that continued for four hundred years. In turn, the Fujiwaras were supplanted by military families, who produced the Shoguns who ruled the Empire from 1600 until the Restoration of full secular power to the Emperor in 1867–1868.

Whatever may have been their origin, the Fujiwaras were of patrician class with that distinctive oval face, slanting eyes and thin nose that modern Japanese actors endeavor to emulate when they take the rôles of noblemen and heroes. The small, almost delicate hands of the Fujiwaras were never adapted for brandishing two-handed swords or bending the long bow. Instinctively they turned to the arts of statecraft

---

* An excellent picture of Kamatari appears on all ten-yen banknotes in Japan.

and administration, to dalliance in poetry, painting and the sensual pleasures of the Imperial Courts. They never gained their ends by fighting — an immense distinction in the history of Japan's usurpers, and one that left its indelible mark not only through the long line of Fujiwaras but on through the Mitsuis down to the present day.

Besides blood ties, clannishness of the Mitsuis is due in large measure to the unique family Constitution, which has existed in one form or another since 1694. As each male member of the family comes of age he is required by the Constitution to take this oath, amid elaborate Shinto rites:

In obedience to the precepts of our forefathers, and in order to strengthen the everlasting foundation of the families of our House and to expand the enterprises bequeathed by our forefathers, I solemnly vow in the presence of the August Spirits of our ancestors that, as a member of the House of Mitsui, I will observe and follow the regulations handed down in the Constitution of our House, and that I will not wantonly seek to alter them. In witness whereof, I take the oath and affix my signature thereto in the presence of the August Spirits of our ancestors.

Today the affairs of the family are in the hands of the Family Council set up under the revised Constitution of 1900. The Family Council replaced the old *Omotokata*, the central administrative body which was instituted at the time the original Constitution was drawn up on the basis of the will of Hachirobei, son of the Founder. *Omotokata* is a difficult word to translate, even into modern Japanese. The general meaning as given by classical scholars is "central order of direction." The main difference between the *Omotokata* of the early days and the present Family Council is in administrative details.

The *Omotokata*, until 1900, served the family as a directional group, originating business enterprises and taking a guiding hand in their conduct. Most of its functions passed into the hands of the *Mitsui Gomei Kaisha* when that main holding company was formally organized. Today, the Family Council, replacing the *Omotokata* in part, takes a back seat in Mitsui business, as little more than a sanctioning body for decisions of the *Mitsui Gomei Kaisha*; but it still rules directly on personal affairs of the family.

It is noteworthy that these changes correspond in general to those of the Imperial Dynasty itself. Once the Imperial Household was a directional body in the affairs of the Empire; today it is little more than a sanctioning force.

The Family Council is composed of two groups, first the Family Heads, the active heads of the eleven constituent families, and next the Associate Members, or retired heads of the same families and such of their direct heirs as have attained their majority but are not yet heads of family branches. Provision also is made that "In case there be at any time among the regular members anyone under age, or one adjudged incompetent or quasi-incompetent by the unanimous vote of the remainder of the Council, he is to be represented by some other regular member appointed by the Council."

Baron Takakimi, as head of the main family, presides at the monthly meetings. Only the eleven Family Heads are entitled to vote, and the Baron's vote is equal to that of each of the others. The Associate Members may take part in discussions, and are entitled to advance their opinions on all matters before the Council, but they do not have a vote. All meetings are secret, but transactions are amply recorded and preserved in the Family Archives.

Marriages, adoptions, accessions, retirements and the course of individual business careers are the principal topics on the agenda of the Council meetings.

In spite of the iron-bound authority of the Council, young Mitsui scions are given considerable latitude in picking their brides. Actual love-matches are reputedly frequent in Mitsui history, but the Family Council has the final word. In this there is a slight departure from usual Japanese custom. Parents commonly contract marriages for their sons, through formal matchmakers, but with the Mitsuis it is the Council that acts as marital negotiators, rather than the parents. The Council similarly would rule on divorces, but the Mitsuis say there have been no divorces before the Council in two generations.

In all such matters the family Constitution prescribes policy in detailed form. The present-day Constitution was drawn up largely by Kaoru Inouye, the distinguished statesman who was Mitsui's right bower in the government of the Meiji Era. Inouye worked for several years on the document, seeking the advice of both foreign and Japanese legalists, and following as closely as possible the original Constitution. When finally drafted, and accepted by the Mitsuis, the "promulgation" took place in a solemn ceremony in the Mitsui Council Hall on July 1, 1900.

The heads of the eleven families, retired Family Heads, those who helped draft the instrument, directors of the various companies, and important firm members all gathered for the occasion. The ceremony started with Shinto memorial rites in honor of the Founder. Then, after a reading of the Constitution and a few speeches, all members of the family, one by one, pledged themselves to observance of the new Constitution.

The full text never has been published, for many passages

are held secret. There are ten "Chapters" and more than one hundred "Articles."

Chapter One specifies the six main families and five branch families by name, and prescribes that branch families may not be elevated to the status of main families, nor may any future branch families be admitted to the Council.

It is characteristic of the spirit of the document that Chapter Two expressly defines the duties of the family members before there is any mention of the rights and prerogatives of these members. In this chapter are laid down these principal points: —

1. Members of the family shall respect the rules prescribed by the Founder, associate with each other as brothers, co-operate in all things, work together to enhance the prosperity of the House and to consolidate the foundations of each family.

2. Dispense with excessive luxury and practise simplicity and economy in living.

3. When of proper age, sons and daughters of the eleven families shall study in good institutions of learning.

4. No debts shall be incurred by members of the Family nor shall any one member guarantee the loans of others.

5. All special actions require the consent of the Family Council.

6. The Family Heads shall observe the various contracts and indentures in transacting their various businesses, shall take turns in inspecting the business conditions of each of the firms and establishments of the House of Mitsui, shall submit reports to the Council, shall call the Council whenever it is found that any officer of any firm of the House of Mitsui is undertaking or attempting to undertake dangerous plans, or if he is found committing some wrong so as promptly to adopt means of dealing with the offender and set about rectification or prevention of similar acts.

* * *

Chapter Three outlines the prerogatives and duties of the Family Council, voting rights, and general agenda of Council meetings. The second article of the chapter gives to the Council the right of "distribution of profits, earmarking of reserves, budgeting of expenses and payments of the various firms of the House, and distribution of property in case any of the companies of the House should be dissolved." Actually these details are handled in general by the *Mitsui Gomei Kaisha*, but the Family Council acts as sanctioning body.

The Fourth Article of the chapter specifies that the Council shall determine the household budgets of each of the eleven members of the family; and this is religiously followed, even to the extent of "entertainment allowance."

Chapter Four concerns marriage, adoption, and regulations about collateral branches. It has never been published in detail.

Strict rules are provided in Chapter Five for clamping a heavy hand on "those members of the House who misconduct themselves or who squander money or property." It is a matter of record that these regulations rarely have been invoked.

The Mitsui clan has been singularly free of wastrels, spendthrifts and hell-raisers. The tongue of scandal has never touched Mitsui private lives in at least two generations. Japanese newspapers are notoriously given to scandalmongering and rarely spare those in the high places, but a cursory glance through the clippings of one leading Tokyo newspaper gives the Mitsuis a generally clear record.

One of the younger Mitsui scions reportedly is the owner, under an assumed name, of one of the night-life cafés of Tokyo. He is frequently seen in the café, and is known to have a weakness for the unusually pretty waitresses that staff his place; but still he manages to avoid scandal. Few of the patrons who observe the quiet-mannered habitué who customarily occupies one darkened corner surrounded by two or three girls know that he is a Mitsui, and if they did it would matter little — for he never drinks excessively or otherwise puts himself in evidence.

Others of the Mitsui family may keep mistresses, — a very common practice in Japan, — but they never get in the headlines. A veteran Tokyo editor could not recall that a Mitsui "love nest" ever had been exposed. He was equally certain that papers would print anything of a Mitsui affair with a geisha if rumors ever reached them; but the Mitsuis apparently are unduly circumspect. Their record for sobriety is similar. The Mitsuis have too much respect for the benevolent despotism of that Family Council.

Chapter Six in essence is the original Sixth Precept of the Founder's Constitution, and is characteristic not only of the spirit of the entire document but of a three-hundred-year-old Mitsui Principle. It specifies that "Retirement shall never be permitted unless it is unavoidable," and includes a maxim of Hachirobei: "The lifework of a man lasts as long as he lives; therefore do not, without reason, seek the luxury and ease of retirement." The rest of the chapter deals with inheritances in the event of compulsory retirement.

Chapter Seven details the duties of the directors of the Mitsui firms and lays down a code, mostly secret, "to assure perfect contact among them so as to obviate friction."

Chapter Eight is held in extreme secrecy. Only family members and the higher directors of the business organization know its provisions. In general, it sets strict limits to various capitalizations, specifies common property and the property of each family. It details the handling of reserve funds, classified as "common reserves, preparatory reserves, extra reserves, outlay reserves and descendant reserves." The descendant reserves are set aside whenever a son or daughter is born into any of the families.

Contractual safeguards among family members are dealt with in Chapter Nine, which asserts that "Violation of rules or contracts by any member of the main and branch families is punished by reprimand, disciplining, and more severe methods under the Civil Code, if necessary." It is evidence enough of the strength of the Constitution as a force of law on the family members to observe that the Mitsuis have never gone into civil court against each other.

The final chapter provides for necessary supplementary rules and amendments with the provision that "Should there be changes in the law of the land which makes the foregoing Constitution of the House of Mitsui infringe them, changes shall be made in the Constitution, but in such a way as not to lose the spirit of the original Constitution."

In no other large business institution in the world is the power and unity of family so firmly entrenched and safeguarded as in the House of Mitsui through this rare document.

Chapter II

WEALTH FROM THREE WELLS

THE NAME MITSUI MEANS "Three Wells." When the political fortunes and influence of the great Fujiwara family began to decline in 1100 A.D., one of the descendants of Kamatari Fujiwara looked about him and wisely decided there was no future for his branch of the family at the capital, Kyoto.

He settled in Omi Province and took the surname Mitsui. Name-changing was not uncommon then in Japan. It was a custom that extended with diminishing practice to modern times. Both geographical and family names were changed with the utmost abandon. Men would alter their names at any crisis in their careers. A decision to settle in some new locality and begin life anew was a common excuse. Members of military expeditions bent on conquest in the remoter provinces, a growing preoccupation of the times, would follow their successes by establishing themselves permanently in their acquired domains and assuming new names, frequently from surrounding place-names.

It is a tradition of the Mitsuis that the ancestor who first bestowed that name upon himself had found three wells on his fief.* In one of the wells he discovered a gold hoard, evi-

* The original Three Wells of the Mitsuis cannot be found today. Presumably, they were somewhere on the Mitsui landholdings in the vicinity of Lake Biwa. The site of the original Mitsui home is now covered with mountainous underbrush, and the only buildings are of comparatively recent origin. The Mitsuis, however, have three wells carefully preserved on their ancestral lands in Matsuzaka, Ise Province,

dently deposited there by brigands who never returned. The first Mitsui claimed the gold, and it was a providential steppingstone to early rehabilitation of the family fortune which had suffered after the Fujiwaras were eclipsed at Kyoto. Recalling that his great ancestor, Kamatari, had taken the name Fujiwara ("Wistaria Field") because an auspicious career was launched in a wistaria field, the first Mitsui saw good omen in "Three Wells." It is perhaps significant that no Mitsui has found it either necessary or propitious to change the name, in nearly one thousand years.

The Three Wells today are incorporated in the Mitsui trademark: a diamond with three horizontal bars in the center. You do not have to go to Japan today to see the Mitsui crest. It appears on many objects that find their way to foreign

on the site of the first business house of the Mitsuis, a sake-shop and pawnshop in the heart of Matsuzaka city. A high wall surrounds the otherwise vacant area, a rectangle about fifty yards wide and seventy-five long. The three wells form the points of an equilateral triangle. Only one of them is still functioning. This one, walled up with concrete and covered over with a roof today, is supposed to be the one that started the Mitsuis on their way to wealth — but not because of a gold hoard found at the bottom. The more likely story is that the well yielded such excellent-tasting water, ideal for sake-brewing, that the Mitsui sake became famous. That may have been the origin of the "gold hoard" tradition. When the writer visited Matsuzaka in 1938, a caretaker of the Mitsui estate there exhibited the well and laughingly recalled the treasure tale. He lowered a bucket and scooped the bottom, bringing up only a clear springlike water. "You see," he explained, "there is no gold. If ever there was any gold in that well, the Mitsuis got all of it out years ago." But there is still confusion in the legend. While the three wells at Matsuzaka are preserved as a bit of family lore, it is obvious that they were not the three that gave the Mitsuis their name. The Mitsuis were the Three Well family several hundred years before they went to Matsuzaka early in the 1600's. Apparently, then, there have been six wells in Mitsui history — the original three, from which they took their name, and the three they conveniently found later at Matsuzaka and adopted as part of the family tradition.

shores — from Hiroshige prints to ocean liners, from insurance policies to tea.

The fact that the Mitsuis had a family name at the dawn of feudal times in Japan is assurance enough of their patrician origin. Only the Emperor and the peasants had no family names in early times. The Emperor needed none. He was above ordinary mortals, and no family name was necessary to distinguish him from other men. He needed only to be distinguished from the gods from whom he sprang, and this could be done by a single name. On his death it was believed, and is today, that he returns to the company of gods. He is then deified under some new name, with *Tenno* added. The *Tenno* means "Heavenly Emperor."

An early custom with regard to family names merged the personality of the individual with his official position in the state, a practice that tended to bestow on certain families an acknowledged hereditary title to some posts. Family names, therefore, were not the heritage of commoners who had not been admitted to state offices, and it was not until 1872 that the peasantry was allowed to have family names, further to set off the individual.

At the time when the first Mitsui was changing his name from Fujiwara and setting up an independent family, Japan was entering upon its Dark Ages, a period of turmoil that had much to do with the subsequent course of the Mitsuis. For it was toward the end of this era of strife and constant civil wars that the Mitsuis saw, as no others of their caste did, that the real master of the Empire was to be, not he who was strongest with sword and bow, and could partition out the land among his military retainers, but he who could excel in the arts of peace and best propitiate the gods of commerce and finance.

The military families of Taira and Minamoto rose and displaced the Fujiwara at the capital, but not without a bitter struggle among themselves. The Tairas were first to seize control of the state, but even then — so strong were the seeds of the Great Reform sown by the early Fujiwaras — the Tairas had no thought of upsetting the Imperial Dynasty. In any other country, such seizure of ruling power at any time would have resulted in a new dynasty on the throne. But in Japan throughout the Dark Ages the Emperors remained above civil strife, puppets though most of them were. The great leader of the Tairas was Kiyomori, who was the son of one of the Emperor's favorite palace ladies. Kiyomori's father carried on his affair with the beauty until he was discovered by the Emperor himself, but the benign sovereign valued his friendship with Taira more than he did his lady so he readily forgave the errant warrior and promised that if the child were a girl he would adopt it and if it were a boy it might be a Taira. It was a boy; and Kiyomori in 1167 achieved the office of Chancellor, never before given to a military man, and the revenues of thirty provinces for his war chest.

Kiyomori proved an able administrator, but in putting down the early threat of the Minamotos he had neglected an important matter. He had brought about the destruction of the head of the Minamotos and his two eldest sons, but had spared the youngest son and three half-brothers. The youngest son, Yoritomo, proved a great warrior, of whom it is said that he once fought all day and fell asleep on his horse and awoke to continue fighting. In an eastern province the Minamotos regained their strength until finally, under Yoritomo, they renewed their war with the Tairas. It was Japan's War of the Roses — for the Tairas fought under a red banner or flower, and the Minamotos under a white.

The bitter forty years' war ended in the Battle of Dan-no-ura, in 1185, one of the three or four decisive battles in Japan's history. The battle was won by the Minamotos, who virtually exterminated the Tairas, handing over their surviving women into prostitution at Shimonoseki. To this day the prostitutes at Shimonoseki claim descent from these ancient noble ladies and affect a distinctive style of headdress reminiscent of the Tairas.

The victorious Minamotos formally set up that unique system of dual government which lasted until 1867 when ruling powers were restored to the Emperor. The name given to this new form of government was *Bakufu*, literally "Curtain Government." It was a Chinese word, like most military terms of the time. The commanding general in both China and Japan customarily surrounded his tent or headquarters with a *baku* or curtain, and its use in this connection denoted "administration from the tent," or field, rather than from the Imperial Court.

Yoritomo, the Minamoto leader, took the title *Sei-i-tai-Shogun*, or "barbarian-repressing Great General." It was not the first use of the term "Shogun," a title that caused so much confusion to the first foreigners who arrived in Japan and conceived it to mean "secular Emperor." "Shogun" means simply "General," a designation conferred by previous Emperors upon distinguished soldiers. But Yoritomo gave the title a new meaning, for he took with it authority to appoint high constables in each of the provinces, tax collectors and other representatives, until gradually the Shoguns acquired the position of *de facto* sovereigns, while the Emperors for the ensuing five hundred years came more and more to be only names of sacred personages living in the growing seclusion of their courts. Not all of the Shoguns lived up to the precedents of Yoritomo, some failing to maintain their authority outside their own capital, but it was the beginning of an institution that had far-reaching effects on Japan's subsequent course in history. Primarily, the establishment of the Shogunate riveted the fetters of feudalism. And because the Mitsuis threw off these shackles even before Japan itself did, it is necessary to look further into the state of government and society of that period to understand the importance of the step taken later by the Mitsuis at a time when every circumstance mitigated against it.

Feudalism was foreshadowed by the rule of the Fujiwaras. In spite of the tenor of their "reforms," heavy rates of taxation were necessary to support the extravagances of the luxurious courts which delighted the hearts of that effete family. As a result, to meet the taxes those who tilled the lands and produced were forced to borrow money or its equivalent, rice, from the provincial magnates or from Buddhist priests, and the only security they could offer was their own small landholdings. Consequently the nobles and temples — just as did Europe's princes and Church — began to add to their estates. The Great Reform had prescribed repossession of the lands for the farmers, and sought to end the nefarious practice of seizure for taxes, but the Government lacked power to enforce the edicts and the farmers slipped gradually into a state of actual serfdom.

The only semblance of authority that could be maintained in the provinces was that instituted by such powerful local land magnates as could defy restrictions against the bearing of arms and, themselves, recruit small standing armies to preserve their fiefs. Many of the peasants became soldiers, being supplied by their creditors with armor, horses and weapons. Petty tyrants soon were at the head of small autocratic states, and so helpless were the capital authorities that provincial governors dared not molest these warriors or try to force their obedience.

Provincial magnates made alliances with court nobles and by one means or another escaped taxation by the Central Government. Imperial Inspectors, sent out to verify reports of drought, flood, or storms, — which were common excuses for forwarding no taxes to the capital, — could be bribed, or, in cases of extreme honesty, could be intimidated. What taxes were collected were deflected into the treasuries of local rulers, and near-anarchy prevailed. The daimio ("great names" or feudal barons) built medieval castles and strongholds, mounted night-and-day guards, and occasionally sallied forth for new conquests. The Shoguns, instead of venturing to put them down, were content with cementing certain ties with this rising military feudalism — keeping the capital, then at Kamakura, for its metropolis, and allowing a rapid decentralization of power.

Then came separation of the peasant-soldiers from the professional soldiers — those who had begun to hand down their arms from father to son, in contrast to those unwilling levees called up from the rice-fields for brief campaigns. This was the birth of the samurai, or *bushi.* Just as in Europe where almost at the same time the professional fighting men of the Middle Ages were perfecting their knighthood or chivalry, the military men of Japan evolved their own rude sort of chivalry and strict code of honor, known as *Bushido.* It constituted their own moral precepts, the *noblesse oblige* of the warrior class. *Samurai,* literally, means "attendants," or "guards," and *bushi* "fighting gentlemen"; but the terms came to be used indiscriminately. It must be borne in mind, however, that the later wide distinction between samurai and commoner did not arise as is often presumed from caste or conquests, but was the natural development of organization and the increasing importance of the soldier, who in this military era and under the guiding star of *Bushido* invested his profession with undeserved honor.

Like their forebears, the Mitsuis were never great fighters. The only individual of their long line who achieved any fame with arms was the high-born son of another family adopted into the Mitsuis. But the Mitsuis held the places in the patrician class and followed, if reluctantly, the Way of the Knight. One of the first distinctive physical marks of the samurai was his hairdress. He shaved the hair from his temples and from the middle of the scalp, binding the remaining hair into a topknot, which was turned forward and laid on the scalp. This was a practical measure, the warriors believed, to keep the hair out of their eyes during combat. Early paintings of the Mitsuis show that they conformed, but they were discovering a better way of keeping the hair of feudalism out of their eyes. Much has been written about the samurai, his stoicism, his self-control, devotion to ideals, fortitude and bravery, and some of these virtues the Mitsuis may have shared; but the samurai also regarded money with the greatest of contempt — and the Mitsuis stopped considerably short of such rashness.

A crude system of commerce was now taking shape in Japan. The Shogun Yoritomo had laid down a highly organized system of government at Kamakura, his capital, even if it did not extend to the whole country. There were rice, silk, timber, charcoal, horses and other staples to be bought and sold. The number of tradesmen was definitely limited in Kamakura. Official stations were established for control of transactions in these commodities, and this resulted in the formation of Japan's first companies with share-holding members in the provinces and their representatives enfranchised for business in the feudal capital. A spasmodic commerce with China already had been going on, for China had brocades, damask, stoneware and matting to sell to Japan in exchange for rice and marine products.

Yoritomo had lived fourteen years after he reached the height of his power. In 1199, he had fallen off his horse and was killed as he rode at the head of a regal procession opening a new bridge. Descendants of Yoritomo had proved too weak to carry on in the name of the great Minamoto family; and another family, the Hojos, kinsmen by marriage, promptly usurped the central authority and were outdoing all predecessors in ruthless rule.

Nevertheless the ships that were plying between China and Japan undoubtedly gave a good account of the trade possibilities in this island Empire, with its population then of 15,000,000; and that led to a historical event of tremendous psychological influence upon the Japanese people, bringing as it did new factors to bear upon the trend of national life.

In China the great Mongol Emperor, Genghis Khan, was extending his sway from the Dnieper to the China Sea. It is a legend now in the Mitsui family that an early ancestor traded with Genghis Khan, which is probable, in view of the commerce known to have been going on at that time, but the Mitsuis as a family were not yet in trade.

The grandson of Genghis Khan, Kublai Khan, hearing glowing tales of Japan across the narrow sea, turned his ambition in that direction. He sent an ultimatum to Japan, demanding that the island Empire yield peacefully or face invasion. Tokimune, seventh of the line of Hojo usurpers, a bold soldier and huntsman, with great physical courage, tore up the ultimatum and decapitated the envoys of the great Khan. The Khan tried another embassy of nine envoys, but these met the same fate. The Mongol was aroused, but he lost none of his caution, and essayed a small trial expedition to Tsushima, the island lying in the straits of Korea, where later the great Russian fleet of 1904 met its fate. The Khan's ships were driven back with heavy losses. He then spent two years preparing an armada of three hundred great ships and an army of one hundred thousand.

The Mongol invaders descended on Japan in 1281, but the Japanese intelligence system was functioning then as well as in 1904, and the Empire was ready with a fleet of light ships and an army temporarily unified. It was the first time in history that Japan was invaded by a foreign army, and as the enemy approached all internal strife was forgotten. The Mongols' ships were armed with apparatus for hurling great stones, while the Japanese, until they came to close quarters, had only their arrows. The enemy lined up its ships off Kyushu, fastened them together with chains, and heaved barrage after barrage of stones at the shore defenses. The Japanese sought to close in, and were harrying their foe with great effect when a timely hurricane came up, a "divine wind" that played havoc with the chain-linked ships of the Mongols. Even the Emperor, as the forces of united effort moved the country, had gone in person to the sacred shrines of Ise to invoke the aid of his divine ancestors. Thousands of Mongols were drowned, their ships tossed on the rocks, and only a few survivors of the once-proud armada lived to tell their story to Kublai Khan.

The Mongol Armada and its rout frequently has been compared with the defeat of the Spanish Armada by the English, but victory was almost incomparably more important to Japan than to England. The historian Nitobe summarizes: "Few things knitted all ranks of society more firmly, and so stimulated the spirit of co-operation and self-sacrifice, of devotion to a common cause and of confidence in their own strength. China and Korea, upon whom the nation had hitherto looked with reverence, had betrayed the trust and forfeited their claim to respect."

It was a hundred years before trade was resumed with China to any great extent. The Ashikaga Shoguns came into power, replacing the Hojos, and ushered in the darkest period of Japan's history. It was a period when even the Mitsuis, as gentlemen, had to fight to survive. Poverty and misery were widespread, and the feudal lands constantly were changing hands by right of conquest.

The Mitsuis were holed-up in a castle stronghold at Namazue near Lake Biwa. Night and day armed men guarded the entrance, challenging all unfamiliar faces. They wore armor of thin scales made of iron, steel, hardened hide, lacquered paper or sharkskin. Their helmets were of iron, lined inside with buckskin and with a shawl-like flap of iron rings drooping down over the shoulders. Some of the guards were further equipped with a false mustache, a custom of the day, calculated to increase the fierce appearance of warriors. For the gate guards, a variety of weapons were at hand specially devised for the reception of those a little slow in making known their peaceful intentions. One was a sort of grappling-iron — ball-shaped, with cruel barbs turning in every direction.

It was mounted on a pikestaff some ten feet long and designed to be thrust quickly outward to catch the loose clothing of a suspect and snare him until he could explain his presence. Two more weapons, one like a double rake and the other in the nature of a pitchfork, were at hand, the first to thrust between a man's legs and trip him and the second to pin him to earth. Retainers and servants who were authorized to pass in and out of the castle were supplied with wooden tickets with their names burned into them. On entering the castle the name cards were turned over to the guards, who posted them on rows of pegs, a procedure used in modern clubs.

The Ashikagas, ruling in Kyoto, began a merciless exploitation of the trading class. They were the first to introduce a practice later widespread in Japan: the sale of monopolies of principal staples to individual merchants or associations of merchants, at prices highly remunerative to the Government. These merchant guilds had been started in an earlier era, but their enforced purchase of monopolies was strictly a device of the Ashikagas. As joint stock companies, their shares in the guilds were transferable by sale or passed from father to son in inheritances. It was a system which the Mitsuis employed to their great advantage in later years.

An old record states that there were seven guilds in Kyoto during the Ashikaga Period, holding monopolies in as many branches of commerce: silk, charcoal, rice, joinery work in wood, fuel, fish, salt and horses. Other cities had as many as eight or nine, according to their trade potentialities. Market places were set aside in the cities, and a crude form of merchandising began to evolve. Formerly merchants had transacted their business literally standing on the road at *tachi-ba*, or standing markets. When the market places of the town were demarked, the merchants took quarters, displayed their wares in safety and sat waiting for customers.

A regulation issued in the year 1493 illustrates the hereditary aspects of commercial monopolies of the period: —

The brewing of sake shall be conducted by the authorized person, and no sons of his shall be allowed to brew sake while their parent is manufacturing. After the death of the parent, the right shall be given to one person, either to the son or daughter, or even an adopted son. You shall understand that the matter has been decided as above upon general consultation.

*August 7, Second year of Meio.**

Under such regulation and assurance of monopoly, the Mitsuis eventually went into trade, choosing sake-brewing as their commodity.

As the Government was decentralized and anarchy spread, powerful local families set up barriers along the roads approaching their lands and collected high taxes from all travelers. This was a further exploitation of the trading class, and a hindrance to commerce that in time led to a resumption of trade with China. An example of this abuse is seen in the diary of a famous temple at Nara, which sets forth that when two messengers in 1479 were sent with two packages of waterpots to another temple less than one hundred miles distant they had to pass through twenty-eight barriers, or local customs posts, and pay a total tax of 1 kwan, 496 mon (approximately $3.00). The harassed merchants resorted to all sorts of means to break up the barrier posts along the highways. With silver, gold dust and rich merchandise they tried, successfully in some cases, to buy the customs posts from the

* Quoted from *The Economic Aspects of the History of the Civilization of Japan*, by Y. Takekoshi. Macmillan.

feudal families. In extreme cases, the worm actually turned, the despised merchants banded together and moved aggressively in surprise attacks on the outposts. Some they burned, others they took by force, until in the end they themselves gained control of the highways — and then proceeded to highjack each other.

The principal medium of exchange was gold dust or silver, and the difficulty and hazards of transporting money under such circumstances may be imagined. In time the system of "bills of exchange" was evolved, — and the Mitsuis credit themselves with originating it, — but for the moment it was obvious that a system of coins was the immediate need of the merchants.

Japan had had three kinds of coins from a much earlier era: copper, gold, and silver. The turmoil of the early Ashikaga Period caused virtual extinction of the gold coins through hoarding. Silver coins likewise became scarce, or were debased, and only the copper were left for general circulation. Use of copper coins proved adequate enough until one Emperor, a devout Buddhist, ordered each province to build an appropriate temple and enshrine a great copper statue of Buddha. The current Shogun gratified his whim, but it set an unfortunate example of temple- and image-building. The result was an increased demand for copper, which more than exhausted the output of the copper mines in Musashi Province and brought about the disappearance of copper coins.

Coinage by the Government virtually had ceased. Merchants of the port cities were dealing with Chinese coins. Lords of various provinces tried minting their own coins without uniformity of size or value, weight being the deciding factor. The copper coins obtained from China were in Japan intrinsically more trustworthy than those minted in Japan and usually circulated at four times the exchange value of Japanese coins.

So desperate was the situation that one Regent sent an envoy to China to buy copper coins with gold dust — a most impractical arrangement, but the coins on being distributed in the market places provided a temporary inflation that vitalized trade.

That, seemingly, was the cue for a curious development which in final analysis proves to be the actual beginning of Japan's foreign trade. It laid the groundwork for a commerce that, in spite of all drawbacks, reached no less than twenty foreign markets between the coming of the first foreigner in 1542 and the complete closing of Japan to the outer world in 1637.

This train of events began with piracy. As we have seen, Japan lost all fear of her mainland neighbors with the defeat of Kublai Khan and the Mongol hordes. The Japanese built larger boats and experimented, profitably, with private descents upon China and Korea for plunder. For the lower-caste warriors, who had little to gain by the constant internecine wars, new adventures at sea beckoned, and there sprang up innumerable armadas of freebooters, unrestrained by any central authority. Chinese historical accounts of the period attest to the fear with which these pirates were regarded. The Chinese erected forty-nine fortresses along the eastern littorals, and drafted one man out of every four of the maritime population for coast-guard duty, but the Japanese apparently were either better fighters or more crafty for they carried their raids far inland, pillaging towns and countryside.

With the scarcity of currency at home and the high exchange value of Chinese coins, it became apparent to these privateers that coins were a more profitable prize to take back to Japan than other loot. They bent their efforts toward that end, until eventually China was compelled to treat these pirates as a great national enemy.

At this psychological point, there stepped into the picture Japan's greatest Sinophile, a character whose subsequent actions still bring blushes to subjects of Nippon. Yoshimitsu, third in the line of Ashikaga Shoguns, was not satisfied with the greatest commoner titles that Imperial Japan could bestow upon him, or that he could seize. He aspired to royalty. But hardly daring to trespass on the sacred rights of his own Emperor, in 1368 he looked to China for satisfaction of his royal ambition.

Taking advantage of the helplessness to which China had been reduced by the harrying of Japanese pirates, Yoshimitsu sent a mission to the courts of the Ming, offering to bring an end to piracy if China would agree to a formal resumption of commerce and intercourse between the two countries. As evidence of his good intentions, Yoshimitsu arrested twenty Japanese pirates from the islands of Iki and Tsushima, near China, and had them transported to the Ming Court.

The Chinese ruler was pleased with the gesture and graciously ordered the pirates returned to be dealt with as Yoshimitsu saw fit. The Japanese large-handedly took the pirates as far as Ningpo and boiled them alive in cauldrons of oil.

Yoshimitsu sent another embassy to the Ming Court, with a personal present for the Emperor consisting of (according to an old record) : "1,000 ryo of gold, 10 horses, 1,000 leaves of silver, 100 fans, 2 gold-foil folding screens, 1 suit of armor, 10 lances, 1 sword, 1 inkstone and 1 inkstone box."

Yoshimitsu was dealing with a personage as ambitious as he. The Ming Emperor, Taiso, founder of the Dynasty, was anxious to make Japan a tributary; and Yoshimitsu wanted to be a King. With the latter's connivance, if not actual supplication, the Ming Emperor declared Japan a tributary of China and gave Yoshimitsu the title of King of Japan. It was the first and only time that any person held such tributary title, and it is a chapter in the Empire's history that brings the greatest indignation to this day to any subject of Japan who lets his mind dwell upon it. Japanese historians are inclined to gloss over it with the assumption that Yoshimitsu had a deeper underlying motive: trade profits. Others boldly pronounce Yoshimitsu a naturally ignorant person who had no understanding of the Imperial background and destiny of Japan. But there is every evidence that the Shogun was capable and strong and had an honest respect for the great glories of the Ming Court. It is known that he affected a Chinese costume and one Imperial maple-viewing party arrived in a Ming palanquin carried by Ming servants.

Whatever may have been the motives of Yoshimitsu, his actions did result in the restoration of trade with China and the arrival in Japan of plenty of *Eiraku*, or Chinese coins, so badly needed to facilitate the commerce of that country. Furthermore, it opened Japan's eyes to the fact that foreign commerce, hitherto regarded as a means of enriching individuals, could be an important factor of national wealth.

And that was the state of affairs when the first Europeans came to Japan.

Europe first heard of Japan through Marco Polo in 1298, but the first European did not reach its shores until 1542. This seems to have been one Mendez Pinto, a Portuguese: he told such amazing stories on his return to Europe that he won the title "Mendez the Mendacious," and his claim of the "discovery" is a doubtful one. It is certain, however, that the first white men in Japan were Portuguese who landed at the island of Tanegashima. Portuguese adventurers and merchants had been roaming the Eastern seas, and these newcomers to Japan are believed to have been traders blown far off their course between Macao and Siam. They had ancient arquebuses with them, and the immediate effect of their arrival was the start of a firearms factory; for the Japanese, always quick to gauge the worth of a foreign importation, saw the potency of the gun, which was theirs ever after.

Provincial chiefs of Japan, hearing of this startling new weapon, thereupon vied with each other in attracting the foreigners to their shores, with the idea of getting more guns or wealth by trade, thus improving their local positions.

The two great maritime nations of 1500 were Spain and Portugal; to keep peace between them in their bitter rivalry for commerce, Pope Alexander VI had issued his famous Papal Bull which divided the world into two parts, the Western part going to Spain and the Eastern to Portugal. That accounted for the prevalence of the Portuguese in Eastern waters.

Whether or not Mendez Pinto was the first white man in Japan, when he left he carried with him an important stowaway. A highborn Satsuma clansman who had killed a man escaped from Japan aboard Pinto's boat and eventually reached Goa, Portuguese colony in India. There he met Francis Xavier, one of the original members of the Jesuit order founded by Saint Ignatius de Loyola under whom Xavier had studied at the University of Paris. The Satsuma clansman was baptized into Christianity, and upon being asked whether Japan might ever accept Christianity he replied in these words, which Saint Francis himself recorded: "His people would not immediately assent to what might be said to them, but they would investigate what I might affirm respecting religion by a multitude of questions, and, above all, by observing whether my conduct agreed with my words. This done, the king (daimio), the nobility and adult population would flock to Christ, being a nation which always follows reason as a guide."

The words proved prophetic, for Xavier, taking the Japanese convert with him as an interpreter, sailed for Japan and set about to Christianize the country. Within some thirty years after Francis Xavier's first preaching the Catholic church counted over a million converts in Japan. Among them were several princes, large numbers of daimios, men high in official position, and generals in the army.

Thus within a short period Japan had Christianity, firearms and a booming foreign trade, all three enthusiastically accepted.

Firearms and trade undoubtedly had much to do with the rapid strides of Christianity, which brought both. The gun stimulated progress of the industrial arts, notably building, for its introduction revised the tactics of the feudal wars and new castles had to be constructed with different ideas of defense. The strongholds of the Fujiwara age, with mud walls, wooden fences and moats, gave way to stone fortifications, towers and citadels. The construction of cannon began, at first from hollowed-out bamboo, good for only one shot, and then from bronze and other metals.

The foundation for modern civilization and the House of Mitsui was laid.

Chapter III

THE MITSUIS SHEATHE THE SWORD

JAPANESE FAMILIES
are subject to the usual biological laws, but you would never suspect it. They can die out, but not many of the great families do, for long ago they discovered the convenient system of adoption. A little judicious limb-grafting here and there has preserved that youthful bloom in many a family tree creaking in the wind as the sap ran low.

In early times perpetuity of the family was essential chiefly for two reasons: to carry on ancestral sacrifices and devotion without which the home was disgraced; and to preserve ownership of land fiefs, because land being held only on condition of military or other services reverted to possession of the feudal lord if a vassal died without male heirs.

The family naturally became the basis of Japanese life, and the unit of civilization and society. This gave rise to the much-praised virtue of "filial piety," the religious root of the family system, which spread to the very state itself, fostering that loyalty or childlike obedience rendered by all subjects to the Emperor, the "father of his people."

From *The Four-and-Twenty Paragons of Filial Piety*, it would appear that the term in Japan has come to mean considerably more than an annual flower-offering observation of Mothers' Day. The Paragons are of Chinese origin, but still are classic moral tales of copy-book tenor in Japan. Here are three of them, in brief: —

One youth had a stepmother whose heartlessness and cruelty were notorious. Most of her evil deeds, as is charged to so many stepmothers, were directed toward the boy himself. But he, long-suffering, thought only of trying to please her. Her weakness was a great appetite for fish. One wintry day when there seemed no prospect of getting fish for her table, the pious lad lay naked upon the ice of a lake until the heat of his body melted a hole through which he snared two fish to set before his harsh parent. The tale is further pointed because the recipient of such devotion is a woman rather than a man.

A second youth of the PARAGON series customarily slept naked near his parents with the idea of inviting mosquitoes to feast on his own tender skin, so that his parents' slumber might not be disturbed.

For sheer inventiveness, one Roraishi outdid them all. His filial piety won him fame at seventy, when he solemnly conceived the idea of dressing in infants' clothes and crawling about on the floor prattling baby talk — to convince his very aged parents that they were young because Roraishi obviously was a baby.

In feudal times, last wills and testaments had little legal standing and the simplest way of leaving money or lands to a promising youth, whether a distant relative or mere friend of the family, was to adopt him. The adopted son always took the name of the parents, and if there were a daughter in the family it was usually arranged for him to marry her. Only an adult person could adopt another, unless the actual head of the family happened to be a child and then the child could do it unhampered by any age restriction. If an infant head of the family appeared unhealthy and unlikely to reach ma-jority, it was no uncommon occurrence for a lusty male adult to become the baby's adopted son, thus providing a little more insurance for the family succession.

The practice has extended to modern days, when the head of a business with a minor son may adopt his chief clerk to induce a new personal interest in the firm, and then have the clerk in turn adopt the son, with the provision that the clerk shall retire when the son has reached suitable age to carry on the business. It is a curious system of alternate headships, to prevent any serious lapses of family activity and directing genius.

The Mitsuis resorted to adoption with most beneficial results at an early stage in the family career.

Inconsequential, undistinctive descendants of the indolent Fujiwaras, the Mitsuis in the Fifteenth Century were settled in Omi Province as retainers of the powerful Sasaki clan. Omi is a rich, picturesque province of some nine hundred square miles in the southern central part of the main island. Its most famous geographical feature is Lake Biwa, the largest inland body of water in Japan, so named because it is shaped like the *biwa*, ancient musical instrument resembling a lute.

Most of the southern half of the province was owned or controlled by the lusty, hard-fighting Sasaki family, who had erected a score of castles and strongholds at the most advantageous spots around Lake Biwa.

In the middle of the Fifteenth Century, by a stroke of luck, the Mitsuis were enabled to adopt Takahisa Sasaki, son of the daimio who was head of the Sasaki family. Mitsui records do not give the precise reason for the adoption. Whether it was because there was no male heir at the time in the Mitsui family or because they desired to instill a little fighting blood in a line descended from the *fainéant* Fujiwaras is a matter left to conjecture. Most likely, Takahisa had other commendable qualities. One Mitsui account describes him simply as "one of those younger sons who need but opportunity to become founders of families themselves."

The Mitsuis provided the opportunity. While they were nominally retainers of the Sasaki family, they were of more patrician descent and the inducement of becoming a Mitsui, taking with him his native talents, swayed the youth to change his name and enter the Mitsui family. It was an advantageous alliance. Takahisa roused the lethargic Mitsuis to a realization that the rigors of the times demanded that the sword be taken up to survive. With his skill at arms and the enthusiasm of the Mitsuis over their new fighting man, Takahisa became one of the legendary "seven chieftains" of the Sasaki clan, and carried the Mitsuis onward and upward for forty years through the darkest of Japan's Dark Ages. When he had established a measure of peace and security about him, Takahisa built a strong castle on his hereditary fief at Namazue, near Lake Biwa, and there he and his descendant lived in a respectable state of belligerency until in 1560 they crossed the path of Oda Nobunaga, one of the three greatest warriors in Japanese history.

The swashbuckling Nobunaga, with his long, trailing sword and wild traits that earned for him the name "Lord Fool," came on the scene when anarchy was at its height, when complete disintegration of the country seemed certain. Through eight generations of Buddhist priests, Nobunaga was descended from the Taira family. His father, however, had left the monastery to carve out a name for himself as a warrior, and to his son, Oda, he left not only a sizeable estate in Owari Province that he had won by the sword, but also an undying hatred for Buddhism. This Oda was to take all the fight out of the Mitsuis in one brief campaign and then perform a further favor for the family by altering the course of the Empire so that it was respectable to be peaceful.

Gathering a small army of hard-bitten fighters, Oda Nobunaga at an early age instinctively took to the sport or pastime of fighting other feudal chiefs, and within ten years was master of the whole province of Owari. Under the decadent Ashikaga Shoguns such feudal chieftains as emerged from the welter of provincial fighting inevitably set their course toward Kyoto, the capital. If their conquests led them that far they stood a good chance of making themselves masters of the weakening Shoguns, which would have the effect of legalizing any further wars to widen the domain of their influence. Kyoto was a natural springboard for any militant parvenu.

Nobunaga encountered the Mitsuis on his way to Kyoto, through a devious bit of politics. The fourteenth Ashikaga Shogun was Yoshiteru, who killed himself as a rebellious element in 1565 attempted to set up a rival Shogunate. His younger brother, Yoshiaki, escaped to the provinces and began a campaign with no resources other than his name to establish himself as the rightful Shogun. The first powerful clan to whom he appealed for help was that of the Sasakis and Mitsuis of Omi Province, directly north of the capital.

It was a poor choice, for one of the rebel leaders was an ally of the Sasakis. Yoshiaki not only was rebuffed by the Sasakis and Mitsuis, but barely escaped with his life. Then he heard of the rising Nobunaga, and he went to him with his story. By this time another military genius of the era, Hideyoshi, had attached himself to Nobunaga's retinue and was a trusted adviser. Hideyoshi was impressed with the pretender's claims, and he was versed in the politics of the times. Hideyoshi told Nobunaga that, though he had progressed convincingly enough so far, he could hope to go little farther without a name for his escutcheon, while by espousing Yoshiaki's cause he could conduct subsequent wars clothed with the authority of the rightful claimant to the Shogunate.

Nobunaga saw the wisdom of that course and adopted it. This made him the natural enemy of the Sasakis and Mitsuis, and pointed his campaign in their direction. His one-man intelligence staff, Hideyoshi, went out and scouted Omi Province and came back with the word that it was a favorable time to attack. So Nobunaga went to war with the Sasaki-Mitsui clan for two allied reasons: because they stood between him and Kyoto, and because ostensibly he was fighting a war for Yoshiaki who had been rebuffed by the clan.

The Omi clansmen had been doing some scouting of their own and were ready for the invader. Nobunaga was met with stiff resistance. For a time it appeared that the military career of Nobunaga would be cut short right there in his neighboring province, for the Mitsuis and Sasakis were fighting with courage and audacity, and on their home grounds.

Momentarily halted, Nobunaga resorted to another familiar device of the period. He sent emissaries to the Asai family, which controlled the other portion of Omi Province immediately to the north of the Sasaki-Mitsui clan. Offering his sister as a bride to the youthful head of the house of Asai, Nobunaga appealed for aid. Whether the Asais were moved by the beauty of Nobunaga's sister, or saw prospects of a profitable alliance with the rising young warrior himself, the Asais were won over to an alliance against their southern neighbors. Most probably Hideyoshi, the fixer, had a hand in it.

With his new forces, the intransigent Nobunaga renewed the assault. The Mitsuis quickly had enough of it. Their adopted warrior chief, Takahisa, had died fifty years before and the head of the family, Takayasu Mitsui, was of lesser mettle. The Mitsuis retired to their castle at Namazue, and Nobunaga laid siege. The Sasakis, fighting the Asais, were unable to help, and after only a brief further resistance the Mitsui stronghold fell to Nobunaga.

Taking pity on the head of the house, Nobunaga refrained from putting the clan to the sword, but he deprived them of their extensive lands. Thoroughly frightened at his narrow escape, Takayasu Mitsui gathered what belongings he could, and with his kinsmen and servants, migrated to Ise, farther south on the coast, and there settled in what obscurity he could achieve, determined never again to fight in Japan's civil wars. And that decision on the part of Takayasu was the first step toward the founding of the Mitsui House as we know it today.

Before the actual transformation of the Mitsuis from noble to merchant class, much spadework was to be done in Japan, and Nobunaga was the first of three great contemporary figures to begin it. The Mitsuis didn't wear the sword long enough to help pacify and unify Japan. But by the time it was done by others, around 1600, the Mitsuis were ready and waiting to take their place in the Empire wrought by Nobunaga, Hideyoshi, and Iyeyasu Tokugawa.

Nobunaga probably never heard of the Mitsuis again, but he marched on to the capital, maneuvered the Shogunate to his own designs and by 1573 was the actual ruler, issuing decrees in the name of the Emperor.

His first step in laying the groundwork for the rise of the

House of Mitsui was to open free trade and introduce the principle of equal opportunity in the commercial world. Nobunaga was no economist, but he applied some well-learned principles of military leadership to the field of commerce and they proved an eye-opener. He was the first leader in Japan to discover and put into practice the theory — startling to the Japan of that day — that a competent general need not be of patrician birth. He was as quick to recognize the ability of a subordinate who might have come from the gutter or from a bandit gang as he was to make use of the best talents of a hereditary chieftain.

Nobunaga's four great generals were nicknamed Cotton, Rice, Attack and Retreat. The names were expressive, and caught the popular fancy. The great Hideyoshi was Cotton, so nicknamed by Nobunaga himself because he was as versatile as cotton which even then was put to innumerable uses in Japan. Goroza was Rice, an absolute necessity in any operation. Shibata, "the Jar-breaker," was Attack, skilled in assault and pursuit. He was also called "the Jar-breaker" because in one famous siege he ordered his men to drink what water they could and then break their water-jars preparatory to advancing, to victory or death.

Ikeda was Retreat, a general who excelled in the art of removing a force from the field of action with the minimum of losses — and it is noteworthy that the man who took over the managing directorship of the House of Mitsui after the assassination of Baron Dan in 1932, at an explosive moment when orderly retreat from the aggressive Mitsui policies was expedient, was an Ikeda.

Nobunaga, firmly entrenched in the capital, soon became known as "the Great Leveler." After establishing the principle of free trade, his next efforts were directed toward breaking up the power of the Buddhist priests and temples, and tearing down the barriers to commerce erected on the road-sides by merchant guilds that had gained power by taxing travelers and merchandise. Others before Nobunaga had tried it unsuccessfully. Some of the principal highways of the country were under absolute control of the guilds or temples. The guilds allowed only their members to pass, while others were forced to pay exorbitant duties. Nobunaga, by issuing decrees and threats, and in some cases by sending military expeditions, finally eradicated the barriers and tax stations, and issued new decrees declaring all commerce might be carried on without fear of molestation.

There had been free ports in Japan before Nobunaga's time, — by 1500 there were ten, where no taxation of any kind was levied on commerce, — but their effectiveness in improving the trade of the country was considerably handicapped by the fact that the moment the commodities left the free cities they encountered the road taxes almost at the outskirts. Nobunaga doubled the number of free ports and saw to it that no adjacent feudal lord extorted any protection tax, or tried any highjacking. Regulations * — still preserved — of one free city, Matsuyama, show the extent to which Nobunaga's principle of free trade applied: —

On the day of the market all goods shall be allowed free egress.

All goods on sale in the market shall be free from any service. Those who come to this market shall not be pressed for the return of borrowed money and rice. No market goods shall be impounded as security.

On the day of the market, whatever dispute the merchants may have, the retainers of the lord shall not interfere, and the townspeople shall settle it.

The above provisions shall strictly be obeyed, and should any-

* Quoted from Takekoshi.

one disobey, the deputy and the townspeople shall immediately announce it.

Another free port, Setagaya, added this curiously modern rule to its market regulations: —

Should anyone enter a tavern and act violently [on market day] he shall be arrested and his name placarded.

Further to facilitate commerce, Nobunaga built roads on a grand scale and ordered the minting of gold and silver coins. Important commercial highways still existing in Japan stand as a lasting memorial to Nobunaga. In spite of the fact that wheeled traffic was practically unknown, Nobunaga built roads twenty-one feet wide and planted rows of pines and willows along their sides so that travelers might not stray when deep snows covered the roads in winter and so they might be afforded protection from the summer sun. Nor did Nobunaga stop with roads. He built bridges, and where bridges were impractical, he improved ferry service with larger vessels, firmer slips and convenient approaches.

Before Nobunaga, the gold used in trade was largely dust or bullion cut up or packed in small bags as required to meet each transaction. Copper coins, either imported from China or minted without uniformity by local lords, were still the principal medium of exchange. There was no legal tender and the ratio of exchange between gold and silver was not fixed. Nobunaga remedied both of these defects, fixing the gold-silver ratio at approximately twelve to one, and issuing strict orders proscribing indiscriminate minting by provincial magnates.

Improvement in the social status of the merchant was a natural outcome of the commercial reformations.

By example and by act, Nobunaga had made significant inroads on the old tradition that heredity, custom, precedent and even superstition were the determining factors in the business of getting ahead. For the first time it was dawning upon the Japanese that sheer ability was an asset.

For the first time, also, Japan was showing evidences of being ready to throw off ancient shackles and take its place in the family of nations of that day. But one momentous episode forestalled this, and that was the complete seclusion that shortly was to be proclaimed.

A consistent foe of Buddhism, Nobunaga gave every aid and encouragement to Christianity. He never became a Christian himself, significantly, but long before he had risen to power he had summoned Portuguese missionaries from Kyushu to his home province and arranged a debate between them and near-by Buddhist priests. He studied their arguments deeply, but the debate served to impress him more with the political potentialities of Christianity than with its merits as a religious creed. As long as his power lasted, however, Christians in Japan were safe.

Nobunaga's rule was cut short by one of his military captains, Akechi, who for years had brooded over a bit of horseplay with Nobunaga. The traitor was one with whom Nobunaga had been on the friendliest of terms for sexual perversion was practised in Japan as in other countries among military men deprived of the companionship of women for long periods. While romping in the palace on one occasion, Nobunaga thrust the head of Akechi under his arm with something of a headlock and playfully tapped a tune on the imprisoned head with his fan. He remarked that it was like playing on an empty drum.

Akechi submitted to the drumming with ill grace and brooded over loss of "face" until he found opportunity for vengeance. It came at a time when Hideyoshi was off on an expedition, and becoming hard pressed, asked Nobunaga to send relief from the capital. Nobunaga named his erstwhile playmate to head the relief. Akechi marched his men to the outskirts of the capital, and encamped overnight while he plotted to return and kill his chief. To his officers he denounced Nobunaga as a usurper and promised plenty of booty if they succeeded. Early the next morning they marched back, and while Nobunaga was still asleep surrounded his quarters in an old temple. The noise awoke Nobunaga, who pushed aside his sliding window and saw the traitorous force in the courtyard below him. A shower of arrows greeted him and one lodged in his shoulder for a mortal wound. Seeing that it was useless to resist, Nobunaga set fire to the temple and committed hara-kiri. The burning building provided his pyre.

The man who rushed back to the capital and avenged the death of Nobunaga was, by a stretch of the imagination and the exigencies of adoption, a kinsman of the Mitsuis. But the Mitsuis have never exerted any claim to the kinship. The man was Hideyoshi, the General Cotton of Nobunaga's incomparable staff, a military genius and a genius of statecraft, generally acknowledged to be the greatest man Japan ever produced.

Born into the lowest class of peasantry, a pithecanthropoid child, he proved so unmanageable in youth that his father, a peasant without the luxury of a family name, sent him to a monastery. He rebelled against discipline and was thrown out, after which he was apprenticed to thirty-eight various trades without success. The youth took to roaming the countryside impudently picking fights and joining robber bands. Looking farther afield he concluded that Nobunaga, then the feudal chief of Owari, showed the greatest promise of reaching the heights. Hideyoshi stormed his way into Nobunaga's presence and talked himself into a job as sandal-bearer, later groom, for the warrior chief. From these low menial tasks, he fought his way upward into the confidence of Nobunaga. One biographer cites a characteristic bit of impudence. In his zeal for soldiering, Hideyoshi habitually would mount guard at Nobunaga's castle an hour before his regular turn. Once when Nobunaga rose early to watch a storm, he noticed a lack of sentries and cried: "Is there no one on guard here?" Hideyoshi showed himself and suavely replied: "Yes, the only one in your whole army that matters."

His gross features had won for him the nickname "Monkey Face" — until it was changed to "General Cotton." A reliable leader in battle, a staff man who could carry a detailed map in his head, a political adviser of the sharpest acumen, this vainglorious bumpkin who rolled his eyes and grimaced as he talked became Nobunaga's right-hand man. Hideyoshi was forty-six years old when his chief died. The traitor responsible for Nobunaga's death almost trapped General Cotton in a western province where he was besieging a current enemy. Caught alone in a rice field, Hideyoshi amid a shower of arrows turned his horse down a narrow path where his foes could follow only in single file. He dismounted, stabbed his horse in the flank, frightening it into backward flight among his pursuers while he fled into a near-by temple. He found the monks at their bath. The warrior quickly shaved off his top-knot, disrobed, and jumped into the water with the monks. When his enemies appeared, he was lost among the sea of bald pates sticking up from the steaming waters. The ruse was successful.

Hideyoshi quickly rallied his forces, and in a pitched battle defeated Akechi. He fought and won two more campaigns famous in Japan's history before he became acknowledged master at the capital. Then, when he had full power, precedent forbade his becoming Shogun because he was not highborn. Advisers suggested a lesser title, the old *Kuambaku*, or Regent; but again precedent stood in his way, for none but the famous Fujiwara clan had ever held that high office.

Hideyoshi promptly resorted to adoption to clear the obstacle. The illustrious Fujiwara family, forebears of the Mitsuis, was now in straitened circumstances. Pedigree was their only asset. They were content to adopt the low-born Monkey Face, for he now had more than half the country under his absolute rule and excellent chances for getting the rest. To overcome any further objection on the Fujiwaras' part, Hideyoshi did a little genealogical research in his own mind and announced that his mother was a descendant of a collateral branch of the Fujiwaras, and that she had fled the capital in a previous generation and, reduced to distress and poverty, had married his peasant father. Furthermore, Hideyoshi maintained, she had conceived him before her marriage, and he was by all odds partly Fujiwara.

A long argument ensued at court, principally between nobles who disputed the headship of the Fujiwara family. Someone had to give the formal consent for the adoption. The contestants brought in their family heirlooms and drearily compared genealogies for hours, seeking to distinguish between the main and branch families. Hideyoshi was attentive enough for a time, but finally his impatience overcame him and he stalked out of the room announcing that to settle the dispute he would take a name of his own, and they could settle the adoption question to suit themselves. The monkey-faced one chose Toyotomi for his family name, and the Emperor formally bestowed it upon him. Hideyoshi then took office as *Kuambaku.*

The stories of Hideyoshi and his precedent-breaking regency are endless. His building of the colossal image of Buddha at Kyoto to rival the huge bronze statue still standing at Kamakura was typical of his grandiose accomplishments. He was in too much of a hurry to have it cast in bronze. He ordered it made of wood and blackened with lacquer. Twenty thousand bushels of oyster shells were requisitioned to go into the image, and the services of 62,700 men were levied upon the feudal lords. The men were divided into thirteen groups of 5,000 to work a month each. Soon after the image was completed, the great earthquake of 1596 leveled it. The disgruntled Hideyoshi impatiently shot an arrow into the crumbled remains, crying: "Look at the expense with which I built you, and you cannot defend even your own temple!"

An ardent follower of the tea-drinking ceremony, he held a famous ten-day tea party at Kitano, issuing a state ordinance inviting the attendance of all people, irrespective of rank, and including "foreigners, if they be men or women of artistic taste or devoted to the tea ceremony." His Osaka castle, built by 80,000 workmen in three years, still stands in part a huge monument to the largeness of Hideyoshi and a symbol of the new era he introduced.

For it was Hideyoshi who first conceived of Japan as a nation that ought to take its place in the world rather than be forever a battleground for rival military chiefs. There had been other "unifiers" before him, notably Nobunaga, but their motives for conquest lay largely in the direction of self-aggrandizement rather than unity as a nation. Nor did the visions of the other unifiers go beyond the Empire's horizon.

Hideyoshi adopted an aggressive foreign trade policy, sending ships bearing his prized vermilion stamp to Macao, the Philippines, China, Cambodia, Annam, Siam and Formosa. By his encouragement of trade, and demonstration of its profits, he converted the armada of Japanese pirates that had been harassing the China coast into a first-rate commercial fleet. A Japanese expedition of twenty-six ships went to the Philippines early in Hideyoshi's regency and attempted to establish a trading outpost. But the Spanish, already settled there, turned their warships on them and drove off the Japanese after a fierce battle. It is recorded in Spanish accounts that the Japanese fought hand-to-hand so valiantly, as they came over the sides of the men-of-war, that the Spanish resorted to oiling the muzzles of their cannon so the Japanese could not grip them. Other Japanese expeditions returned to gain new footholds, and for a time Hideyoshi seriously considered a military expedition to take over the Philippines at one stroke. But an invasion of Korea, nearer home, with the object of improving trade relations and communications with China, diverted him at the time; and the Japanese adventure in the Philippines was left to run a more leisurely course.

Meanwhile, at home the problem of Christianity was approaching a crux. For the first five years of his rule Hideyoshi, like Nobunaga, had turned a tolerant eye on Christianity, even permitting his son to embrace the new creed. Then, almost overnight, Hideyoshi turned on the Christians.

A wide variety of reasons has been adduced as to the cause of Hideyoshi's precipitate change of heart. One missionary historian suggests Hideyoshi was incensed because he could get no Christian convert to enter his private seraglio of three hundred women which he maintained at Osaka. But there were many weightier reasons, and Hideyoshi undoubtedly "possessed the gift of measuring with precision the strength of offense or defense that a given combination of men or things would develop under certain contingencies." An opportunity for exercising that gift was undoubtedly at hand. Hideyoshi overlooked none of the sectarian rivalry that had begun to manifest itself in Japan. As has been stated, the Pope in 1585 vested the sole right to preach in Japan with the Jesuits. The Franciscans, jealous of the spiritual monopoly held by the Jesuits, arrived in Japan in 1593 with an embassy sent up from the Philippines by the Spanish Governor-General there. The Franciscans got around the Papal Bull by pretending they were ambassadors, not missionaries; but once they arrived the field appeared too tempting.

The Franciscans, in fact, had no sooner landed than they began saying mass and preaching to street crowds. Said the Governor of the capital to Hideyoshi: "I fear those priests who call themselves ambassadors intend both to preach and baptize like the rest." "They won't," the Regent retorted in anger, "if they be wise; for if they do I'll make examples of them." Thereupon Hideyoshi issued orders expressly directed against the Franciscans' preaching. The orders were ignored, and the friars happily continued their labors — for Hideyoshi, intent upon his Korean invasion, forgot them. More and more Franciscans came to Japan, and services soon were being conducted openly in Kyoto, Osaka and Nagasaki.

Then came a further "incident" that led to seclusion. A Spanish galleon, the *San Felipe*, was caught in a typhoon and disabled off the coast of Tosa. The Tosa men promptly boarded the ship and took possession. The captain protested in vain against such a violation of international law. Then, thinking to overawe his adversaries, he produced a map of the world and pointed out Spain's vast possessions, with the warning that his capture would be avenged. The Tosa clansmen, who distinctly had no reputation for quailing in front of threats, were impressed, but not in the way the captain desired. How, they asked in wonderment, did a nation or King go about such business of winning new territories beyond the seas?

To this the captain replied in words famous not only for their immediate consequences, but as a formula followed by white imperialists from the earliest times to the twilight of empires: "Our kings begin by sending into the countries they wish to conquer priests, who induce the people to embrace our religion; and when these have made considerable progress, troops are dispatched who combine with the new Christians, and then our kings have not much trouble in accomplishing the rest."

The Tosa clansmen knew they had something there, and they made all haste to report the exact words to Hideyoshi. It may or may not have been an eye-opener for that statesman, but certainly on hearing the report he bethought himself of first the Jesuits and now the Franciscans loosed upon his country. He burst into a great rage, and as an example condemned to death twenty-four Christians, six of them priests and the rest native converts. The tips of their ears were cut off and they were crucified, in a manner representing Japanese refinement of the Roman method, at Nagasaki on February 5, 1597.

It was the first of a long series of Christian persecutions. Japan feared Christianity not as a creed, but as the precursor of an unpredictable force — the wholesale descent of barbarians upon their beloved nation. She tried to drive out the

Christians; and when it became difficult to distinguish Christians from ordinary foreigners, she went to the extreme and drove them all from her country, in edicts promulgated over a period of years, turning her back upon the world and deliberately choosing the life of a hermit nation. For two hundred and fifty years, a nation of thirty million persons closed its doors, "the world forgetting and by the world forgot."

It was a seclusion that set Japan back — and put the Mitsuis ahead. Complete political metamorphosis was achieved within one hundred years after the first foreigner reached Japan in 1542. The nation now entered upon an amazing period of tranquillity and internal development, a period unique in the histories of the great powers of today. It was a period ideal for the development of the House of Mitsui.

Chapter IV

TWO STRONG=WILLED WOMEN

画 IN THE ECONOMIC VER-
tigo that seized the country immediately upon its seclusion
and forced suspension of foreign trade, the Mitsuis began
to emerge. It was a period that saw a feudal agricultural economy break down and give way to a mercantile economy more
dependent on usury than on a healthy development of domestic trade. This mercantile economy in turn inaugurated
an artificial capitalism that could not be maintained without
reopening the country.

The seclusion era of 1638–1853 was ideal for the founding
of the Mitsui family fortune, based as it was on mercantile
and trade-usury enterprise. Historically, the rôle of the Mitsuis
in this period is comparable to those hooded figures in the
classical drama of the country. The mechanics of the Japanese
stage were such that the presence of attendants or property
men sometimes was necessary on the stage in full view of the
audience. Japanese formalists of the drama were severely
obedient to the verities, and this was a problem solved by
typical procedure. A system was evolved whereby the stage
attendants were garbed in black, supposedly an invisible color,
and wore peculiarly shaped hoods that concealed their heads
and faces. In such dress they might appear openly on the stage
and by common agreement the audience would not see them.
They would bob up from behind hedges and hand the actor
a "prop," or assist in changing a costume, move furniture, and
rearrange falling trees. In the event an actor was "killed" in

the progress of the play, the hooded attendant would slip out to the foreground and lower a small black hand-curtain between the prone body and the audience, to allow the "corpse" to rise and make his exit still covered by the curtain. These veiled persons became popularly known as *kurombo*, or "blacks." What they did was seen but not looked at. The Mitsuis became the "blacks" of the later seclusion period.

When Japan was closed to the outside world in 1638, the Mitsui family was living in Ise Province. They were still of the patrician, or warrior, caste; but they had renounced the sword and were living upon what they had salvaged from their defeat at the hands of Oda Nobunaga in the campaign in Omi Province, their old home to the northward. Takayasu Mitsui, head of the family, having been spared by Nobunaga, on moving to Ise Province had ordained that the family take no further part in Japan's civil wars.

These wars now were at an end, and the *Pax Tokugawana* had set in. When Takayasu died, his son Sokubei succeeded to the headship of the family.

It was the bald-headed, fat-faced Sokubei Mitsui who launched the family upon its commercial career. Had he not taken a drastic step at the propitious opening of the Tokugawa era, the Mitsuis might have sat back on their haunches through succeeding generations, poor but proud, and wound up as army men or second-rate politicians of modern Japan.

The Mitsuis had migrated from Omi, famous for its early peddlers, and their new home province was scarcely less known for its small merchants. The Omi peddlers had established a reputation for wandering. They were thrifty, energetic and enterprising. They formed an association for the purpose of improving the roads over which they traveled and establishing their rights on those roads, permitting others to use them only for a fee. A proverb of the times was that the "carrying-pole of Omi men was worth 1,000 ryo of gold," which meant that these small entrepreneurs would rather shoulder a pole loaded at both ends with merchandise, making their tortuous way over upland roads to sell their wares, than to own 1,000 ryo and remain comfortably at home.

The reputation of Omi and Ise men reached the ears of the Tokugawa Shogun, then establishing his new capital at Yedo (the old name for Tokyo) in the eastern part of the Empire, and it was only natural that he chose them to come to Yedo and set up shop.

Humble and obedient, they flocked to the capital; and, by ironical fate, within fifty years had so penetrated the economic state that the Shogun's own feudal lords as well as the Government itself were caught in the toils of the system they evolved — a self-invited incubus for Japan's ruling powers.

Sokubei Mitsui was alive to the trend of his times. He looked about him and saw Ise Province almost denuded of merchants and tradesmen, now launched upon prosperous careers in Yedo. By the time the present moats of the Imperial Palace in Tokyo were laid down, the Ise merchants had so thronged the capital that shop curtains stamped with the characters Ise-ya (Ise House) were waving in the breeze from almost every block in Yedo.

Sokubei made several trips to Yedo and what he saw there fortified a decision that was forming in his mind. Something of home-town — or home-province — pride must have stirred him. The Japanese, always realists with their epigrams, had a saying of the time that the commonest things to be found in

Yedo were Ise houses and dog manure. Still wearing the two swords of the samurai, Sokubei was received, with some wonderment on his part, in the homes of the Ise merchants, rivaling the richest establishments set up by the feudal lords themselves.

When Sokubei returned to his home town, Matsuzaka, he took the step that started the Mitsuis on their way.

"With remarkable moral fortitude," says a sparse record of the family's beginning, "he decided to abandon all rank and class and enter a commercial career."

The "remarkable moral fortitude" necessary for such a step lay in the fact that a wide gulf still separated the merchant caste and the rank that Sokubei was giving up. Nobunaga had successfully demonstrated that a man of low estate might rise to the highest, but he had given neither hint nor example of the more difficult and almost unprecedented action of stepping from high estate to low. Society had crystallized into a rigid system of ranks and there was little passing between. Highest were the old "court families," or *kuge* — those who, in the belief of the Japanese, had descended from Heaven with the ancestors of the first Emperor. The Fujiwara, from whom the Mitsuis were descended, had held such rank; but now the court families, congregated at Kyoto with the secluded Emperor, had no landed estates and lived on pensions granted by the Shogun, or on petty revenues still accorded the Imperial House.

Next in rank stood the daimio, or feudal barons, who had extensive landholdings; and then the samurai, or hereditary fighting men who had been granted the right to carry two swords. The samurai lived on dispensations from the feudal lords, who maintained them as small standing armies, or as warriors who might be called up for fighting in emergencies.

Not all of samurai rank, of course, were actually fighting men, for the rank extended upward from the warrior, to include all of good family, descendants of warriors and several classes of retainers that lay somewhat loosely between daimio and the fighting men.

Below the samurai, in order came the farmers and artisans and then the merchants. It is noteworthy that the farmers and artisans stood above the merchants because they produced, whereas the merchants simply dealt and profited by the products of others. Actually many samurai particularly in the South were farmers, but they looked with the utmost contempt on the tradesmen. The samurai class was encouraged by its leaders to despise money and all forms of commercial transactions. One celebrated representative of the class, Takeda Shingen, issued an order forbidding his samurai even to discuss matters relating to purchases or sales outside his family circle.

In the social scale, the merchants stood lowest but one — the Eta, who were the real outcasts. They were the people who handled dead bodies: the skinners, tanners, leather dressers, gravediggers and undertakers. They owed their low position to the fact that the Buddhist religion prohibited the eating of animals as food.

But, as we have seen, the hundred years of embryonic foreign and domestic trade, prior to the Seclusion Period, had begun to better the position of the merchants. By the time of the Tokugawa usurpation of 1603 the merchants, although their social niche was unchanged, were beginning to pull themselves up by their boot-straps. They were getting their hands on money, and were learning how to handle it to their own profit.

*   *   *

All this, Sokubei Mitsui took into consideration when he decided to enter the commercial class. But what would he sell? Again, his trip to Yedo helped him decide. While in the capital, he was struck with the sensuous living that had taken possession of the idle feudal lords and their retainers who were required to live there certain portions of the year. Sokubei visited the Yoshiwara, Japan's most famous district of licensed prostitution, which had been started in 1590 when Yedo was still an embryo city. He saw on all sides evidences of wild drinking, licentious reveling, and luxurious eating. He talked with his merchant friends from Ise Province, and came to the conclusion the most profit and quickest turnover were to be had by dealing in sake.

Summoning members of his family about him, Sokubei gravely took off his two swords and ceremoniously announced he was to become a commoner.

"The Mitsuis," his proclamation began, "are a proud and old family, descended from the Fujiwaras whose ancestor stood on the right side of the Heavenly Grandchild when he was commanded by the Sun Goddess to go to the land of the Luxurious Reed and establish an everlasting rule. . . ."

He traced the heritage of the family and its vicissitudes down through the centuries of civil strife that had culminated in the Battle of Sekigahara. He recounted its defeat in war at the hands of Nobunaga, and recalled within his own memory the forced migration from Omi Province to Ise.

In the future of the Tokugawa Shogunate he expressed the utmost faith.

"A great peace is at hand," said Sokubei. "The Shogun rules with firmness and justice at Yedo. No more will man be required to live by the sword. I have seen in Yedo that great profit can be made in the field of commerce and that it can be made an honorable profit. I have seen in Yedo the merchants being accepted in the highest position, sharing the confidences of the great daimio and by lending them money putting even the mightiest under their obligation."

He called attention to the low fortunes of the Mitsuis at that time and avowed he saw no chance of betterment so long as they clung to their caste and depended for livelihood upon the rice-doles they rated.

"The Mitsuis," he said, "must get money" — a startling pronouncement, almost heresy, for one of his rank. "We can get money only by entering the field of trade. That I propose to do. As a commoner, I shall brew sake and shoyu sauce, and we will prosper."

Sake is a fermented rice drink that must have existed in Japan from the very earliest times, judging from the fact that ancient religious rituals contain frequent reference to its use. It is still the national drink and in spite of its generally low alcoholic content — from eleven to fifteen per cent — it is a rather heady tipple for the Japanese, more so than for Westerners. It is normally served hot, before and with meals, although in recent years an effort has been made to introduce a cold sake to compete with the rising consumption of beer. In taste, it baffles comparison with Western drinks, but Chamberlin's classic description is still as good as any. It reminded him of a weak sherry that had been kept in a beer bottle.

Shoyu is a sauce made of fermented wheat and soya beans, with salt and vinegar added. It is a standard condiment that adds piquancy to many of the flat and tasteless Japanese dishes. Western epicures who have had plenty of time to explore the native foods of Japan have found few worth importation, but foreign experimenters in sauces were quick to discover that

HACHIROBEI MITSUI AND HIS WIFE JU-SAN

(From a Contemporary Painting)

Japan's shoyu made an excellent base for their own sauce products.

Sokubei Mitsui called his shop *Echigo-ya*, or "Echigo House," in honor of his father Takayasu, who had held the nominal title of Lord of Echigo before he removed to Ise Province.

While it is true that Sokubei Mitsui launched the family on a commercial career, he is not looked upon today by the Mitsuis as the Founder of the business House. That honor and reverence is reserved for his youngest son, Hachirobei.*

In all truth, Sokubei cannot be credited with any more than a firm resolution to throw off all rank and enter the merchant class. He picked his field, but once in it he found he knew uncomfortably little about commerce. But he was fortunate in having for a wife one of two remarkable women who had much to do with the destiny of the House of Mitsui.

Sokubei's wife, whom he married after moving to Ise Province, fortunately was of the merchant class herself. She was the daughter of one of the richest men of the province. Her family name was Nagai, but her given name was lost to the records when she became converted to Buddhism in middle age and took the religious name Shuho.

Shuho married Sokubei Mitsui when she was thirteen years old. From her father she had inherited decision, firmness of character, and something of a commercial instinct, but apparently there was no financial help forthcoming from her

---

* Both Sokubei and Hachirobei bore the name Takatoshi but the son became more commonly identified after he entered business as Hachirobei. His posthumous name was Soju Koji, in accordance with the custom of Buddhist priests' giving another appellation immediately after death for inscription on the funeral tablet.

family when her husband set foot on the rocky road of commerce.

When the sake shop of Sokubei was slow in starting, Shuho opened a pawnshop on the same premises. Mitsui business picked up almost immediately, for Matsuzaka was a lively provincial town offering diversion enough to milk visitors of ready cash on short order. Moreover, Shuho instituted the first Mitsui price-slashing of record, by undercutting her pawnshop competitors on interest rates. She not only made the rates inviting, but added a personal touch to the business by listening to the stories of patrons, occasionally serving them a cup of sake from her husband's casks and, in the case of habitual customers, a free meal when they were short of cash.

The Mitsui sake store and pawnshop quickly became one of the most prosperous institutions of the town. Shuho's thrift became a legend of the Mitsuis. In a privately printed pamphlet, *The Life and Deeds of Shuho Taishi,** it is recorded that she was a string-saver. She would pick up bits of string as she walked through the streets, tie them together in a continuous line and accumulate innumerable balls of twine. She converted a bowl with the bottom broken out into a rain pipe funnel. A damaged ladle was converted into a teapot stand — and so on. "To her all things were useful," says her biographer.

Shuho's influence in leading her husband, and the Mitsuis ever afterward, into business is debatable. Her anonymous biographer asserts that she "encouraged her husband to open some trading business so that the family might prosper," but there is considerable evidence that Sokubei Mitsui independently had made up his mind to enter business.

---

* It refers euphemistically to Shuho as "the real Founder of the Family," partly substantiating a popular legend in Japan that the House of Mitsui was founded by a woman.

Sokubei Mitsui died in 1633, at the age of forty-five. He left his wife with four sons and four daughters. From then on, until her death at the age of eighty-seven, Shuho assumed full responsibilities as head of the House, and saw to it that the Mitsui sons stayed in commerce.

With what savings she could accumulate from the brewing business, Shuho waited until the eldest son, Saburozaemon, reached a responsible age; and then she packed him off for Yedo, where he was instructed to open a small drygoods shop. The other boys she kept at home and trained in the precepts laid down by their dead father, who in effect had told them to "get money" and "work together."

It was early apparent to the strong-willed Shuho that the youngest son showed the most promise. This was Hachirobei. When Hachirobei reached the age of fourteen, Shuho, with no thought of a mother's sacrifice, dispatched him to Yedo to enter his brother's shop for further training in the new business code that was flowering in the capital. Shuho outlived her husband by forty years. Always exerting a firm, guiding hand on her sons, before she died she saw Hachirobei successfully started on the business and banking career that was to lay the foundations of the Mitsui family fortune.

Hachirobei even as a boy showed quick intuitive ability in the art of handling money. Japan had had copper and silver money, and some gold, as early as the Seventh Century, but not until the Portuguese and Spaniards introduced foreign trade did its general circulation receive any stimulus. Rice was the common medium of exchange even as the Tokugawas gained the Shogunate, but it was a cumbersome medium. Now the Shoguns, following the example of Hideyoshi and Nobunaga, were minting more money and encouraging its use in business transactions. In Hachirobei's youth, the country seems to have been adequately supplied with metal currency, but there was an unfortunate looseness or fluctuation in its day-to-day value, due to the insistence of certain powerful daimios on coining their own money — a practice subsequently proscribed by the Shogunate.

In Yedo, money was rapidly displacing rice and young Hachirobei watched the operation with instinctive understanding. His eldest brother, Saburozaemon, not content with the profits of a fast turnover in brocades, silk and cotton goods, was tempted to set aside a part of his savings as capital from which small loans could be advanced to temporarily impecunious dignitaries awaiting funds from distant provinces. For these resident feudal lords and their retainers, ready money was a necessary adjunct to the ostentation that became the fad of the capital. Interest rates for such loans were high and the profits substantial, but Hachirobei had an instinctive fear of these loans. It was too easy for the samurai class to default; and in such instances, the low-caste merchant-lender had no recourse in court. But Hachirobei perceived that if the same principles could be utilized in another field, where the risk was less, he could make money.

In the end, Hachirobei and his brother parted company over that issue. The younger boy constantly admonished Saburozaemon against such loans to samurai, but his advice went unheeded — and in later years Hachirobei had the dubious satisfaction of seeing his brother almost bankrupted by an incautious loan to a feudal lord. Hachirobei rushed to his rescue, however, and thus established one of the guiding principles of the House of Mitsui: namely, that one Mitsui rises or falls with the other Mitsuis.

Hachirobei stayed fourteen years in Yedo and then at the age of twenty-eight left the capital to start in business for himself. He returned to his home town of Matsuzaka as his father did a generation before — and modestly set up business as a private moneylender. It was a characteristic bit of shrewdness that sent Hachirobei back to Ise Province to start his career. There he would be surrounded by a commercial class of his own fellows whom he might meet with equity in court and who were good risks in their own small enterprises.

Hachirobei Mitsui remained in Matsuzaka for twenty-three years, accumulating capital and perfecting a commercial *modus operandi* which he applied with unerring skill later in a wider sphere.

Hachirobei married a girl hand-picked by Shuho, the Mitsui matriarch. She was Ju-san, whose domestic virtues are celebrated even today in Japanese school primers. Ju-san was the second Mitsui woman who did so much to shape the course of the family. She was only fifteen years old when she married. Like her mother-in-law, she was the daughter of a wealthy Ise provincial family. Shuho took particular care in training the wife of her favorite son, and the two women formed a strange, purposeful unity in setting the House of Mitsui on a firm foundation.

Ju-san bore six sons for Hachirobei, the forebears of the six main family branches in the modern House of Mitsui. The five other branches were added later.

In 1673, when Hachirobei was fifty-two years old, he packed up his family and moved from Matsuzaka to Kyoto. There, with carefully laid plans, he opened a drygoods store and hung out the famous Mitsui sign. In bold Japanese characters, surmounted by the Mitsui three-bar crest, it read: *Genkin Kakene Nashi*. Translated tersely, this was: "Cash payments and a single price."

The sign, a heavy six-foot slab of *Keyaki* wood, four inches thick, with the characters carved deeply, is preserved in the private Mitsui library in Tokyo today. It is rarely brought out for visitors to inspect.

The two principles emblazoned on the family shingle were drastic innovations. The "single price" precluded all the bargaining which has been seemingly the inalienable birthright of the Oriental from time immemorial. It was an innovation that came to be adopted in time by all Japanese shops and to this day even the most casual visitor to the Orient inevitably returns with one firm impression: that you may haggle over prices everywhere from Suez to Peiping, but once you set foot in Japan you pay the same "single price" that Hachirobei Mitsui introduced to an amazed commercial world two hundred and fifty years ago.

The cash-payment principle utilized the method well-known and widely practised by modern Western retailers. Before the time of the Mitsuis, retail business, at least in the articles in which Mitsuis dealt, was conducted through long-term accounts. Customers therefore had to bear the burden of interest and losses on unpaid bills as well as the normal profit required by the merchant. The Mitsui cash-payment plan permitted marking-down of prices and business flowed into the Mitsui establishment.

Hachirobei introduced still another innovation that met with immediate popular response. He abolished the custom of selling silk and other fabrics in standard lengths, usually sufficient for one kimono. Cloth could be purchased at the Mitsui store from the bolt in any quantities his customers desired.

Soon after he opened his Kyoto shop, Hachirobei, never forgetful of that boom town to the north, Yedo, started a branch at the teeming metropolis. The same business principles he ordained at Kyoto were laid down for his Yedo branch and both became prosperous. Correlating his two shops, he found it advantageous to buy Nishijin brocades at Kyoto and transport them to Yedo, where they were sold at a high profit to the dandies of the capital. The Mitsui store in Yedo, with warehouse added to warehouse until it finally covered a huge area in Suruga-cho, became one of the sights of the city and a favorite theme of the color-print artists who portrayed in the current language of the day the ukiyoe or "the floating world." This was the world of theaters, restaurants, wrestling booths and brothels, with their colorful population of actors, dancers, storytellers, courtesans and bath girls who filled the profligate lives of rich merchants and dissolute samurai.

Within a short time, more than a thousand men and women were employed in the Yedo store under a paternalistic system which permitted a certain amount of profit-sharing among the higher classes of employees, and strict rules governing rest periods, health, sanitation and hygiene for all others. Dormitories were set up, and the private lives of the employees were carefully looked-after. They were coached in proper speech and required to be neat and clean in attire. Another forerunner of modern practice which the Mitsuis introduced was their own system of bookkeeping by double entry.

Mitsui was a pioneer in mercantile advertising, but idealized accounts of the firm's beginning overreach a bit in ascribing to him the reputation of being Japan's first advertiser. This honor seems definitely reserved for a contemporary, one Kinokuni Bunzaemon, a Jack-of-all-trades who made and lost fortunes in a half-dozen different lines.

Bunzaemon went up to Yedo from Kii Province, and started as a dealer in teakettles. Then he tried a small hotel. Both failed and he went back to his home province, where he conceived the scintillating idea of buying up all the *mikan*, or small Japanese oranges, for which his province was noted. He proposed to ship them to Yedo for house-to-house sale. To insure an enthusiastic reception for his oranges he had the forethought to employ a popular song-writer to compose a catchy piece on the theme that old Bunzaemon's orange ship was coming to town soon and that it was something worth waiting for. The song caught on so well that it was sung not only throughout the capital but all over the country — and the "*mikan-buni* song" is still sung in Japan today. Needless to say, a thirsting metropolis was waiting for Bunzaemon's ship, and he sold out his cargo almost overnight for an estimated profit of 50,000 ryo, which would be about $5,000 in today's values.

Such advertising methods proved an eye-opener to the observant Mitsui, opening his dress-goods shop in Yedo. While competitors disdained the romping antics of old Bunzaemon, Hachirobei adopted the same general policy of broadcasting his name, but he was more subtle and covered more ground.

Hachirobei was aware most of his trade was to come from housewives, who customarily do the purchasing for Japanese households. With that in mind, he had made a large stock of the oil-paper umbrellas for which Japan is famous. They not only turn the rain but are picturesque and attractive, and have changed little in design in their long history. Instead of adorning them in the usual delicate brushwork symbols, however, Mitsui had bold characters painted on them advertising Mitsui's shop as a treasure-trove for thrifty buyers. The advertising message, as usual, was topped off with the familiar three-bar

Mitsui crest. On rainy days, or when sudden showers caught shoppers unprepared, each would be given these umbrellas free. When this word spread about, most of Yedo's house-wives managed to be caught in Mitsui's on days that free umbrellas were given out with each trifling purchase. There-after, when it rained, a veritable canopy bearing thousands of Mitsui trade-marks almost covered the capital to the further glorification of the shop.

Theaters, formerly despised as a vulgar pastime, were now attaining brilliance in Yedo and attracting throngs from all classes of society. Mitsui saw a further field for advertising on the stage, and he subsidized playwrights to mention the Mit-sui shop in favorable fashion in the dialogue.

Then, for fair days, Mitsui had wood-block handbills printed, to be pasted up on hoardings, vacant buildings, stone walls or any other surface that would hold them. Mitsui's ad-vertising scheme did much to stimulate the production of the Japanese prints with which the Western world is familiar. Some of Japan's best prints were produced during this period. Hiroshige, one of Japan's greatest artists, was hired by the Mitsuis at a later period to paint their Yedo shop with the mountain, Fujiyama, in the background. That print is a prize of modern collectors.

Chapter V

THE FIRST MITSUI EXCHANGE

~~~ HACHIROBEI MITSUI
established the prototype of the modern Mitsui Bank in Yedo
about ten years before the Bank of England opened for business.

The Mitsui Bank began modestly as a money exchange department in the dress-goods shop that Hachirobei had opened
in the capital as a branch of his Kyoto store. It was customary
at that time for stores of good standing to operate a money
exchange department on the premises, constituting, in effect,
a small private bank. But Mitsui had no idea of remaining a
store banker. In those days exchange houses of two kinds were
operating in Yedo: the *Zeni-ya* dealing only in subsidiary
money, and the *Ryogaye-ya* handling gold and silver, accept-
ing deposits and making loans. The *Ryogaye* houses were the
higher type, and through the influence of the guild system
which already has been described they operated on a monopolistic basis. It was difficult for a newcomer to break into their
circle.

The profession of money-exchanging in Japan dated back
to the beginning of the Fifteenth Century; but while rice
remained the principal medium of exchange, there was not
much business for the money-exchangers. At that early period
the profession was in the hands of peddlers who went about
the market places carrying strings of copper coins with holes
in the center, which they offered in exchange for gold and

silver coins, then in rare circulation, or for packages of gold dust. Small currency transactions of the day were largely in copper coins.

When Yedo became the capital and the migrations of tradesmen to the new boom town set in, the itinerant exchange men flocked in their wake. Then, instead of tramping about the market places they settled down in their own shops and waited for trade to come to them. As the Tokugawas revived and encouraged the guilds of Yedo, the vogue of trade associations spread rapidly to the capital. Hairdressers, saucemakers, carpenters, bathhouse keepers, artisans, tradesmen and merchants of all classes were organizing. It was, incidentally, a day of horizontal unions. There is on record a complaint filed with the Shogunate by the sawyers, who charged the carpenters were sawing too many of their own timbers in building up the capital. The exchange men were caught up in the sweep toward guilds and six hundred of them formed their own organization which was duly licensed and no unlicensed person was permitted to operate an exchange.

Though of independent origin the operations of the Yedo exchanges soon fell under the influence of those in Osaka which had had an earlier start. The people of Osaka and vicinity, the so-called Kamigata people, seem to have had a special bent toward commerce through all eras in Japanese history. The economist Takekoshi calls them "the Jews of Japan." He points out that they had the oldest civilization in the nation, and the provinces in which they lived long had been the most densely populated. For centuries they had seen their territory overrun by clashing factions in continual warfare. They saw the Imperial Family thrust into seclusion and one ruling power give way to another. On all this they turned their backs and, never resorting to violence, always obedient to the regency in control, they spent their time developing their talents for trade.

Then during the hundred years Japan was in full contact with the foreigners, the Kamigata people were strategically located for observation and acquiring the finer points of commerce as practised by the Westerners. When Japan isolated herself and foreign trade was cut off, it was only natural this class should turn its attention toward internal trade.

The first manifestation in this direction was the development of Osaka's flourishing rice exchange. To meet the needs of a city of 280,000, Hideyoshi, the regent of the preceding generation, summarily ordered a feudal chief, Lord Maeda of Kaga, whose landholdings included large rice-growing areas, to supply 100,000 *koku* of rice a year for Osaka. Lord Maeda could produce the rice, but he had little knowledge of economics. He, in turn, called upon a merchant to work out a system for handling the rice he poured in to the market and determining the prices for which it was to be sold.

The first rice exchange grew out of the merchant's efforts, and within a decade there were 1,300 rice brokers and some fifty money exchangers operating on that exchange. The money-exchangers took the name *kake-ya* or "agents." Their functions rapidly evolved into those of private bankers. The feudal lords would forward their rice and other commodities to the agents and entrust them with the business of disposing of the product on the exchange at the highest price. Then the agents would hold the proceeds or forward them by installments either to Yedo where the landowners were in periodic residence or to their home fiefs. At the end of each year they would render full accounts, deducting from two to four per cent as commission. It was a position of trust and confidence, and the merchant-bankers established valuable reputations as dependable bankers for the wealthier samurai. Sometimes in reward for exceptional services the feudal lords would grant them a hereditary pension or allowance such as minor samurai received. Occasionally an official title went with the grant. The Mitsuis in time became among the best known of the Osaka commission-merchant-bankers, controlling the finances of whole provinces.

In the middle of the Seventeenth Century Osaka was particularly fortunate in having a governor who sought to increase the element of credit in commerce and promote wholesale transactions. With a view toward improving the conditions of the money market, he selected ten leading money-exchange merchants to exercise control over all the others in that business and oversee transactions in general. These ten, ex officio, became accountants for the Shogunate; and at the same time they carried on a general loan business on the side. In recognition of their services, the Shogun permitted them to wear two swords and exempted them from taxation and from being liable to render public services to the city. They were called junin ryogaye or "ten exchange merchants," and formed an association among themselves, with power to permit or prohibit the establishment of new exchange houses in their city. Under them was a guild of twenty-two exchanges, whose members readily honored each others' vouchers — to the general speeding-up of commercial transactions. Bills of exchange in kind were passing as readily as currency or coin, and advances could always be obtained against them from pawnbrokers.

The exchange houses then opened a central currency mart for purely monetary transactions. This was called the Kin-gin Baibai Tachiai-sho, or "Meeting-place for Sale and Purchase of Gold and Silver." Business began at ten o'clock and closed at about noon each day. The period of the business was determined by lighting what the Japanese called "a slow-match," which burned for about two hours. When it went out, the exchange closed. The practice has long since ceased; but to this day the closing hour on stock exchanges in Tokyo and Osaka is called *hinawa*, or "slow-match hour." Those early exchange dealers probably never heard of the Royal Exchange in London, but by interesting coincidence in the same century the British were lighting a candle and the period that it burned determined the length of trading time on the London exchange. The caretakers of the exchange hall were called *mizukata*, or water-men, because in their impatience to get about their work they would boldly invade the premises and sprinkle water on the floor as soon as the slow-match burned out, to get rid of traders who lingered to carry on private deals.

Transactions in gold and silver on the exchange were in actual cash, so at first there were no frequent or big fluctuations. Gold prices usually climbed precipitately in June and December of each year because of nation-wide religious festivals when the public needed ready money. It was not long, however, before speculation set in. The debasement of gold and silver coin by the Shogunate in an effort to replenish the Government Treasury gave impetus to speculative transactions. The Osaka rice exchange already was showing the way. The commission merchants operating on this exchange had learned to rig the market. When there was no contest between buyers and sellers on dull market days, these merchant bankers would "jiggle" the rate of exchange between rice and silver for an occasional coup. This naturally resulted in flyers in gold and silver by speculative merchants.

The evolution of simple rice sales into a widespread system

of trading in margins and futures in this early day, and in this country completely cut off from foreign intercourse, reflects the maturing commercial mind of the Japanese. When the Osaka rice exchange opened, the mechanics of transactions were relatively simple. As shipments of grain arrived, notices were posted inviting bids up to a specified date for each shipment. On the date set, the bids were opened in the presence of agents and exchange officials and the highest bidder was proclaimed. Thereupon he was required to make a deposit for his purchase and stamp his seal on a statement of the transaction. Ten days of grace then were allowed for payment of the rest of the money, unless the bidder had a bad credit rating. In such case, he was required to pay immediately. Failure to pay within the grace period brought confiscation of the purchase as well as of the deposit, and the dealer would be dropped from the exchange. Proper payment, however, entitled the buyer to a ticket, which permitted delivery in such amounts as he chose up to the third month of the second year after the sale. There was no fee for storage.

The exchange in time began to attract such shipments that large granaries were built to accommodate the dealers. With the grain safely stored and the offerings increasing, it was a natural step for the agents to begin to deal in shipments that were to arrive after periodic harvests, in other words to deal in futures. The next step was to defer cash payments for delivery tickets and merely register the transaction in the exchange records. The money exchanges operating in close connection with the grain exchange readily received the tickets and made advances against them.

Speculative operations spread on both exchanges and frequently caused crashes. Just as in 1929 in America, when market prices rose to an abnormally high figure, public opinion in Japan in the Seventeenth Century rebelled against the speculators; the Shogunate was obliged to intervene and issue orders to curb them. Several of the more daring brokers were arrested and tried. Largely because of lack of legal precedent they were acquitted, but the Central Government forbade dealings in margins, required transactions on the money market to be done in cash only, prohibited all speculative transactions and compelled traders to have a license from the governing authorities.

This was in 1696, two hundred and thirty-seven years before Roosevelt established the Securities Exchange Commission in America.

The exchange houses operating in Yedo at the time the Mitsuis started banking took on the same general characteristics and organization form as those of Osaka. The houses of the Ryogaye type soon were performing most of the functions of the modern Western bank, with the additional practice of issuing a form of trade voucher which played an important part in the commercial transactions of the period.

The voucher was an expediency that arose from necessity as far back as the fourteenth century. It first made its appearance in the Yoshino market of Yamato Province. Transportation of copper money was so arduous in that hilly district the merchants began to substitute written receipts or vouchers which gained ready circulation. Next came a type of joint voucher or kumiai-fuda which were signed by several persons, any one of whom was pledged to redeem it. In 1636, this type of trade voucher gained official recognition when the third Tokugawa Shogun selected thirty substantial merchants and formed them into three guilds, each permitted to issue vouchers. He

GENNOSUKE MITSUI
Vice-President of Mitsui Gomei Kaisha

GENEYEMON MITSUI
Late Vice-President of Mitsui Gomei Kaisha

improved upon the idea, however, by requiring each guild to deposit a certain sum by way of security.

This paper performed all the functions of the modern bank-note, but appears to have no more than a local circulation until Hachirobei Mitsui evolved the idea of a country-wide system of bills of exchange.

Studying his immediate mercantile problems, Mitsui perceived the immense amount of waste motion in the flow of goods and money between Osaka and Yedo. The Mitsuis and other Yedo merchants were buying their wares in Osaka and Kyoto and transporting money there, while the Shogunate was moving tax collections and other moneys from its treasury sub-station in Osaka to Yedo.

This movement of money in two directions involved not only loss of time and transportation expense but risk of highway robbery. The Tokugawas had built a network of good roads to connect with the capital, but they were careful to route them across steep defiles and bridgeless rivers as part of the defense plan of Yedo. In the event of rebellion it would be easier to stand off invading armies, but in times of peace the Tokugawas paid for their caution. Rapid transportation from Osaka required frequent changes of pack-horses and coolies.

Mitsui went to the Shogun's finance ministers with his plan. He would agree on his own responsibility to receive the Shogun's gold and silver collections in Osaka, and repay them to the Government in Yedo within sixty days. The Shogunate thus would be relieved of all expense and risk of transportation, while Mitsui, in return, would have the use of the money for buying goods in the Osaka district where the wholesale markets were operating.

*   *   *

The efficacy of the scheme at length was apparent to the ministers and it was forthwith adopted. For Hachirobei Mitsui it proved a veritable springboard from which he was able to leap into the highest circles of Yedo banking and merchandising.

To carry out the plan, the Shogunate at first selected ten financial agents who were at the head of the exchange guild in Yedo. They were the *Junin-Gumi* or "the union of ten," similar to the Osaka organization. Subsequently, in return for having presented the scheme to the Shogun, the Mitsui firm was added, but instead of joining the "union of ten" the Mitsuis, operating independently, took the name *Ninin-Gumi*, or "two men union," and afterward with the addition of a third branch, the Mitsuis became the *Sanin-Gumi*, or "three-men union," all of which united in time to become the *Mitsui-Gumi*, finally the modern Mitsui Bank.

Successfully launched as a banker, Mitsui now opened a separate exchange house of the *Ryogaye* type next door to his dress-goods shop in Suruga-cho, Yedo. Similar houses were established in Kyoto in 1686 and in Osaka in 1691. The two branch houses were headed by two sons of Hachirobei who thereby established one of the founding principles of the House, the requirement that only members of the Mitsui family could succeed to the headship of the branches. Thus the firm or branch name in each locality became permanent and hereditary, and for a time the respective heads of the branch houses customarily took the same first name. The hereditary chief in Kyoto was Saburosuke, and in Osaka, Gennosuke.

In the merchandising end, Hachirobei Mitsui made use of his bills of exchange in this fashion: He took the cash turned over to him in Osaka by the Central Government and purchased goods for his stores. The bills to the government were repayable in sixty days, but it required only fifteen or twenty days to move his wares from Osaka to Yedo. Within a short time, Mitsui, having demonstrated his reliability, was granted one hundred and fifty days between collection and repayment. Now he was able to make short-term loans at a remunerative interest rate with the Government's money. In addition, he was able to undersell other Yedo stores by his cash-price, quick-turnover system which fitted in very nicely with his collaboration with the Government.

Mitsui's cash-sales plan worked to his profit in still another direction. Yedo's stores previously operated on a credit basis largely because the Tokugawas paid off their thousands of retainers only three times a year. Between times, the Tokugawa samurai, as well as others dependent upon provincial nobles, supplied their needs from merchants who would give them credit, but added a good percentage to prices to cover the risk of bad debts. When the Mitsuis demonstrated that cash sales could bring lower prices without sacrifice of profit, other merchants gradually adopted the practice. The samurai accordingly were forced to find more cash between paydays, and had to resort to short-term loans. In effect, the Mitsui banker-merchant plan had them coming and going.

The Mitsuis then introduced so-called "wrapped money" to quicken the flow of commerce. They would wrap up uniform quantities of gold or silver coins in the durable paper which the Japanese already were adept in making. On the cover would appear the Mitsui signature and crest, together with a notation of the amount of the contents. The tiny parcels very much resembled the present-day usage of banks in handling coins in quantity. But modern coin packages are opened. The early reputation of the Mitsuis was such that their wrapped money was rarely opened and counted. It was readily accepted and exchanged at face value.

Early Mitsui records still treasured in the family museum reveal numerous other elements of modern banking practice. Terms that might be translated as "the shop's foundation" meant working capital; "cellar silver" and "lay-aside silver" were reserve funds, and "business profit toll" was clearly interest on loans.

Meanwhile, the evils of Japan's debased coinage were being eliminated, helping to establish all banking on a firmer foundation.

The genius who discovered for Japan the principles of Gresham's Law — "bad money drives out good" — was Arai Hakuseki, who was born soon after the Great Fire in Yedo in 1657. In memory of that conflagration he was named "Arai," which means "spark." As a youth he was thoroughly educated in the Chinese classics, and for a time operated a private school in the capital. Then he became tutor of the Tokugawa heir, nephew of the Shogun, Tsunayoshi. When Tsunayoshi died in 1709, his nephew, Iyenobu, succeeded him. Iyenobu named Hakuseki his Chief Councillor, and entrusted him with most of the administrative duties.

Hakuseki had never heard of Sir Thomas Gresham, the financial adviser called in by the English Government in 1551 to raise the value of the pound sterling on the "bourse" of Antwerp and discharge the debts of Edward VI. But Hakuseki and Gresham were faced with somewhat the same predicament — and Gresham didn't invent Gresham's Law. The principle that the worst form of money in circulation regulates the value of the whole currency and drives out all other forms is a timeless one. It had been set forth centuries earlier by Copernicus, and Gresham simply demonstrated it as he started financial house-cleaning in England.

To meet the problem of debased coinage and consequential high prices, Hakuseki applied a fundamentally sound and thoroughly modern line of reasoning. It was all the more remarkable because Japan was then in the transition period that saw rice as a medium of exchange being supplanted by metal money under pressure of the Central Government. Europe in the Middle Ages underwent the same transition but rice held on as the exchange medium in Japan longer than similar commodities in Europe, because the irrigation system behind Japan's rice crops operated for more stability. There was less fluctuation in supply than in Europe, where the size of crops was more dependent upon weather.

Under Tsunayoshi, debasement had been carried out on the fallacious theory coins received their value solely from the official stamp they bore. Hakuseki quickly perceived that coins themselves were being dealt in because they were as negotiable as the merchandise they purchased. He reasoned therefore that in commercial transactions the value of the coins had to be equal to the value of the goods for which they were exchanged and that coins were used in trade not only because of convenience but because they were priced goods. It was his contention, in other words, that the gold piece that passed for one ryo did so not because it was a coin so stamped but because it contained gold worth one ryo in the market. Consequently Hakuseki had the gold and silver pieces recoined with metal in them that was enough to make them pass in the field of commerce but not of such quality as to cause hoarding. Within a short time the currency of the Empire was again on a sound basis.

By this time, during the latter Seventeenth Century, besides conducting the exchange work for the Government the banking house of Mitsui was building up a sound private-banking business and was in a position to supply capital to many promising enterprises. Loans to feudal chiefs, however, were still ruled out by Hachirobei — who held by his decision that they were poor risks. (One economic historian of the day has estimated that by 1700 the debts of the feudal lords alone totaled one hundred times all the actual money in the country.) However high their social and military standing, the credit rating of the daimio in the Mitsui black book was nil, for the Mitsuis well knew the merchant class had no standing in court against two-sworded men of the Empire.

Hachirobei's own observations on the folly of lending to the non-producing class were recorded by his son, Takafusa Mitsui, in his book *Chonin Koken-roku* which circulated for many years in manuscript among business families in Kyoto and Osaka. Codifying some of the business axioms of his father, Takafusa wrote:

It is a common practice of the feudal lords nowadays to tempt the merchants, when the latter are well-to-do and able to lend as much money as the lords are anxious to borrow, by making them a yearly allowance of rice, and even granting them samurai rank. All goes well so long as the merchants are prosperous, but directly they are unable to lend more money, the lords change their attitude, grudging them the allowance of rice, or stopping it altogether.

In fact, the feudal lords are very much like anglers, decoying fish with destructive bait, and that is why I warn my fellow-merchants not to be desirous to become purveyors for feudal lords, receiving from them a yearly allowance of rice, or the temporary rank of samurai. The sole business of a samurai is to know the military art and gain a victory over the enemy. However desirous the merchant may be to take advantage of the samurai's lack of economic knowledge, to make money out of him and withdraw just at the right moment, it is very difficult, or rather impossible, for the merchant to get the better of the samurai in their commercial or business warfare, for the samurai is at the head of the four classes of people, and his wisdom and sagacity are far above those of the merchant. [Was this a bit of sop to rank?] He is acute enough to see into the mind of the merchant, and, feigning to be duped by him, borrows as much money as he can, and when he finds he has squeezed the merchant dry, he refuses payment of the money he has borrowed.

In business warfare between samurai and merchant, the samurai handles a very sharp sword and the merchant has only a bamboo spear. The result can easily be foreseen. Only a fool would believe that the feudal lords would permit the merchant to make unreasonable profit. These lords promise to send their rice to the merchants in Osaka, and on that security borrow money in advance. For the first year or two they appear to be willing to deposit more and more money in advance from the merchants. Never will they pay back their debts by sending the promised amount of rice to the merchants, but sending their rice to another quarter where they expect accommodation, they refuse the payment to the merchants from whom they have already borrowed large sums, and by whose help they have been extricated from financial difficulties. The *Book of Strategy* instructs us that a good general is careful to be informed about the conditions not only of his own army but also of the opposing army, and therefore the merchant is greatly mistaken if he deals with samurai as he would with his fellow merchants.

There is an abundance of evidence to bear out Hachirobei's advice to his descendants. Under the Shogunate, samurai who repudiated debts escaped punishment, but ill-fared the merchants who borrowed too extensively to extend their businesses. There is of record the case of a Kyoto merchant operating a wholesale business with goods imported by the Dutch at Nagasaki. Finding himself temporarily hard-pressed, the merchant borrowed 1,500 *kwan* of silver. He was unable to pay when the loan was due, and the moneylender, having influential connections, succeeded in bringing the case to court. The court verdict, with a reasoning typical of many later commercial cases in litigation, was that no mere merchant should ever have borrowed so large a sum. Exemplary punishment therefore was decreed, — and the borrower was crucified. Still another Kyoto merchant, similarly bankrupt, was beheaded and his head exposed in the streets as a warning.

It was years before the moneylenders of commoner rank established any general standing in the courts. The magistrates themselves had no law precedents to guide them and were reluctant to take cases arising from money difficulties. Accustomed to handling disputes over rice fields, rice taxes and payments in kind, they were slow to assimilate the complexities brought on by the metal money economy. Early records of magistrates' courts reveal that they were frequently exchanging letters of consultation among themselves concerning the new type of litigation.

One moneylender who had been elevated to samurai rank in return for loans to Lord Mori of Mimasaka Province took his plea to court when the lord repudiated a sizeable debt. He not only failed of any satisfaction, but was severely reprimanded by officials of the Shogun's court for having brought suit against his lord.

As more and more creditors clamored for adjudication, courts urged private settlements on the ground that "Money loans owe their origin to the integrity and mutual fidelity of the parties, and if they continue to exercise those virtues, all such transactions can be privately settled without difficulty and the aid of public officials need not be sought. The recent increase of such suits is due to the absence of generosity and gratitude among lenders and borrowers." *

The Central Government at Yedo finally was obliged to order the courts to accept money cases along with other litigation, and set aside certain periods each year for review of money cases.

However annoying this may have been to the magistrates and however disagreeable the penetration of money economy may have been to moral leaders of the period [Takizawa summarizes], money economy had securely taken root in Japan. By the end of the Genroku Period rice and metals had completely changed their positions. Metal money had become the pivot of the economic life of Japan and it became impossible to live without it, no matter how great an amount of rice one might have in his storehouses. Thus the feudal institutions based upon rice economy were gradually undermined by the new forces brought into action by money and in course of time new institutions were created to take the place of the old.

The Tokugawa Shoguns were not blind to the fact that the rising status of the merchants and moneylenders was menacing the samurai class and tending to fuse the two. The Yedo Government had looked benignly enough upon the profits of commercial houses. But when wealth accumulated to a point where it might prove mischievous and threatening to the peace of the realm, the Shoguns had a way of cracking down. To this end they maintained spies in the larger cities who watched the private lives of wealthy citizens and reported

* From Takizama's "Materials for Study of Private Laws in Old Japan" in the *Transactions of the Asiatic Society.*

on any spectacular flights into higher finance. Iyeyasu, the founder of the Tokugawa line, laying down a course of policy for his successors to follow, had enunciated the principle that whenever any citizen had gained such opulence as to attract attention, the Shogun should impose upon him the task of carrying out some great public work.

The case of the Nawaya brothers of Kyoto provided an example of amusing results of an effort to carry out that injunction. The brothers were moneylenders who by services rendered to a feudal lord had won some rank and took to wearing swords and riding horses down the main streets of Kyoto with spear-carrying servants at their back.

Such ostentation was deemed a proper bit for punishment. The Shogun's court at Kyoto called the brothers before the bar and the Nawayas barely escaped a precipitous and exemplary beheading. Instead, for punishment, they were ordered to make extensive and lasting repairs to one of the main bridges of the town. The brothers, in their joy at escaping the headsman's axe, pitched in on the bridge-repairing job so fulsomely and with such lavish expenditures that they outdid all expectations of the court. For when the bridge was finished the imposing structure became known all about the countryside as "the bridge of the Nawaya brothers." This advertised the business of the Nawaya brothers more than they had counted upon, and within a short time their wealth was climbing back to the danger point. The perplexed court was at the point of summoning the brothers back for what would amount to modern "contempt of court" when the Nawayas stumbled into a 50,000 ryo debt loss which sent them sprawling. Within a year the house was bankrupt — another object lesson for the fledgling House of Mitsui.

Takafusa Mitsui recorded numerous instances in which re-

MITSUI BANKING OFFICE IN YEDO

fusal by feudal nobles to repay loans spelled disaster for their creditors. Some passages in his book are merely terse records of such bankruptcies, but they constituted what was probably Japan's first *Bradstreet's*. Some of the daimio who achieved a very poor credit rating in the Mitsui black book of that early day are ancestors of great industrial families of modern Japan. Takafusa did not hesitate to name two of his uncles, Saburozaemon and Rokuemon, as victims of bad debts, but apparently they were the only two Mitsuis so enmeshed. They had loaned considerable sums with the usual prospect of profitable interest to Lord Tokugawa of Kii and Lord Hosokawa of Higo. Certainly the Tokugawa loan seemed safe enough as the lord was a close relative of the Shogun but even he exercised the prerogative of high caste and defaulted on the Mitsuis. The family fortune was nicked for a time, but Hachirobei, the head of the House, rushed to the rescue of his brothers and preserved the solvency of the family.

Hachirobei Mitsui, business genius of the House, died in 1694 at the age of seventy-three. He had lived to see the Mitsuis safely launched in the dual business of banking and merchandising. His last twenty-one years had been a period of sound calculation mixed with bold enterprise. The Mitsui shops of the feudal era were the foundation for the great importing and exporting business carried on by the House today, and the early money-exchange in one corner of the drygoods shop became the modern Mitsui Bank.

Before he died, Hachirobei saw his six sons formally installed as the heads of collateral families and placed in charge of the various branches of his business. A strong believer in the strength of Japan's family system, he determined to utilize its every merit for the perpetuation not only of family but of the industrial House of Mitsui. Hachirobei left a remarkable will which minutely prescribed the relations among the members of the family and allotted each branch its portion of inheritance and sphere in the fraternal copartnership of managing the Mitsui enterprises.

A contemporary account, written about 1725, of the early operations of the Mitsuis from which stemmed the present business relationship states: —

In the Mitsui (house) there were six brothers or six families who owned together the head office and branch houses, none of which belonged to any of the six individuals. The profit or loss of each of their stores was divided among or borne by the six families together, and no one of the six took more profit or bore more loss than the others, all six assuming equal responsibility for loss and taking an equal share of profit.

The employees of Mitsui were the employees of the whole family, and were not distinctly assigned to any individual family of the six. In Yedo there were six managers who were in charge of the main store at Suruga-cho and at other places. These six men did not attend to the daily business at the stores, but held a conference six times a month at which the policies, method of business and so forth were discussed. Each family received a certain fixed annual income for living and so on, and not even the heads of the families were allowed to spend more than what they were given. On account of such rules governing the Mitsui organization, these six Mitsui families will prosper forever, and none of them will decline.

On the basis of Hachirobei's will the original family code was drawn up by his eldest son Takahira.* As drafted by Taka-

* Takahira worked ten years on drafting the family code, completing it at the age of seventy. Before it was adopted he called his five younger brothers before him and ceremoniously illustrated an

hira, the first family code, fructifying the wisdom and observation of the founder, read: —

1. — The members of the House should deal with one another in close friendship and with kindness. Beware that contentions among the kin would in the end ruin the entire House.

2. — Do not needlessly increase the number of families of the House. Everything has its limits. Know that over-expansion, which you may covet, will beget confusion and trouble.

3. — Thrift enriches the House, while luxury ruins a man. Practise the former but avoid the latter. Thus lay a lasting foundation for the prosperity and perpetuation of our House.

4. — In making marriages, incurring debts or underwriting others' debts, act always according to the advice of the Council of the Family.

5. — Set aside a certain part of the annual income and divide it among the members of the House according to their portions.

6. — The lifework of a man lasts as long as he lives. Therefore, do not, without reason, seek the luxury and ease of retirement.

7. — Cause to be sent for auditing to the main office the financial reports from all branch houses; organize your finance and prevent disintegration.

8. — The essential of a business enterprise is to employ men of great abilities and take advantage of their special talents. Replace those who are aged and decrepit with young men of promise.

9. — Unless one concentrates, one fails. Our House has its own enterprises which are ample to provide for any man's life. Never touch another business.

10. — He who does not know, cannot lead. Make your sons begin with the mean tasks of the apprentice, and, when they have

ancient Japanese homily: that it is easy to break one arrow, but difficult if six arrows are tied together. In accordance with another Japanese custom, he left a scroll bearing his motto in his own brushwork: "Prudence is the source of happiness." Takahira died at the age of eighty-five on November 27, 1737.

gradually learned the secrets of the business, let them take a post in the branch houses to practise their knowledge.

11. — Sound judgment is essential in all things, especially in business enterprises. Know that a small sacrifice today is preferable to a great loss tomorrow.

12. — The members of the House should practise mutual caution and counsel lest they blunder. If there be among you any evildoer, deal with him accordingly at the Council of the Family.

13. — You who have been born in the land of the gods, worship your gods, revere your Emperor, love your country and do your duty as subjects.

Chapter VI

THE INEVITABLE AMERICANS

A FAVORITE THEME of the after-dinner speakers who gather around Tokyo's public tables today in the wake of ship arrivals is "the reopening of Japan" in 1853. It makes excellent hands-across-the-sea fare. The argument is that America reopened Japan, thereby creating eternal bonds between the two nations.

These speeches have been dragging on with dreadful monotony for years. They are varied only by the metaphors of the more gifted orators whose fanciful figures of speech take on a wide range. Some are pretty, some questionable and none very accurate. All show fruits of hasty research in ships' libraries. The religious speakers are fond of allusions to the walls of Jericho and Joshua's (America) blowing of the ram's horn. One speaker before the American-Japan Society (in America the same society is courteously designated Japan-American Society) depicted Japan as something of an idiotic child — certainly one of arrested development — wandering around the fringe of the "family of nations" until a kindly physician (America) laid on healing hands. Another speaker once envisioned Japan as a brave crew of seamen in a sunken submarine. Divers (again America) could hear tappings from within and knew life still existed. The rescue was dramatically accomplished; but somehow the simile did not sit so well with Japanese. Unknown to the speaker, only a week before there had been a similar disaster in Japan and the seamen weren't rescued.

No one ever dwells on the fact that the American naval commander, Commodore Matthew Perry, was at the point of blasting Yedo with his thirty-two-pounders when he "reopened Japan." Not that Perry went over with that intention, but he did have a formidable force of warships and a very accurate suspicion that Japan did not want to be reopened. When he dropped anchor his decks were cleared for action, and if someone on shore had shouted "Boo," the chances are Perry would have replied with a broadside.

America's policy was clearly one of caution and a determination not to arouse the hostility of Japan. This is borne out in part at least by the actions of a naval predecessor of Perry's. When he arrived to "knock at the door of Japan" he had only one warship. On trying to go ashore, he got as far as the dock but when a Japanese soldier gave him a gentle shove he scurried back into his boat and ordered his men to bend oars. He left without sounding the much-belabored ram's horn.

Actually, as has been indicated, there was nothing so simple as showing up with a naval squadron and clearing for action off Yedo to frighten or even to blow Japan out of her isolation. If such a phenomenon must be reduced to a few words, there is no better summation than that of the historian Griffis, whose impressions were first hand. "Impulse," he wrote, "not impact, opened Japan."

The forces behind Japan's termination of her self-exile and the Restoration of secular rule from Shogun to Emperor are inextricably interwoven. They were a combination of economic and intellectual impulses.

In both events — Reopening and Restoration — the Mitsuis backed the forces that won, and emerged in the customary Mitsui position — on top.

*   *   *

The reader who turns the pages of the last period of the Tokugawa Shogunate, between 1770 and 1867, will be struck with the number of peasant revolts growing out of the system whereby merchants and bankers exploited the territorial nobles and they in turn squeezed the farmers. The rising standard of living in the towns, increasing tax rates and the substitution of metal money for rice, all contributed to the calamitous state of the farmer. In the last hundred years before the reopening of the country an economic war had been going on between the two main classes, merchant and noble, both unproductive, while the farmers footed the bill and lacked the natural means with which to do it.

When, in 1932, the Roosevelt Administration inaugurated an agricultural policy of plowing up every fourth row and slaughtering pigs, the thought was readily translated into Japanese by the term *mabiki*. In Japan's dark days of the latter half of the Eighteenth Century, the starving farmers on their own initiative resorted to a sinister *mabiki*. Japanese is an euphemistic language. The direst, darkest actions often are clothed in almost elegant terms. *Hara-kiri* means "belly-cutting" in literal translation but its connotation is "the happy dispatch." Similarly, *mabiki* is a term used by farmers when they thin out rows of vegetables by uprooting, but in those days it meant killing little children so there would be fewer mouths to feed. Sometimes they called it *kaeshi* or *modoshi* with an even more tender meaning: "sending back."

Of the many agrarian revolts of the period, one that occurred in the province of Hizen, in 1771, was not only typical but bears a striking resemblance to militant tactics of modern labor uprisings. The Lord of Hizen, acting in conjunction with a district representative of the Shogun, had sought to increase taxes and compel the planting of 30,000 mulberry trees. The farmers called a mass meeting and passed around word that anyone who failed to attend would be visited by the "red ox." That was the equivalent of the "black spot," or more literally meant that the dissenter's house would be burned.

The meeting was attended by ten thousand peasants. The Shogun's representative boldly faced them and commanded that they disperse. He was answered with a taunting laugh. Other officials addressed them. They were greeted with loud hand-clapping; and hand-clapping wasn't cheering. The speakers then retired in confusion. Having gained no satisfaction, the farmer-army began moving on the provincial chief's castle. It is recorded that they advanced in orderly fashion with ample space between ranks so that spies or informers might be more easily detected. They were under a pledge of silence and, according to rules previously drawn up by their leaders, would "not fight among ourselves whatever be the circumstances."

By the time the march was well under way, the army had increased to 23,000, including several thousand fishermen who had joined up in the hope of forcing suspension of a recently enacted fishing duty. The provincial lord was thoroughly frightened and sent out new representatives to meet the rebels before they reached his castle. A halt was called and the farmers presented their demands again. This time, to their surprise, every demand was met and they in turn agreed to disperse peacefully. A few months later their leader was arrested and beheaded, but there was no further uprising as the farmers were satisfied with the concessions made to them. They secretly gathered their leader's remains and enshrined them in the village of Heigen-mura, where an appropriate marker may be seen today.

Farmers who resorted to *mabiki* or infanticide went unpunished, but finally when the practice became so widespread that it approached a national calamity, the Shogunate saw fit to issue another of his wordy edicts importuning against the practice. The Shogunate, in fact, frequently was given to such decrees in time of stress, always attempting to solve the growing economic difficulties with a newly enunciated system of philosophy and ethics calculated mostly to preserve the existing caste distinctions and *status quo* for the Tokugawas, rather than to attempt any practical steps toward relief.

Corruption and profligacy of the Shogun's court continued apace.

Extravagances and maladministration brought new financial straits. By 1813, the Shogun's coffers were so drained that the Government again resorted to debasement of the currency, and made a temporary profit of 9,000,000 ryo by re-minting gold coins. This tided over the Shogun for a time; but in 1836, when Iyenari desired to retire in favor of his son, Iyeyoshi, there were no funds in the treasury to pay for the usual festivities of succession and he was forced to borrow from a relative to install the fourteenth Shogun.

In 1837 a significant revolt broke out in Osaka, resulting from a combination of circumstances, — including debased coinage, a poor harvest, rice speculation which sent the price up while thousands starved, — and a growing indignation over the general misrule of the Tokugawas.

The Mitsuis had a narrow escape in this revolt. It occurred almost a hundred years before another uprising growing out of agrarian discontent led to the assassination in 1933 of the managing director of the wide Mitsui interests. The 1837 revolt was led by a patriotic police sergeant of Osaka, one Heichairo Oshio. Oshio apparently was no ordinary policeman. He was accounted a scholar given to deep thinking and an eloquence of expression which won him many disciples. Oshio's principal preachment was that much of the current misfortune of the people was due to usurpation of the secular powers of the Emperor by the Tokugawas. This was an ominous new note in popular uprisings and it boded evil for the declining Shoguns.

In the midst of hunger and starvation, with the support of an increasing number of poverty-stricken people, Oshio appealed to the Shogun's commissioner at Osaka for direct aid. The commissioner stood on rules of formality, replying that he could do nothing without sanction from Yedo, whereupon Oshio laid careful plans for his rebellion. First he sold his valuable accumulation of books and his house furniture and bought rice, doling it out to as many as he could, which gained him numbers for the onslaught. Then he constructed four copper and wooden guns. They were primitive field pieces, good for about one shot apiece, but Oshio believed they would be shots that would be heard around the Empire. Then he turned to his propaganda department and drew up manifestoes calling for dire punishment of corrupt and selfish officials and immediate direct relief.

With his army at his back Oshio set fire to his own house as a signal for assault and began a destructive march in a wide swath upon the homes of the wealthy and the Shogun's officials in Osaka. The homes of the Osaka Mitsuis were in the path of the mob, but the clan rallied with all their retainers and employees and fended off the horde, which was more intent upon reaching the homes of officialdom. They had not gone far, however, before they were surprised by an ambush of soldiers and were thrown back with heavy loss of life. Oshio was seized and executed. All that remained to show for the premature uprising was the embers of 18,000 houses.

*   *   *

In spite of this and other sporadic rebellions, there was no evidence that any in the Shogun's administration had even a dream of practical reform. The only efforts in this direction which achieved any degree of success at that time were sponsored by Sontoku Ninomiya, a great agricultural reformer and sage who had much to do with the development of Japanese agricultural resources around 1850. Literally a man of the people, he formed the Hotoku Society (or Cooperatives), which venerated the virtues of thrift and disseminated practical information to increase the products of the land.

The place where the people began to think and attempted to rationalize their wretched conditions has been called the "Boston" of Japan. This was the province of Mito, which long had been noted for the number, ability and activity of its scholars. The "real author of the movement which culminated in the Revolution of 1867" was the second prince of Mito, Mitsukuni, who was born in 1622 and died in 1700. Early in manhood he collected a group of scholars from all parts of Japan and began writing in classical Chinese — which is to Japan what Latin is to Europe — the *Dai Nihonshi* or "History of Japan." By the time it was finished, fifteen years after his death, it filled 243 volumes. All in all, Mitsukuni's philosophical history came to one indisputable conclusion: that the Emperor was the true and only source of authority in Japan and the Tokugawa Shoguns were military usurpers.

This was not exactly heretical but it was a dangerous thought for the peace and well-being of the Tokugawas. The Tokugawas had always exerted a careful censorship to prevent any such seeds from being sown in the minds of the people, but the Prince of Mito was allowed some liberty at the time he was compiling his documents because he was a grandson of the great Iyeyasu, founder of the House of Tokugawa. Moreover, since the voluminous history was kept in manuscript and never published, there seemed less likelihood of its conclusions becoming known. Other scholars found it readily accessible and were producing shorter works of similar theme. Finally a wide demand forced this publication in print in 1851. This was a critical time, and for those who could read between the lines of Mitsukuni's great work and give a thought to the political future it was apparent that a showdown was approaching when the weakening Shogun would be obliged to restore his stolen properties to the throne and submit to its authority.

The Emperors had been living immured in the seclusion of their Kyoto palace in the society of women, courtiers and a few underpaid nobles. Someone suggested that if anything was going to be done toward restoring the secular power to the Emperor the word should be passed along to Kyoto and an effort made to interest His Majesty in his own cause. To this end there went to Kyoto one Shikibu Takeuchi, a scholar and disciple of the new thought and, incidentally, an expert on military tactics. He gained the position of retainer to a prominent Kyoto family and began lecturing on military tactics. Then gradually and cautiously he worked around to advocating restoration of power to the throne. He drew crowded audiences of Kyoto nobles. The monarchists, seeing their star in the ascendancy, agreed to aid him in getting his views before the Emperor.

Secrecy was to be maintained at all costs, for the spies of the Shogun were everywhere, even in the Imperial Palace. Takeuchi accordingly wrote out his lectures and one at a time they were passed on to the Emperor. All was going well, and there is reason to believe that the Emperor was being fortified with the wish to regain power, when there was an unfortunate slip-up. One of the ladies of the palace observed His Majesty assiduously studying the smuggled-in communications and she, not unnaturally, conceived the idea that they were love letters. She contrived to read one and, discovering its purpose, in a fit of pique she revealed the plot, thereby spiking the monarchial movement at that time. The whole affair was told to the Shogun, who promptly exiled the luckless Takeuchi to a lonely island.

But the tide of imperialism was not to be stemmed. Another current of thought flowing in the direction of a restored Emperor was the revival of the study of pure Shinto, the ancient religion of Japan, which had been modified or corrupted by Buddhism, Confucianism and Chinese philosophy. The new and virtually subversive historical school stirred into activity by the teachings of the Prince of Mito was responsible for the revival of pure Shinto. Under its tenets, Japan is preeminently the Land of the Gods and the Emperor is their vice-regent and Divine Representative upon earth. Therefore, it is the implicit duty of all Japanese to obey him. In the view of the Shintoist, Buddhism and Chinese philosophy and the Shogunate usurpation were all of a piece.

After the scholars of the new historical school, the next to show an interest in the revived doctrine were some of the great territorial nobles who had never quite composed themselves to the spectacle of one of their own rank, as the Tokugawas were, lifting himself by his boot-straps to a position of power and domination over the Emperor and imposing social and political difficulties upon themselves. These forces, the scholars of the historical school and the restive nobles, together with the oppressed peasants, with no conscious direction in time became enlisted on the side of the Restoration. They were the progressives of Japan. Among them were the first thoughtful persons to foresee that the military dictatorship and stubborn seclusive policy of the Tokugawas could not be maintained. They were the instruments of the "impulse" that reopened Japan, the forces operating from within to effect a change.

Concurrently the seas surrounding Japan that once were thought of as a wall helping to enforce seclusion were becoming a highway for the new steam vessels that were making their appearance in the middle of the Nineteenth Century. America's acquisition of Oregon and California gave Japan restless, vigorous neighbors to the East. American whalers already were cruising Japan's waters operating within sight of her coast. On the north, Russia, having marched across Siberia, was descending on Saghalien. The English and the French, no longer occupied with Napoleonic wars, were paying more frequent, though unsuccessful visits to Japan in an attempt to tap a new trade area. As early as 1811 a Russian naval captain, Golownin, boldly sailed up to Japan's northern coast and began a survey. When he ventured ashore he was seized with several of his crew and imprisoned for two years. Eventually other Russians arrived with sufficient representations of Golownin's peaceful mission and he was freed, but he remained in Japan long enough to write in a two-volume work in 1811 an observation of such prescience that it might be applicable to the Russia of today: —

What must we expect of this numerous, ingenious and industrious people, who are capable of everything and much inclined to imitate all that is foreign . . . should they ever have a sovereign like our Peter the Great . . . and build ships on the model of those of Europe? . . . I therefore believe that this just and upright people must not be provoked.

Within a century Japan did have a sovereign like Russia's Peter the Great, and Russia did provoke them — with results that amazed the world.

Yet in the face of all these indications that Japan was soon to have a foreign problem, the Shogunate neither made preparations to resist an invasion nor showed any inclination peacefully to give up the seclusion policy.

The Dutch still trading at Nagasaki, and serving as Japan's sole outlet to the foreign world, gratuitously provided an intelligence system for the Shogun after 1638. From their vantage point in Europe they kept informed of all intended voyages to Japan and tipped off a growingly nervous Yedo. The motive, of course, was to arouse Japanese suspicion against all foreigners so that the Dutch might retain their monopolistic trade. In 1846, the Netherlands, perceiving that other nations were going to use more pressure to extract Japan from her exile, sent an impressive map of the world together with scientific books and other presents to Yedo, with the suggestion that Japan abandon her isolation peacefully and mark the event by giving the Dutch the first favorable trade treaty. But that approach was too timorous to make an impression upon the Shogun. Three years later the Dutch intelligence service notified the Shogun an American fleet might be expected in Japanese waters the next year. The Dutch ruler even enclosed in his dispatch an approximate draft of the treaty that would be sought by the Americans. Thus Japan had ample notice of the coming of the Americans, and it must not be supposed that she was required to make any sudden decision in renewing her relations with the outer world.

When Perry and his fleet sailed into Yedo Bay in July, 1853, and dropped anchor, the first intelligible words to reach the visitors from small boats swarming alongside were: "Are you the Americans?" The query was delivered in Dutch, but an interpreter aboard understood it and translated the words. The Americans were considerably taken aback, but they admitted their identity, to the disappointment of those who believed they would be taken as men from Mars.

Perry was by no means the first American in Japan, nor was his the first official expedition.

History has not done well by the first American resident in Japan. He was exhibited in a cage. Full recognition of this pioneer was given only a few years ago when patriotic residents of Ferry County, Washington, communicated with Japanese officials and confirmed through old Tokugawa records another of the long series of dramatic episodes in the background of early Japanese-American relations. The man belatedly honored was one Ranald MacDonald, born in Astoria, Oregon, the son of a Scotsman and an Indian princess. As a youth he became interested in the suggestion that his mother's race came from the same stock as did the Japanese. To investigate that theory, MacDonald at the age of twenty shipped on a whaler ship in 1848, with the understanding that he would be allowed to leave the ship at the nearest point to the coast of Japan. At the proper destination young Mac-Donald went over the side and put off alone in a small boat, bearing his trunk containing his books and writing paper. Within swimming distance of shore, at the northern end of Japan, he capsized his boat and floated in with the tide astride his trunk. He feared that if he arrived by boat he promptly would be dispatched by the same vessel.

MacDonald immediately was imprisoned and the Shogunate ordered him removed to Nagasaki at the other end of the island, the only place where foreigners were permitted to tarry. To keep the youth confined during the long, tortuous journey, the Japanese constructed a portable cell of wooden bars. The prison procession stopped for a time at Yedo, where the exhibit attracted considerable attention. On reaching Nagasaki, MacDonald's fortunes took a turn for the better when samurai and other dignitaries engaged him to teach them English. One of the interpreters who hid behind a screen as a double-check on the negotiations with Perry a few years later learned his English from MacDonald. The American remained a prisoner at Nagasaki for seven months. The Dutch meanwhile had informed the American naval squadron in China that MacDonald and several other American castaways were held in Japan and Washington ordered Commander Glynn in the *U.S.S. Preble* to proceed to Nagasaki and take off the Americans. Glynn dropped anchor off Nagasaki and sent a note ashore demanding the prisoners. The Japanese were obdurate until the *Preble* moved in and cleared for action with guns trained on the city. There was no polite knocking at the door then, in 1849. The Americans were delivered to the naval commander, who promptly cleared for China.

Another American naval commander, Commodore Biddle, cautiously stood in to Uraga and at the behest of Washington sent a note ashore seeking communication with the Emperor. He waited ten days for a reply and then, when he attempted to land to see what was going on, a Japanese soldier pushed him. The Commodore, who was of considerably less naval stature than Perry, hastened back to his ship and departed, leaving the reopening to his brother officer.

Perry's expedition was the result of a resolution passed by Congress in 1845 asking that "immediate measures be taken for effecting commercial arrangements with the Empire of

Japan." Mercantile interests in New York and New England, fearful that other nations would gain a more auspicious start in the race for Japanese trade, had pressed the bill through Congress with no great support or even interest from the rest of the country. The Japanese historian, the late Inazo Nitobe, on looking through American newspapers and periodicals of the time wrote that he was "struck with the absence of public sympathy covering an enterprise of which the United States can be so nobly and justly proud." The *New York Herald* ironically remarked at the time: "The Japanese expedition, according to a Washington correspondent, is to be merely a hydrographical survey of the Japanese coast. The thirty-two-pounders are to be used merely as measuring instruments in the triangulations; the cannon balls are for procuring base-lines. If any Japanese is foolish enough to put his head in the way of these meteorological instruments, of course nobody will be to blame but himself." And *Punch*, in London, observed: "Perry must open the Japanese ports even if he has to open his own."

Perry, a big, imposing-looking naval officer with a gift for showmanship and a born diplomat, spent long months in preparation for his voyage. He sent to the Netherlands for charts and descriptions by foremost Dutch authorities; he studied all the written accounts and heard the stories of castaways who had been in Japan, and he went to the whaling ports of New England to interview captains and seamen who had cruised Japanese waters. He acquired considerable useless information and some actual misinformation — he left America completely in the dark as to current policies and politics in Japan, and did not know that the Shogunate ruled the country instead of the Emperor. But his research provided him with one valuable idea: that if he were to make progress with the Japanese he had to match caste with caste. He determined that he would create for himself a position of the highest rank and inaccessibility. His staff and other officers were graduated downward, corresponding to their own naval rank. On the long voyage over, by way of Madagascar and Hong Kong, he carefully rehearsed his gigantic piece of foolery to instill in his men what he conceived to be the same sort of awe the Japanese had for caste. Perry afterward admitted he put on his show with considerable trepidation, fearing that Congress would hear about it and make him a laughing stock; and there was some discomfiture in the fleet as democracy gave way to a new social order, but Perry's plan was carried out.

Perry's four ships, bearing five hundred and sixty men, rounded Cape Sagami and entered Yedo Bay on July 7, 1853. The flagship ran up the signal "Clear for action." Ammunition was broken out, gun crews took their stations, and marines were posted to repel boarders; "in short all the preparations made usual before meeting an enemy." But nothing untoward happened.

The first minor Japanese official who appeared was permitted to converse only with a low-ranking officer. Perry kept out of sight. The Japanese sent out a higher rank. He got only one step up with the Americans. A vice-governor rated a flag lieutenant; the Governor rated a commander, and so on. The Japanese were agreeably surprised. This barbarian lord apparently knew how to do things. Previous visitors had been trying to send mere orderlies to see the Emperor.

The plan worked to perfection. Within ten days, a Prince with Imperial credentials was on hand and Perry emerged from the Forbidden Interior of his ship with great ceremony. Assured at last that he had been properly received, he consented to go ashore, where a gorgeous pavilion had been erected for the rites. Still Perry took no chances. Moving his fleet in close, so that his guns would cover his landing, he went ashore and after considerable ritual he handed over to the proper officials President Fillmore's letter to the Emperor respectfully asking a treaty of friendship and commerce with Japan.

Then Perry re-embarked and cleared for China. It was another inspired act, in that he did not insist upon immediate conclusion of the treaty. The Japanese breathed easier, believing he would never come back. But he did the next spring, this time with seven warships instead of four. During the six months he was away much had happened in Japan. The progressive forces and Restorationists were gaining strength. The Shogun Iyeyoshi died, and was succeeded by Iyesada, the last and one of the weakest of the Tokugawas. Fortunately Iyesada was surrounded by far-seeing ministers. An effort to mobilize for resistance to the Americans failed because of the growing disunity of the forces working toward the downfall of the Shogunate. Moreover, a Russian admiral was descending from the north to keep an eye on the American visitors and try for a commercial treaty of his own. A French frigate was in the vicinity and the British were outfitting still another treaty expedition.

The counsel of the Shogun's progressive ministers finally prevailed. After some weeks of face-saving negotiations on both sides, Japan was ready to sign. Perry put on his last show, going ashore while his band played "Yankee Doodle," frightening horses and little children. Two giant Negroes bore the American flag. Seamen unloaded an imposing array of presents, including a miniature steam locomotive, complete with car and rails, a telegraph set, agricultural implements, a lorgnette and toilette set for the Empress, perfumes and wines. It was a small World's Fair.

There was much conviviality, both sides got drunk and tried on each other's clothes — but the important fact was that the treaty was signed, and Japan was open again to the outer world. The stage was set for the last act featuring the old, feudalistic Japan. Only the brief struggle for Restoration of the Emperor lay between Perry's drama and the actual emergence of the modern nation.

The Mitsuis, as the next chapter will show, were enlisted on the side of imperialistic forces. The now prosperous firm, unlike the Shoguns, was quick to see the potentialities of the new foreign trade that Perry was bringing to their door, and before the treaty was signed the Mitsuis had sent staff artists out in small boats to make almost photographic sketches of the huge foreign steamers.

One Mitsui artist, a scion of the family, drew a celebrated portrait of Perry, giving him fiery red hair and a nose longer than Cyrano de Bergerac's.

Chapter VII

THE MITSUIS DESERT THE SHOGUN

THE HOUSE OF TOKU-gawa was once the greatest and most powerful in Japan. The House of Mitsui after 1852, however, played a long shot on the overthrow of the ruling Tokugawas, and won in 1867.

The histories of great financial houses invariably are marked by such vital ventures against the odds. At a time when all Europe trembled in fear of Napoleon, Nathan Rothschild staked the interlocking fortunes of that great family on the overthrow of the man who had returned from Elba. When the English Government could not meet the financial obligations undertaken by the Duke of Wellington, Nathan Rothschild stepped in and successfully floated loans that led to victory at Waterloo. The Mitsui gamble was not unlike that of the Rothschilds.

In the space of a healthy man's lifetime, the Mitsuis and Tokugawas for all practical purposes have swapped positions in Japan. Today, it is the Mitsuis and their astute financial chiefs who are called in to talk with Cabinets and leaders of the military clique, while a pudgy-faced old gentleman with benign eyes makes the rounds of diplomatic luncheons and lends his name to prefaces for international "good will" publications. He is Prince Iyesato Tokugawa, sixteenth direct descendant of the great Iyeyasu, who sturdily but unimportantly carries on the line of Tokugawas who ruled Japan when the Mitsuis were fledglings stirred up by the plowshares of commerce.

From 1903 to 1932 Prince Tokugawa served as president of the House of Peers, presiding at the august ceremonies each year when the Emperor opened the Diet. On such occasions it is to be wondered if he did not speculate on the turn of fortune that made him a mere herald in the political presence of the Emperor. But for the successful Restoration movement that came on the heels of Japan's reopening, in other words between 1852 and 1868, this complacent old remnant of a great House might today have been the actual ruler of Japan, and the Emperor monastic head of the State religion still in seclusion at Kyoto. Tokugawa's title of Prince is little more than courtesy. With their overthrow as Shoguns, the Tokugawas reverted to their true status of feudal vassals on a par with other baronial retainers of the Emperor. When the present Prince dies, the line will be carried on by a son who has ambassadorial ranking in the Foreign Office.

Until the coming of Perry, the House of Mitsui had run on a confluent course with the House of Tokugawa, but on a much smaller orbit. As we have seen, it was the promise of a peaceful era at the very outset of the Tokugawa rule in 1603 that had diverted the Mitsuis from the unprofitable sword-swinging of the patrician class to an uncharted, untried industrial and commercial career.

Under the Tokugawas, the Mitsuis not only had founded their bank but had expanded a small-time haphazard venture into the responsible and money-making position of fiscal agent to the Shogun's Government. Indeed the Mitsuis had found most things to their advantage under the system of government carried on by the Tokugawas. It did not matter if some of the Tokugawas in the long line were weak, dissolute and reckless with state finances. The Mitsuis were on an inside beat, and sailed a safe course. It was knowing when to veer off that mattered.

Archivists and historians of the House of Mitsui today disagree with the conception that any great decision was involved in the Mitsuis' switching from Tokugawa allegiance to aid the forces working to restore full administrative control to the Emperor. But their protestations may be tempered by the fact that they were made in the critical year of 1938, when it was not becoming for Japanese to admit the possibility that they or any of their ancestors had ever questioned the Emperor's political right to rule.

The Mitsuis to be sure always had been devoted subjects of their Emperors. The fifth* commandment of the family code was observed religiously. It read: "Worship your gods, revere your Emperor, love your country and do your duty as subjects." But like all such abstract injunctions, it was capable of various interpretations. The Mitsuis for several generations had demonstrated that they could successfully revere their Emperor while supporting the Tokugawas — especially while the Emperor was in seclusion at Kyoto with only subversive talk of restoring him to political eminence.

It is true, moreover, that the Mitsuis had acted as court bankers while the inconsequential court functioned at Kyoto. On numerous occasions, as may be seen from the carefully treasured Mitsui records written in old-fashioned script but

---

* My translator says that strictly speaking it was not the "fifth" commandment of the family code. He adds: "While the so-called Fifth Article was designated as such by historians of a later date, apparently it was not so specified either by the author of the document or by Mitsui family members. In other words, it must not be assumed too exclusively that the Mitsuis were pouring forth loyalty to the Emperor with consciousness that they were standing by Number Five Article of the Family Convention."

still clear and bold, the Mitsuis advanced funds to construct a few buildings and provide other necessities. For this they received grateful acknowledgment, but for the Mitsuis it must have come under the category of religio-patriotic benevolence. The court was in no financial position to pay interest rates such as the Mitsuis might charge the Tokugawas. Most of the time it could not even return the principal.

What is more significant in the Mitsui records is an exhibit of the journal containing the names of prominent visitors who called on the Mitsuis in Yedo during the period of uncertainty over the possible course of the Restoration movement. On the callers' book, with increasing frequency appeared such names as Saigo, Iwakura, Shojiro Goto and Munemitsu Mutsu. Just the names and dates of their calls, no remarks or other evidence of their missions. But it is well known that these men were spokesmen and leaders of the Imperialist forces then gathering strength for their attempt to throw out the Tokugawas.

Then there is another revealing bit of evidence in the Mitsui archives. In Japan there is a game called *sugoroku*. It is several hundred years old. It is very much like the Western game of parcheesi, or simplified backgammon. A paper is laid out on the floor. Along the edges are placed various stations, denoted by appropriate drawings, of streams to be crossed, mountains and caves, and then when the going gets easier, geisha houses, pleasant inns, and favored villages. The players cast a die and advance along the stations as determined by the numerals on the die. The game is thought to have originated in India, and found its way to Japan in the Eighth Century. It was, according to Brinkley, prohibited for a time on account of its gambling character, but eventually Buddhist priests took up the device and converted it into an instrument for inculcating virtue. The proper path along the board led to Heaven, but unfortunate throws of the die would precipitate the player into Hell. "Young people, therefore, were expected to derive a vicarious respect for ethical precepts that marked the path to victory. The game henceforth became a vehicle of instruction as well as amusement," says Brinkley.

The Mitsuis have always been master propagandists. When the topic of Restoration was still a dangerous one the Mitsui stores in Yedo had started selling *sugoroku* games with the inside picture or Heaven changed to the Imperial Palace at Kyoto. It was clever subterfuge. In the very capital of the Tokugawas no one would have dared to publish a pamphlet or volume putting in words the teaching conveyed on the *sugoroku* cloth. The Mitsuis still pridefully exhibit those *sugoroku* cloths. They probably directed the thoughts of more persons to their secluded sovereign at Kyoto than all the surreptitiously circulated literature of the period.*

* A modern variant of this device was seen in Tokyo in 1938 when the Morinaga Confectionery Company took full-page newspaper advertisements to announce a "drawing competition for schoolchildren of Germany, Italy and Japan." The sugar department of *Mitsui Bussan Kaisha* does an annual business of $45,000,000, and Morinaga's candy is a substantial outlet. Japanese children are remarkable candy-eaters and Morinaga candy wrappers probably reach a numerically greater public than most of Tokyo's newspapers.

Morinaga's proclaimed: "Underlying this competition is the thought that children are the best 'good-will ambassadors.' It is felt that mutual understanding will be cultivated to a certain degree and in the end the cause of world peace furthered by bringing together the children of Italy, Germany and Japan on a common meeting-ground. Nearly all children like to draw; here is an unusual opportunity to stimulate interest and at the same time to plant the seeds of peaceful internationalism.

"In announcing this competition, Mr. Hanzaburo Matsuzaki, president of the Morinaga Confectionery Manufacturing Company, Ltd., said: 'It is a matter for great felicitation that an anti-Comintern pact has been concluded among the three advancing countries of Japan,

The Mitsui inclination to the Imperial cause may be traced several generations back from 1867. It lies in the story of the friendship of two small-town neighbors and illustrates probably the first instance of what later became a truism in Mitsui history: that there have been few great Mitsuis but an almost constant succession of great Japanese who were taken under the wing of the Mitsuis, who either directed the affairs of the House or influenced its decisions.

Matsuzaka is a country town on Ise Bay in Mie Prefecture. A thousand years ago it was a country town, a little smaller perhaps but of no more importance than it is today. A good many people in Japan have never heard of it. The local Chamber of Commerce assiduously puts out booklets and handsomely illustrated testimonials of its provincial greatness. Two spinning factories — one of them a Mitsui concern — produced 900,000 yen worth of cotton products there in 1936. The amount of raw silk produced in a year was worth 400,000 yen; finished metals, lumber, pictures and posters are other important products of the town. There are good schools, historical temples, the preserved castle of the local feudal chief, and a library or two. The population as of 1936 is 36,335,

Germany and Italy for the sole purpose of establishing world peace. Firmly believing that co-operation between the boys and girls of the three countries through the medium of drawings will contribute toward the promotion of friendly relations between the nations, we have decided to hold this competition supported by various circles, and we earnestly hope that this scheme will meet your hearty endorsement.' "

The subject of the drawings to be entered was left to "individual option" of the children, but a broad hint was thrown out in an accompanying drawing of a small Japanese, German and Italian boy, each giving the Fascist salute. The prize-winning drawings of Japanese children were to be sent to Germany and Italy for exhibition and outstanding entries from those countries were to be shown in Japan. The contest offered 75,210 individual prizes and 632 school prizes for a total of 50,000 yen, or about $15,000.

divided in the categorical Japanese mind among 16,553 men and 19,782 women.

Matsuzaka is also a lively town. Its main street is lighted with the same type of standards and fixtures that adorn the Yoshiwara licensed district in Tokyo. But that is just a coincidence, the Chamber of Commerce explains. Perhaps it is more than a coincidence, however, that the smaller town of Tomita, only a few miles distant, for hundreds of years has been known for its beautiful women. When they go to town, they go to Matsuzaka, and they frequently stay. Matsuzaka's large and boisterous licensed district is near the center of town.

Matsuzaka means "Pine Hill" in Japanese. Once it adjoined a flourishing fishing village, and perhaps the fishermen saw pines and a hill, but that was a long time ago. There are few pines now to adorn the flatness of Matsuzaka. But stretching away from the lowlands are the rugged hills of Mie Province, and still farther back the mountains of Omi. They are rugged, jagged hills stacked up in fantastic shapes by the mad forces that quiver beneath Japan. In those mountains water still boils and sulphur seethes at unexpected openings, proof enough that a terrible Fire God is still raging below the surface. Once in those mountains the heroes of Old Japan lived and fought and sometimes the gods themselves took part, ranging first on one side and then on the other, as in the battles of the Greeks and Trojans. It is a land rich in stories of miracles wrought, visions seen of supernatural happenings, and dragons rampant. Little wonder it was that Matsuzaka when the sun went down behind those mountains was glad to turn away and light its candle at both ends.

Out of those mountains came Takayasu Mitsui "like a falling leaf," to escape the civil wars raging around Kyoto.

Three generations after the first Mitsui settled in Matsuzaka, the family had become an important element of the
town's trade gentry. They were moderately successful bankers and merchants in Kyoto and Tokyo, but one branch of the
family remained at Matsuzaka, and the old family home was a
common gathering place of the Mitsui clan on frequent occasions. The home was and still is in a walled compound occu-
pying most of a small city block.

At the back of the Mitsui home, separated by a small stream
crossed by a footbridge, was another compound of much
smaller extent. It was the home of the Norinagas, widow and
son. Like the Mitsuis, the Norinagas once had been a family
of samurai rank who had turned to commercialism.

Young Motoori Norinaga was a thin, sallow youth with a
high forehead, and an avid thirst for knowledge. The Mitsuis
had more books than any of the other trade families in town,
so young Motoori frequently crossed the footbridge from his
home to the Mitsuis' and borrowed Chinese classics and other
reading matter. Anecdotes of his remarkable youth are still to
be found in the children's storybooks of Japan. Even in his
early years he began to exert an influence upon a contemporary of the Mitsui household, Takakage.

When Motoori reached the age of twenty-one he decided
to study medicine. His mother scraped together her savings
and with the advice of the elder Mitsuis sent the youth to
Kyoto. Whether or not the Mitsuis lent any money to finance
the education of Motoori cannot be substantiated from the
family records, but the Mitsuis today are in no wise hesitant
about claiming Motoori as a protégé.

Motoori remained for six years in Kyoto, and in 1757 returned to Matsuzaka to set up as a general practitioner, special-
izing in children's diseases. But his love for philosophical

books lingered, and six years later his course of life was altered by a personal meeting with the great scholar, Mabuchi, one of the leaders of the Wa-gaku-sha School of so-called "pure Japanese thought" which preached loyalty to the Emperor. Mabuchi was then sixty-four, and Motoori only thirty. The younger man spoke zealously of his desire to write a lengthy commentary on the *Kojiki*, or Records of Ancient Events, to advance the cause of the Emperor, whose mythical history and divine origin form a large part of the Records.

Motoori was encouraged and influenced by Mabuchi to carry on the latter's work. Perhaps an even stronger influence had directed the scholar's thoughts toward the Emperor. Matsuzaka is only a few miles from the famous Grand Shrine at Ise, the most sacrosanct and revered spot in all Japan, the shrine to which each new Emperor goes soon after his enthronement to inform imperial ancestors of his accession. Besides the Imperial Family and other State dignitaries, hundreds of thousands of pilgrims pass through Matsuzaka, almost by the door of Motoori's old home — and the Mitsuis' — on their way to this holy place. This spectacle of outpouring devotion to the old Imperial cult, during the period when the Tokugawas were carrying on their high-handed rule, must have made an impression upon the philosophical Motoori.

At any rate Motoori, with Takakage Mitsui sitting at his feet now as a disciple, began a work which the historian Murdoch describes as "pregnant with dire disaster to the Tokugawa supremacy." Motoori's monumental task of commenting on the *Kojiki* occupied him for thirty-four years. His work was completed in 1786, but was not published until 1822, twenty years after his death. In its final form it ran into forty-four large volumes. In addition, he found time to write one of Japan's first grammars, a two-volume work on current conditions and economics with helpful suggestions from the Mitsuis, and a dozen other books on a wide variety of subjects.

The dominant theme of Motoori's works was a belief not only that the Emperor was true sovereign, but that Japan rather than China was the center of civilization of the Universe. He directed his polemics against the Chinese influences so strong in Japan at the time. Some of his writings have a curiously modern tinge, with a theme not unlike the half-mystical announcements circulated by the military group in Japan at the height of the China invasion in 1938. Motoori wrote, in 1780: —

China is a country where the True Way generally has not been handed down. There they do not know that all things are the doings of the gods and therefore resort rashly to innovations. Japan is the country which gave birth to the Goddess of the Sun, Amaterasu Omikami, which fact proves its superiority over all other countries. The eternal endurance of the dynasty of the Mikados is a complete proof that the way called Kami-no-Michi, or Shinto (Way of the Gods), infinitely surpasses the systems of all other countries.

Motoori on occasion could descend from philosophical heights. Invited by the feudal prince on whose fief he was born to draw up a memorandum on how to administer large landholdings, Motoori consulted his more practical-minded friend, Takakage Mitsui, and wrote a two-volume work on current economic conditions. He prevailed against many abuses of the times and reflected an old Mitsui apprehension when he ranted against agrarian uprisings. He insisted such demonstrations shamed the daimio on whose fief they occurred rather than the demonstrators themselves. This was a new and thought-provoking attitude for a contemporary commentator. He condemned the entrenched custom of hara-kiri and called upon the authorities to proscribe the practice whereby trustworthy, honorable men killed themselves in assumed responsibility for some trivial mishap. A lengthy passage against the wasteful system of maintaining feudal retainers echoed an old Mitsui antipathy toward an unbusiness-like custom in vogue among their creditors.

Murdoch sums up Motoori's influence in this wise: —

In his writings and in his teachings we find a chief source of that movement which within three-score years and ten from the date of his death was to sweep the Shogunate and feudalism into endless night. From the beginning of his nationalistic and chauvinistic propaganda in 1771 down to the overthrow of feudalism just a century later his influence, latent perhaps, was in all probability nearly as great as that of any other man of these three generations. It is not indeed given to many of the sons of men who have to eke out an impecunious existence as a medical practitioner of children's diseases to count as a first-class political force in one of the most populous empires of the world for around 100 years. . . . The natural tendency of the Japanese mind, in common with the human mind generally, is to believe too readily and to believe too much, and this tendency is far from being at its weakest when the propositions or theories people are requested to accept as truths are pleasantly flattering to their importance and dignity and national vanity. Of all this the shrewd Motoori was no doubt perfectly well aware; certainly there is no reason to suppose that he was ignorant of the Japanese proverb to the effect that "it is the quality of faith that is important, were its object only the head of a sardine."

For relaxation during his arduous work, Motoori turned to music. He played well upon the *koto*, an ancient Japanese musical instrument now of twelve strings but at that time only five. He found his greatest musical diversion in ringing thirty-six small bells which he had ranged in tonal sequence. The musical Swiss apparently had an early counterpart in Japan. A visit to Matsuzaka today is evidence enough of the high esteem in which Motoori was held. He is accorded all the honor of a great man of Japan, as he truly was. His old home has been removed from the Mitsui backyard and enshrined on one of the town's few hills. It is maintained by a national association for the preservation of historical relics. A few years ago the city widened the road leading to the shrine and in 1938 as the nation began to talk much of the Way of Japan, there was a notable increase in the constant stream of pilgrims to the Motoori shrine. Travelers on their way to Ise in increasing numbers stopped off at Matsuzaka to pay their respects to Motoori who wrote a famous *tanka*, or thirty-one-syllable poem, beloved by all Japan. It runs: —

> *Shikishimano Yamatogokoro wo*
> *Hito-owaba*
> *Asahini niou yamazakurabana.*

> If one should ask you
> What is the heart
> Of Island Yamato —
> It is the mountain cherry blossom
> Which exhales its perfume in the morning sun.

Still preserved are the small bells on which Motoori played. Their tinkling resonance has not been lost. And visitors may see the favorite corner of the author in his study where he sat on the floor and wrote for thirty-four years. Matsuzaka is the Mitsuis' home town, but Matsuzaka takes more pride in Motoori.

The Mitsui love and respect of Motoori is reflected in the relics preserved in the Mitsui family library in Tokyo. Prominently displayed is a *koto* designed by Motoori and given by him to Takakage Mitsui in 1790. It is a magnificent instrument five feet long of highly polished wood. Its thick, heavy strings still give forth the resoundingly deep tones that delighted its designer. But more priceless is the letter written to Takakage to accompany the gift. The letter has been transferred to a *kakemono*, or tapestried piece which the Japanese use as their sole wall decoration above the godshelf or honored part of each room. Still another prized relic is the original of a book of poems written by Takakage, who apparently was a better businessman than a poet, for the manuscript shows laborious corrections in the poems made in red ink by Motoori. Thus Takakage went down in the Mitsui annals as a poet and scholar, but an examination of this work in the original reveals that he like other Mitsuis had a way of getting help from the masters.

Coincident with the arrival of Perry, the weakening Shogunate's financial demands on wealthy business firms became heavier and more insistent. Eight days after Perry left Japan on his first trip, the Shogun Iyeyoshi died and was succeeded by the twenty-nine-year-old Iyesada, who scarcely had the mentality of a child of twelve. Money was badly needed, not only for belated efforts at building up some sort of defenses against the foreigners, but to relieve the populace which had undergone a new series of natural calamities including crop failures, earthquakes and tidal waves. That same year the Shogunate asked the Mitsuis for a loan of 200,000 ryo, citing the dire need of the State treasury.

Very politely the Mitsuis refused to extend the loan. It was the first time the Mitsuis refused to play along with the Central Government. They pointed out that the bad times had affected the Mitsuis' own fortunes, and furthermore the coming of Perry had thrown such a perplexing light upon the circumstances of Japan that they were uncertain of the future. That, however, was only a convenient excuse; for the Mitsuis were far less myopic than the rest of Japan about the coming of Perry. Already they were making nebulous plans for branching out in foreign trade as soon as restrictions might be lifted.

A year later the Imperial Palace at Kyoto burned and the Shogun in a burst of generosity toward the Emperor's court asked the Mitsuis for funds to aid in the reconstruction of a larger palace of finer materials. This time the Mitsuis contributed, but continued to refuse any requests for replenishment of the Shogun's treasury.

As the penury of the Shogunate increased, its ministers had continually resorted to the old device of frequent issues of debased coinage. Premiums were given for older coins which had higher content of gold and silver.

In 1855, by increasing the premium for such exchange and other decrees, special efforts were made to get back all the old coins, in order to have them replaced with the new. As usual, such treasury profiteering resulted in higher prices and greater suffering by the populace.

One of the more startling schemes advanced at about this time to keep money pouring into the Shogun's treasury was that the Government take over collection of "nightsoil" and sell it at higher than prevailing prices.

In Japan human excrement has been something of a standard commodity for centuries. As far back as in the period of the first Tokugawas private companies were organized for periodic collection of "nightsoil" — to use Japan's adopted euphemism — by coolies to be sold to farmers and truck gardeners as manure. When the suggestion for making this business a Government monopoly arose, there was considerable protest, which led to a famous speech comparable to the oration of the American hill-billy legislator on changing the name of Arkansas. Yukichi Fukuzawa, founder of Keio University in Tokyo, which in time came to be looked upon as ·Mitsuis' university, where Family Heads and chief clerks were trained, tells about the speech in his autobiography.

The speech was made by an unidentified authority on foreign affairs at a gathering of fellow protestants. As translated, it read: —

The Government is determined to take over all the profit from the nightsoil, disregarding the rights of the brokers! What is this but downright despotism? In history I have read that the citizens of the American colonies resisted their Mother Country when she imposed a tax on tea.

The ladies of America gave up all use of tea, and even gave up the pleasures of tea parties. Now, let us follow the example of those Americans and give up the entire production of nightsoil, for the express purpose of resisting the despotism of our Government. Do you second my motion?

It was a seriously advanced suggestion, typical of Japanese political psychology. What became of the plan unfortunately was lost sight of in history.

Another scheme revealing the mental caliber of the Shogun's advisers was that a canal be dug through the heart of Yedo so that tolls might be collected for the Government. The canal was to have run alongside one of the capital's busiest streets.

Fukuzawa was sent on a mission to America, in 1867, to conclude the purchase of a warship for the Shogunate. The members of the mission received their allowances in Japanese silver coins which they were to change into American dollars before leaving Japan. Fukuzawa recalls that Hachiroemon Mitsui was the banking agent of the Government, and the mission members went to the Mitsui exchange house at Yokohama.

The wide fluctuations in Mitsui exchange quotations was a little disturbing to the Government officials who were in the mission. But one official had this very neat suggestion: —

"Look here," he said to the Mitsuis, "the exchange rate has been going against us for several days now and we haven't much time before our ship is scheduled to sail. Surely you must have on hand quite a stock of dollars that you took in when the rates on American dollars were better. In other words, don't you have some cheaper dollars that we could buy today?"

The idea was preposterous to the Mitsuis, who were well-versed in the laws of exchange, but they saw it was useless to try to explain the theory to the official, and untactful to go against governmental prerogative.

"Very well," said the Yokohama Mitsui, bowing low, "I imagine we have some cheaper dollars lying around somewhere. We will be glad to make the exchange at the lower rate." And the Mitsuis wrote off the loss.

Altogether, it would be difficult to estimate how much Japan lost when the country was opened to foreign trade — the losses being due to the Shogunate's lack of comprehension of currency problems in international transactions. All advice of the Mitsuis appears to have gone unheeded in this period, and the Mitsuis themselves were making some costly experiments in the new field opened to them.

American traders were quick to see how they could work the Japanese currency most profitably. Under the treaty with the United States Japan was obligated to change the money brought in by Americans into Japanese money. The Shogun's ministers never learned the fact that American silver dollars were no more than silver bullion in Japan. So the Americans worked in this fashion: One silver dollar weighed as much as three pieces of Japanese *ichi-bu* silver and were exchanged accordingly. Domestically four pieces of *ichi-bu* silver could be exchanged for one ryo of gold. When the Americans found out they could in effect get three ryo of Japanese gold for four dollars in silver, they started buying Japanese silver with American silver and then Japanese gold with Japanese silver, which caused considerable gold to leave the country, to the perplexity and dismay of the Shogunate.

The Government resorted to two different types of silver coinage to offset the influx of American and Mexican dollars and loss of Japanese gold, but both were unsound and the Americans kept on reaping exchange profits. For one hundred American dollars they were getting from one hundred and fifty to two hundred and seventy-four dollars' worth of Japanese gold. Eventually the Shogunate allowed the Japanese to pay taxes to the Government with foreign silver, assuring its free circulation in Japan, and in 1859 issued the following public appeal: —

Since the port of Kanagawa was opened to foreign trade the foreigners resident there have desired to get the Koban gold both new and old, and as a result the prices of commodities purchased therewith have gone up especially high. It is learned the foreigners resident in Yokohama often go out into the Japanese towns for the purpose of purchasing the Koban gold, and the Japanese merchants in the Japanese quarters, too, seeing the foreigners are anxious to get the Koban gold, collect these gold coins with a view to using them in their transactions with the foreigners. If that state of affairs continues the Japanese gold will gradually be taken by these foreigners out of the country, which is outrageously against the interests of Japan. The headmen in each street should, therefore, call the attention of the people in their respective streets to this matter, so that they will not act in the manner described against the interests of their country.*

It was soon evident, however, that it would require more stringent measures than sending headmen out into the streets exhorting shopkeepers to circumvent the natural operations of exchange laws in Japan.

The Shogun in 1858 had a Finance Minister named Kozuke Oguri, who, through a combination of circumstances, was to become a finger-man for the Mitsuis.

Oguri reasoned that the best place to find out about foreign currency was its home, and since it was American money that was troubling Japan most he asked permission of the Shogunate to go to America to study modern banking and exchange methods. The Government granted Oguri's request, sending him with the first mission to America in 1860 aboard the *U.S.S. Powhatan.* Altogether there were ninety-three members of the mission, including a dozen or more Japanese whose names long will be celebrated as pioneers in the modernization of the country and the people. The mission had a wide range of purpose, primarily to pay the Shogun's respects to President Buchanan, to observe various aspects of American life, and to bear copies of the ratification of the new treaty of commerce between America and Japan.

It was an exciting trip for the Japanese, all of whom were seeing the Occident for the first time. They crossed the Pacific

* Quoted from Takekoshi.

by way of Honolulu, where they were received by the King of Hawaii, to San Francisco, then sailed down the coast as far as Panama, where they disembarked and crossed the Isthmus in a "land-steamer" (or train) that "sped like an arrow, 57 miles in three hours"; and then they sailed aboard another American warship up the Atlantic Coast to Washington. They were received by the President, saw the sights of Baltimore, Philadelphia and New York, and returned the following year to make known their findings to a Government that was to last only a few years more.

Histories have skimmed over that first Japanese mission to the United States. But Frank Leslie's *Illustrated Newspaper* had staff artists down at the Potomac docks when the delegation arrived, and again must have had a man under President Buchanan's desk to get the impression depicted when the Japanese were received at the White House. And the Japanese themselves brought back five bulky journals of their impressions of America. The most detailed is the diary of the retainer of the High Commissioner of Foreign Affairs.

The diarist* promptly noted that American officers carried only one sword, that America had no beggars, that even the ladies wore watches and were highly honored and that every room in the Willard Hotel in Washington had a bell cord which guests might pull to get attention from the manager's desk. Some other interesting observations, quoted from the diary of this first Japanese impression of America, read: —

When the President of this country is to be elected four or five of the leading men of the Government choose a candidate

* Kanesaburo Masakiyo Yanagawa was the diarist. His journal was translated into English by Junichi Fukuyama and Roderick H. Jackson and published under the title *The First Japanese Mission to America* by J. L. Thompson and Company, of Kobe, Japan, in 1937.

who is nominated by the party convention. This candidate then stands for election. Anyone of good character except a Negro may be elected President. . . .

When the President or other high officials go to a private house they remove their hats. . . .

In order to marry, the man must be twenty-one, and the woman eighteen. As they are not fully grown before this age, if they marry younger they will get sick.

Ladies are very careful not to expose their breasts, so when they wish to nurse their children they do not withdraw their clothes from their breasts but they put the child's head inside their waist so that he may nurse.

The American people are simple and honest like Japanese born in the mountains or on the farm who have never been spoiled by the big city. The English are jealous and have a very bad disposition. Because we came to America they are jealous, hence we are more carefully guarded. A cartoon printed in the newspaper showed a Japanese and an American walking hand in hand while an Englishman stood by looking on, gnashing his teeth.

At the Willard Hotel, there were "many flies, but no mosquitoes or fleas."

In New York the Japanese stopped at the seven-story Metropolitan Hotel, whose manager "was a colonel in the Russian army during the Crimean War and commanded 300 cavalry and 2,000 infantry."

The Japanese had arrived at the Battery and rode up Broadway, "escorted by several thousand soldiers; and policemen carrying sticks about three feet long walked on both sides of our carriages. The spectators carrying flags and waving handkerchiefs or hats welcomed us." This was not more than a half-century before the parade of Channel swimmers and trans-Atlantic fliers up Broadway from the Battery.

Another strictly modern touch: —

"Because many people from other countries live in New York we were heavily guarded when we went out." A Japanese delegation of ninety-three arriving in New York in 1939 might need an even heavier guard.

"Because we were so well guarded while in New York, we gave $20,000 to the authorities." Well, they had come to America to learn about exchange.

They paid a visit to the home of Commodore Perry, who had died only a few years previously. Commodore Perry had brought back to America two Japanese dogs. The diarist with pathos records: "They sniffed our clothes and, realizing that we were Japanese, danced at our feet, leaped in our laps and would not leave us. When we departed they followed us and though they could not speak, they had feelings like men. They showed their affection so plainly by their voice that we were quite sad and shed a tear when we left them."

Meanwhile the Shogun's two-sworded Finance Minister was making the rounds with the delegation, observing that "the price of gold and silver is higher than in Japan but both are used very much." He paid a visit to the United States mint at Philadelphia and saw "mountain-like" piles of gold and silver specie. He talked with leading bankers, Government officials and exchange experts.

When Oguri returned from America in 1861 he had some definite ideas about meeting American traders on a common ground.

He proceeded to carry out his plans through the instrumentality of one of the four most brilliant financiers ever connected with Mitsuis, the first of a long line of illustrious *banto* or head clerks who began managing the affairs of the House just before the Restoration.

This was Rizaemon Minomura, a supple, resourceful financial genius, who piloted the Mitsuis through the uncertainties of the Restoration period and kept their house from going on the rocks with the Shogunate itself.

From the time of Minomura's distinctive service, the actual direction of the firm's business has been in the hands of the chief managing director instead of those of the heads of the Mitsui family as in the past.

Not a great deal is known of Minomura's antecedents. His father apparently was an impecunious businessman who had given up samurai rank on leaving his native town of Dewa to essay a commercial career in Yedo. Rizaemon was born in Yedo in 1821, but started wandering about the country at the age of seven with his parents. He was a penniless orphan in Kyushu at the age of ten, and his movements were obscure until he returned to Yedo nine years later. He became an apprentice in a small banking and textile firm. The youth's industriousness and early adaptiveness to the business won the favor of the head of the firm and when Rizaemon fell in love with the daughter of a neighboring household, Nishimura recommended him so strongly that the girl's father adopted Rizaemon and permitted him to wed the daughter. Rizaemon took the name of his father-in-law, Minomura, and joined the Minomura sugar and candy-making establishment in the Kanda Ward of Yedo.

Young Minomura immediately displayed the same ability and acumen in candy-making that he had shown in textiles. During the day he went about the city drumming up business for his father-in-law, and at night carefully folded up his formal clothes and turned to the menial task of helping the shop employees refine sugar and make candy in the back of the establishment. Minomura showed all the earmarks of an early Japanese go-getter — he was confident, sometimes he was brash, and he was a smooth talker. In personality he more nearly resembled the American type of businessman than perhaps any other Japanese of his time.

By a fortunate coincidence, the home of Finance Minister Oguri was in Kanda, not far from the home of the Minomuras. Meeting Finance Minister Oguri, perhaps in the kitchen, young Minomura attracted the attention of the Finance Minister by his personality, industry and fertility of ideas about business in general. One account says that Minomura became something of a courier for Oguri, and as their intimacy grew Minomura was persuaded to leave the candy trade and set up a small banking and exchange house of his own. There were promises of assistance and Minomura lost no time in making up his mind.

The Finance Minister diverted considerable business to the new firm, and from his close association with Oguri Minomura soon had a better insight as to the actual state of the Shogunate's finances than did most of the businessmen who were dealing with the Government, including the Mitsuis.

The Mitsuis were very early followers of the sound business theory that if you can't compete with a rival it is a good idea to buy him out. The Mitsuis could compete with Minomura, probably, in business; but not in profitable association with the Finance Minister. They sent Junzo Saito, their contact man, to Minomura, and after some negotiation Minomura agreed to scrap his own business and join the Mitsui firm. It was a brilliant business stroke for the Mitsuis.

Minomura came to the Mitsuis just at the right time, two years before the Restoration of 1868. If any further conclusive word was needed to keep the Mitsuis from going down with the Tokugawa, Minomura could furnish it. Besides his actual knowledge of the Tokugawas' financial predicament, he was imbued with new ideas of corporative business brought back from America by Oguri. He needed only the resources of the House of Mitsui with which to work.

This was an infusion of new blood into the Mitsui commercial line, comparable to the adoption of Takahisa Sasaki into the family in the middle of the Fifteenth Century. Minomura did for the Mitsui business what the young, spirited Sasaki did for the family line. And as the Sasakis left their crest with the Mitsuis, Minomura left the indelible imprint of new business policies. Even more valuable was his demonstration to the Mitsuis that talent from outside the family could be hired to conduct the firm's affairs better than could the Family Heads themselves.

As the storm of the Restoration broke Minomura, riding high and dry with the Mitsuis, parted company with his old benefactor Oguri. The Mitsuis now definitely were with the Imperialists. Minomura did not have to be converted. His business instinct simply fortified the Mitsui decision. But Oguri remained loyal to the Shogunate. Even after Yedo fell into the hands of the Imperial Army and the last Shogun, Keiki Tokugawa, voluntarily retired to Mito peacefully giving up his power, Oguri gathered together a band of followers and fled northward from Yedo.

Apparently he had in mind an attempt to set up a new seat for the Tokugawas. A detachment of Imperial troops was close on his heels, and finally caught up with him at a hideaway in a small village at the foot of Mount Akagi in Gumma Prefecture, not far from the present idyllic summer resort of Karuizawa. Oguri and his son were decapitated in that village as soon as they were found.

One story is that Oguri carried a fortune in gold with him when he fled from Yedo, presumably to be used in an effort to restore the Shogun's government. As the chase became too hot he buried it somewhere in the depths of Mount Akagi. This was never verified. Several years ago the legend was printed in Japanese newspapers. Gold hunters swarmed about the mountain seeking the treasure trove. Nothing was found. Oguri's secret died with him.

Chapter *VIII*

THE CHOSHU CLAN

𝄃𝄃𝄃 D̲RESSED IN FORMAL robes, Saburosuke Mitsui, dignified head of the House of Mitsui in Kyoto, sat waiting in silence late on the night of December 26, 1867, in the Mitsui mansion across the street from the Nijo Castle in Kyoto. At his side in a beautifully polished inlaid box was 1,000 ryo in silver and gold. Mitsui men did not often sit up so late at night. Tallow candles were blazing in the main rooms of the mansion. Servants were awake and alert, each man at his appointed post. An air of expectancy hung over the whole compound.

Across the street from the side entrance to the Mitsui compound in the Nijo Castle there was even greater activity. A sixteen-year-old boy only a few months before had become Emperor. He was Mutsuhito, destined to become Japan's most illustrious ruler, the great Meiji. Only a few days before he had signed an imperial edict which opened a new epoch in the history of Japan. Its salient part read: —

Now that Tokugawa Keiki has restored the administrative authority to the [Imperial] Court, the Court directly controls the Imperial polity, quite free from bias, laying great stress on public opinion, and keeping all undisturbed those good customs and usages preserved under the Tokugawa regime. The clans shall be quite bold to fight for justice, on the one hand, and to strive for the augmentation of the glory of the Empire on the other.

That, in effect, was the Restoration. Once again, after seven hundred years, the Emperor was the administrative head of the State, in Japan.

But there was one slight difficulty: The coffers of the new Government were empty. Events had been moving fast during the latter months of 1867. Now that the Restoration, or relatively bloodless revolution, had been achieved and the rule handed over to Meiji, the Councillors of State became aware of the depleted treasury. Informally the word was conveyed to Saburosuke Mitsui that a great honor was to be bestowed upon the family. So the Mitsuis were prepared.

Just at midnight an Imperial messenger, accompanied by a small retinue, crossed the moat at the entrance of Nijo Castle and walked the half-block down the empty street to the entrance of the Mitsui mansion. Heralds stirred up the Mitsui lodge-keepers. The Mitsui servants admitted the messenger straightway to the presence of Saburosuke. After a customary exchange of formalities, the messenger informed Mitsui that his presence at Nijo Castle was desired. With feigned surprise and acquiescent humility, Mitsui announced he would go at once. The messenger left and Mitsui, not forgetting his box of coins, followed the messenger to the Castle.

There, soon after midnight, he was received by officials of the Imperial Treasury and informed that the new Government had no money and that he, as head of the Kyoto *Mitsui-Gumi*, had been appointed Fiscal Agent to raise funds for the Imperial Treasury. Mitsui, with the usual protestations, acknowledged the honor, and begged leave to make a slight present on the spot. Thereupon he produced the box of gold and tendered it to the Treasury officials. This act marked the first instance of the contribution of "the people's money" to the Government in the new regime. It was, moreover, the beginning of a long period of financial service by the Mitsui family to the Imperial Government.

The Mitsuis had watched with approbation and in various ways had contributed to the succession of steps that put young Meiji on the throne again. When a few months earlier Meiji rode in state from the old Imperial Palace at Kyoto to Nijo Castle, where he was to take over rule, the Mitsuis had a grandstand seat. From the side entrance of their home across the road from the new Imperial seat, the whole family gathered to watch the brilliant procession pass only a few yards from the Mitsui gate and turn at right angles to cross the moat into the palace. It was a sight that so impressed the Mitsuis that they had it painted. The resultant piece, by the artist Tomone Kobori, was a large Japanese-style water color, which was presented by the Mitsui family to the Imperial art gallery. It hangs today in the memorial building dedicated to Emperor Meiji in the Outer Gardens of the Meiji Shrine in Tokyo. It was a Mitsui-eye view of a turning in the history of Japan, opening the period of expansion for the Mitsuis.

There have been countless thousands of words written on the cause of the downfall of the Tokugawa Government, but they may be summarized in the statement that the rule of the dictatorship gave way before complications attendant upon the opening of the country to foreign trade. Just as the Mitsuis suffered financial losses, as we have seen, the western clans, principally Choshu, Satsuma and Tosa, feared the vacillating attitude of the Tokugawas toward the foreigner, together with indications that the Tokugawas themselves desired to monopolize the new trade. All of which, the clans believed, menaced the independence of Japan. Meanwhile the clans had grown in military power as the warrior class, no longer awed by the weakening Shogunate, began to desert their lords and take on the status of ronin, or free-lance samurai attracted to the growing power of the clans. There had sprung up in every town and village of Western Japan so-called "Patriotic Schools" with a theologico-military curriculum — widely revived in Japan one hundred years later, when expansion on the Asiatic continent began. These "schools" taught exaltation of the Emperor, — as descendant of the Sun Goddess and therefore rightful ruler of Japan, — destruction of the power of the Tokugawa vassals, and expansion by force of arms of the Japanese Empire into Asia. These courses in chauvinism took active expression in military training, involving both new Western tactics and the old samurai arts.

One clan, the notorious Choshu, in 1864 had become strong enough to attempt a bold plan of kidnaping the Emperor Komei, with his knowledge, if not consent, and of holding him until the Tokugawas were overthrown. The plot failed due to the vigilance of Tokugawa spies. The Shogun sent a punitive expedition against the clan, but not only did the expense of this expedition exhaust the Yedo treasury but its failure erased what remained of the Tokugawa's military prestige.

In the end it was all very simple. On February 3, 1867, the antiforeign Emperor, Komei, died, and Mutsuhito, or Meiji, ascended to the throne. The time was ripe for action. The clans gathered at Kyoto to back the Emperor, but before marching on Yedo they decided to forward a joint invitation to the Shogun inviting him to step down from office. To the surprise of the bristling clans the Shogun, Keiki, harassed by foes and fears on every side, welcomed the opportunity of quitting the job so easily, and on November 3, 1867, sent the following historic reply: —

My ancestor received more confidence and favor from the Court than any of his predecessors, and his descendants have succeeded him for more than two hundred years. Though I fill the same office, almost all the acts of the administration are far from perfect, and I confess it with shame that the present unsatisfactory condition of affairs is due to my shortcomings and incompetence. Now that foreign intercourse becomes daily more extensive, unless the Government is directed from one central authority, the foundations of the State will fall to pieces. If, however, the old order of things be changed, and the administrative authority be restored to the Imperial Court, and if national deliberations be conducted on an extensive scale, and the Imperial decision be secured, and if the Empire be supported by the efforts of the whole people, then the Empire will be able to maintain its rank and dignity among the nations of the earth. Although I have allowed all the feudal lords to state their views without reserve, yet it is, I believe, my highest duty to realize this ideal by giving up entirely my rule over this land.

The Emperor Meiji's reply came nine days later, saying briefly that: "Tokugawa Keiki's proposal to restore the administrative authority to the Imperial Court is accepted by the Emperor."

Nobody protested openly against the Shogun's resignation except the merchants and tradesmen of Yedo, who, fearing their ruin if the seat of Government was removed to Kyoto, inspired citizens of the capital to sign a long document bewailing their plight. This promptly was pigeonholed.

There were a few sporadic outbreaks by lesser retainers of

the Tokugawas, notably an uprising at Toba and Fushimi, not far south of Kyoto, which gave the Mitsuis another chance to come through with "people's money" for the new Imperial Government. The new Government sent out an army to crush the Toba-Fushimi uprising, and, in an engagement lasting less than twenty-four hours, the Shogun's forces, although numerically greater, were decisively defeated. Significantly, the Government's army displayed the Imperial banner in that engagement, a technicality which branded the skirmish as an "attempted revolt against the Emperor."

To finance this brief but significant expedition the Government had to draw on Mitsui resources. An Imperial messenger again rushed to the Mitsuis early in the morning of January 2, and called for 2,000 ryo "in cash, and please hurry."

The Mitsuis, with dubious pride in their new honor of serving as financial angels of the Imperialist cause, brought out the specified amount of silver, loaded it onto a handcart, and rushed it to Sokoku Temple, which was the field headquarters of the expeditionary army.

By a coincidence, the Government escort who accompanied the rumbling Mitsui handcart to the temple was Iwao Oyama (later Marshal Prince), fierce-visaged Satsuma clansman who years later commanded the Japanese forces to victory in the famous Battle of Mukden in the Russo-Japanese war of 1904–1905.

About ten days after the Toba-Fushimi coup, the Mitsuis joined with two other leading Kyoto exchange houses in presenting another "gift" of 10,000 ryo to the new Government. Mitsui historians assert this was the last voluntary gesture of financial assistance to the Meiji Government by the House. Thereafter all financial support was extended in the form of loans. Quickly gaining confidence, the Government in the latter part of January, 1868, levied a "forced loan of 3,000,000 ryo" from the Mitsuis and other wealthy merchant-bankers of Kyoto and Yedo to form a treasury fund and reorganize the currency system.

An expensive item of the new Government's operations was the dispatch of imposing expeditions of Imperial troops into the field, not so much to put down uprisings against the new rule as by their very appearance in the field to dissuade any such opposition at its inception. These expeditions were called *chinbu*, or, roughly, "stabilize-and-comfort" forays. These *chinbu* expeditions quickly became a headache for the Mitsuis, for they were expensively equipped. They traveled about in some ostentation, as they carried the burden of instilling confidence in the new Imperial régime into the populace.

Mitsui records have quite a bit to say about these *chinbu* expeditions, with a bitterness scarcely hidden by the grandiloquence of ledger-language. Apparently, if it had not been for Mitsui resources the *chinbu* junkets would have had hard going. One such expedition, 5,000 strong, became stranded about twenty miles outside Tokyo and rushed back a messenger calling for 1,000 bales of rice to carry on. The Government relayed the requisition order to the Mitsuis, and as usual the Mitsuis made good. Says the Mitsui record, probably written for subsequent official perusal: —

The Mitsui firm this day had the great honor and privilege of receiving an Imperial Government order for 1,000 bales of polished rice. After a hurried conference among the chief *banto* [clerks] a Mitsui representative went to the mansion of Prince Iwakura [commander of the Imperial forces] and was honored to be able to report that the order forthwith would be filled.

After a few more costly experiments in quartermastering for the Imperial Troops, Mitsuis sent another representative to the mansion of Prince Iwakura and asked if they might be permitted to send along a Mitsui man with these expeditions to have charge of the strong-box containing the troops' cash. This was arranged, and the Mitsuis were enabled, with more personal supervision, to keep the *chinbu* expeditions financially in hand. No doubt if the system had kept up for long the Mitsuis could have put it on a paying basis.

Back in Kyoto, *Mitsui-Gumi* was taking the lead in floating the three-million ryo bond issue which may be regarded as the very first national debt raised as such in Japan. It was floated under adverse conditions with the future of the Government anything but secure, the people restive, the *chinbu* marching around running out of food, and the foreigners clamoring for new trade treaties and opening of new ports. Three million ryo at such a time was an unheard-of sum in Japan, comparable to some of the astronomical figures introduced by the New Deal in America in 1932. Moreover, the country at the time had not heard of bonds. But Mitsui's two banking houses, in Kyoto and Osaka, became the headquarters of the new bond campaign, and the equivalent of four-minute speakers were sent around among bankers and merchants, appealing to their religio-patriotic motives. The first big bond flotation in Japan was oversubscribed, in ten months, to the extent of 3,800,000 ryo.

When the Imperial Government put out an issue of paper money the Mitsuis again set the example by prompt acceptance of it at its face value, attempting to induce the public to realize its value and use. But close on the heels of this paper money the Government issued an order for still another 860,-

ooo ryo in hard money, to eliminate some of the difficulties caused by the unpopularity of the paper money. Of this amount Mitsui-Gumi was assigned 300,000 ryo and asked to produce immediately 50,000 ryo. The Mitsuis had to sell all the old gold and silver coins in their possession and the "cellar reserve" of silver to scrape that amount together.

The bewildering diversity of coinage and note issues, together with some counterfeiting, before long had immersed the Government in such difficulties that it was forced, in February, 1868, to entrust the work of transacting the state exchequer business to Mitsui-Gumi in conjunction with Ono-Gumi and Shimada-Gumi, two other big Osaka exchange houses.

"This will give an idea of the extreme financial straits in which the government was placed in those days," Mitsui records modestly recount. "It was, however, enabled to tide over the situation, thanks to the unremitting exertions and intense spirit of patriotism with which Mitsui-Gumi did its part."

Histories of the period seem attracted to the glamor of the Choshu and Satsuma clans and almost totally overlook the unpublicized Mitsuis and the generous assistance they gave to the Imperial Government at its most trying time. On the other hand, it would not be incorrect to say that the Mitsuis had speculated boldly on the success of the Restoration movement. Mitsui leaders must have realized that they were taking a risk that might have ruined three centuries of steady business progress. Although they may be credited with a full measure of patriotic devotion to the Imperial cause, from a business viewpoint it was a gamble of major importance and the returns they won were in keeping with the venture they took.

Mitsui's rewards, in fact, were not long withheld. During the first year of Meiji, 1868, they formed what was later to become a most profitable connection with Kaoru Inouye, the finance expert of the new Government. Thus was achieved one of the typical Mitsui transitions. The House had been linked to the Shogunate's last Finance Minister, but lost no time in gaining an even stronger position in the same office under the new regime.

Inouye, the "one-man Cabinet," and Ito, the "Constitution maker" were two of the most remarkable products of the Choshu clan, and two of Japan's greatest statesmen. The Mitsuis' close connection with Inouye and still other Choshu clansmen has given rise to the traditional belief that the Mitsuis were closely allied with the Choshu in the period of clan rivalry for the domination of the new Government, though Mitsui archivists deny there was any real connection with the Choshu clan, and assert on the contrary that the Mitsui-Osaka branch had close business dealings with the Satsuma, issuing notes for the clan two or three years before the Restoration.

The Japanese are a homogeneous race; but the Irish of Japan, at least in those stirring days, were the Choshu clansmen. In the Donnybrook Fair of factions and fights that preceeded the Restoration in the days between 1852 and 1868, the Choshu alone were willing to fight all comers by themselves or on either side. They tried to kidnap an Emperor, they spat on the ground and went to war single-handedly against the United States, they twisted the British lion's tail and fought an allied naval expedition of five nations before they were subdued.

Perhaps a little more gentlemanly but only slightly less powerful were their rivals, the Satsumas. It is a tradition in

Japan that her army officers for generations, down to the present day, have come from the Choshu clan, while the Satsumas produced the naval officers. When in later years the Iwasakis, who formed the House of Mitsubishi, Mitsui's greatest business rival, joined forces with the Satsuma clan, Japanese politicians were fond of tracing Mitsui-Choshu connections. The same effort continued when clan politics merged into party politics, the Choshu leaders being instrumental in founding the Seiyukai party and the Satsuma influences merging into the Minseito. Commentators profess to see the rise of Mitsui fortunes when the Seiyukai was in power and Mitsubishi gains under Minseito cabinets, down to 1932 when strictly party cabinets virtually disappeared in Japan. Clan influence in the Japanese Army and Japanese Navy thinned out to little more than a tradition, but for fifty years or more the Mitsuis stood in good favor with the army authorities, while the Mitsubishis have done very well with some naval contracts.

Clans in Japan were not exactly analogous to the Highland clans of Scotland, whose members generally claimed common origin or used the same surname. Clansmen of Japan might be of dozens of different families, more intangibly but no less strongly held by ancient ties of propinquity, landholdings and the innate Japanese sense of loyalty. "Clan" is the ordinary English translation of a Japanese word *han*, which Chamberlain suggests might better be rendered by the word *diamiate*, that is, the territory and personal followers of a daimio or feudal noble. It was an influence not so easily abolished as feudalism itself in Japan; and until the founding of political parties under the new democratic rule of Meiji, the clans were reservoirs of opposing political thoughts. Even within the Choshu clan, some were eager for contact with the foreigners after 1853, while others fought them off.

When the "patriotic schools" sprang up prior to the Restoration they uncovered one prodigy in the Choshu clan, Shoin Yoshida, who indirectly contributed to the making of the Ito-Inouye team which was so instrumental in starting the Meiji government on its constitutional path.

At the age of eleven Yoshida was giving lectures on military science and tactics before his clan. Before he was twenty, this combination of genius and fanatic was laying down a program for Japan that included the forceful acquisition of Formosa, Korea, all of Manchuria, and large parts of Eastern Siberia. He conceived of Japan as a great continental Asiatic power, and urged the Choshus to send men to America to study Western methods by which these ends might be achieved.

When the clan was slow to act, young Shoin, who never topped five feet, tried to go himself. Four times this burning zealot with two swords in his belt tried to stow-away on Perry's ships when they were in Japan in 1853. Each time he was caught and sent ashore, for the Shogunate's laws still forbade Japanese from leaving the country. After Perry left, Yoshida continued his subversive lectures against the Tokugawas, until finally he was arrested, sent to Yedo in a cage, and beheaded at the age of twenty-nine.

His clan erected a monument to his memory in 1909, pointing out significantly that Yoshida was one of the first "farsighted men to see that Japan must adopt foreign civilization, or, like India, fall before foreign progress."

And it was a Choshu clansman, Inouye, who at last guided the Mitsuis and the start of foreign relations to success and entrenchment.

In 1863, this future Prime Minister of the House of Mitsui was twenty-seven years old, a strong, sinewy youth full of nervous energy and unabated curiosity about the foreigner newly arrived in Japan. Popular feeling against the foreigner was spurred on by the "*Kinno! Joi!*" ("Loyalty to the Emperor and oust the foreign barbarians!") slogan adopted by all factions against the Tokugawa Shogunate. The year had opened with extraordinarily solemn religious ceremonies by the Emperor, the father of Meiji, for the purpose of imploring divine aid in the current move to drive the foreigners out of Japan, thereby compromising the Shogunate — which apparently had revealed its weakness by submissive yielding to their "knocking at the door." An Imperial Decree was promulgated April 20, fixing May 10 as the definite date beyond which no alien was to be tolerated in the country. But it was a little early for Imperial Decrees to be very effective.

In the midst of such an atmosphere of boiling fermentation, Kaoru Inouye had recalled the admonition of his fellow clansman, Yoshida, and himself had become convinced that Japan needed all the weapons of the foreigner, military, economic and governmental, to cope with his invasion. He believed primarily in a strong naval force, and insisted there was nothing that had been invented or contrived by the Westerners that could not be appropriated for Japan's own use. Only a few days after the Emperor returned from the temples of Kamo and Iwashimizu in pompous cavalcade, Inouye decided to go abroad — with two principal ideas in mind: to study the essentials of a strong defensive naval force, and to confirm his impression that the real foundation of a powerful nation must be laid in economic development.

This was a hazardous resolution, for at this time it was still a capital offense to leave Japan; and the Shogunate's spies were still vigilant, especially against such escapades of the young doctrinaires of the more restless clans. Inouye first approached Prince Mori, head of the clan, and sought to interest him in the project. The clan leaders were strongly opposed to the venture, being unable to reconcile the idea of learning about the foreigner with the business at hand of driving him out of the country. But Inouye continued to exhort and plead until he won over Prince Mori and interested four other young Choshu clansmen in the trip, including Ito, who was to become "the greatest Oriental since Confucius."

Prince Mori went so far as to make a secret donation of 600 ryo toward the expenses of the trip. This reminded Inouye that he had no conception of the money needed to live abroad, so he wrote the British Consul at Yokohama, a Mr. Gower, and asked for an estimate. Mr. Gower replied that it would require at least 1,000 ryo a year for each person. This meant 5,000 ryo, an enormous sum for any samurai family, and one that would strain the resources of the clan itself. By this time Inouye was so set upon going it became apparent to the clan elders that, in true samurai fashion, Inouye, or perhaps the whole five, might commit hara-kiri if the money were not raised. "Officials of the Principality (the clan) thought it too pitiful to condemn to suicide such a spirited and energetic young man as Inouye," wrote a kinsman, "especially as he was now seconded by young Ito and others, all of whom doubtless already had given unmistakable evidence of future greatness."

There were more clandestine conferences, and finally the Choshu leaders agreed that without making public the decision, they would advance the money from a reserve which had been accumulated for guns ordered from America.

The 5,000 ryo secretly was transported to Yokohama and turned over to Mr. Gower, who bought their passage through Jardine, Matheson and Company, the oldest foreign shipping firm in Japan. A month later, the five youths, traveling separately to avoid Tokugawa spies, made their way to Yokohama and presented themselves to the consul. At midnight, May 12, 1863, they were provided with their first foreign clothes and smuggled aboard ship and concealed in coal bunkers.

Just before the ship sailed the spirited Choshu youths dramatically ranged themselves in line and cut off the top-knots of their hair, which they had worn samurai-style. It was symbolic of the step they were taking. The consul had told them samurai topknots would be ridiculed in England. Inouye entrusted his hair to Mr. Gower, with a letter asking his parents to "have pity on this, my unwilling act."

They had taken passage only to Shanghai, where they were to change ships. The busy port of Shanghai with its hundreds of steamers from foreign lands so impressed Inouye that he considered his beliefs about the wisdom of foreign commerce virtually confirmed. He wrote a letter to an elder of his clan, telling him of the obvious advantages of ending Japan's seclusion; but the recipient is said to have tossed the letter aside with the contemptuous remark that Inouye was "out of the country only four or five days and already he has changed his convictions."

At Shanghai the five Japanese called on a Mr. Keswick, head of the Shanghai branch of Jardine, Matheson and Company, and presented their letter from the Yokohama consul. Mr. Keswick spoke to them in English, but only one of the party knew any English at all — some forty or fifty words.

Inouye knew only one English word, and he had that wrong. He had confused the word "nebigation" (navigation), as taken from a primitive English-Japanese dictionary, with "Navy" — which was the idea nearest his heart. Mr. Keswick asked them through an interpreter why they were going to England.

Inouye, with quick understanding, and hoping to make an impression, replied: "Nebigation!" He had no more words to explain and Mr. Keswick, assuming him to be the leader, thought the Japanese wanted to learn the science of navigation. When he shipped Inouye and Ito aboard the schooner *Pegasus* he helpfully told the Captain that these Japanese wanted to learn sailing from keel to truck and to be treated like common sailors. The other three were to sail on another ship.

As soon as the *Pegasus* cleared port the Captain mustered his passengers out with the crew and put them to work coiling lines. Inouye and Ito were a little surprised at this, for they had paid for their passage and had not understood in Yokohama that passengers were supposed to work. All efforts at explaining failed because of their lack of knowledge of English. The Captain helpfully but firmly saw that they were hauled out of their berths regularly to stand watch, and in spite of protestations in unintelligible tongue the youths literally worked their way before the mast from Shanghai to England. Seasickness added to their discomfiture, and in later years Count Inouye was fond of telling how he and Prince Ito passed many a night sitting together in a lifeboat on deck discussing the destiny of Japan between vomiting and tears.

For four months and eleven days around the Cape of Good Hope, these sensitive samurai with their delicate hands stood up to the hard toil of cleaning decks, lending a hand with sails, pumping water and coiling lines, eating salt beef, hardtack and bad tea, until finally they reached London.

They found their other three companions had already arrived, and as they swapped experiences it dawned upon Inouye and Ito what hardships had been brought upon them by Inouye's unfortunate use of the word "nebigation." But now they could laugh about it, and with the same fortitude that carried them through the ordeal aboard ship they could apply themselves to the task of learning about the foreigner.

They started in by learning English and before many months Inouye had progressed to the point where he could read the English newspapers with partial understanding. When delayed dispatches told of the bombardment of Kagoshima, stronghold of the Satsuma clan, by English warships the news meant considerably more to these Japanese in London than to any other reader. It was apparent to Inouye and Ito that the Satsuma clan had sought to enforce the Imperial declaration against foreigners, with the consequent defeat of the Satsumas. Then came news that their own clan had fired on an American vessel attempting to pass through the Straits of Shimoneseki.

Fearing the inevitable for the Choshu clan, and well fortified with their own observation about the power of the foreigner, Inouye and Ito heroically decided to abandon for the present their mission to Europe and hurry home, not only to save if possible their own clan but, by preaching the impossibility of seclusion, to avert a similar fate for the whole country. They believed they could, by reporting on the actual power of Western nations, open the eyes of all Japan to the peril of trying to block the foreigners at its doorstep. They persuaded their three companions to remain behind, to carry on their original course, and they left London in the middle of March, 1864, to return to Japan on a sailing vessel. This time they spoke English well enough to explain carefully to the Captain that they wanted no further instruction in navigation, and they were able to make the trip as passengers, arriving in Yokohama June 10.

It was true that while the youths were abroad the Choshus

had begun target practice against foreign ships and precipitated a small-sized World War in the Orient. With their old
smooth-bore guns in place and a college cheer for "*Kinno!
Joi!*" they drove a row of stakes in midchannel for sighting
purposes and proclaimed the Straits of Shimonoseki closed.
These Straits controlled the principal route between eastern
Japan and the Continent. The action may be likened to a
whim on the part of the Governor of Panama to close the
Canal. When an American steamer tried to go through a few
days later, the Choshu opened fire on her. She escaped by
deft seamanship. An American warship went down from
Yokohama and gave battle to the Choshus, sinking two former
American ships that were part of the Choshu navy, and silenc-
ing a row of batteries.

But the Choshu clan was by no means subdued. They rebuilt their fortifications, mounted new mortars, and continued
to fire at all foreign passers-by. The French tried their hand
at pummeling the Choshu batteries, but only wasted their
shots.

Then foreign nations began assembling at Yokohama an
allied fleet of seventeen ships and 7,000 men from four nations
to send against the Choshus.

In the midst of preparations for the allied expeditionary
force, Inouye and Ito arrived home in Yokohama and looked
up the British consul who had befriended them the year before. He told them that the combined fleet was at the point
of descending upon Shimonoseki. The two youths had come
all the way from England to avert just such a calamity, and
apparently had arrived too late. Nevertheless they made every
effort, not only to get word to the Choshu but to persuade
them to alter their course before the foreign warships arrived.
They were further handicapped by the necessity of moving

secretly lest they be discovered by the Tokugawa agents and decapitated for having left Japan.

Late at night they went to the British Legation and pleaded with the British Minister to delay the expedition awhile, to give them a chance to get home and plead their case before their fiery fellow clansmen. They argued that the Choshu clansmen had been "fighting fools" largely through their ignorance of the actual power of foreign nations and the benefits of foreign intercourse. They believed they would be able to persuade Prince Mori to reverse his policy, if they could only get to him before the foreign warships made it too late.

The British Minister consented to take up the question with representatives of other powers and asked Inouye and Ito to wait until he could give them an answer. As they left the Legation, Interpreter Ernest Satow reminded them of the dangers of exposure as Choshu men and suggested that they go to a European hotel in the foreign settlement and talk only English at the hotel. They applied themselves so diligently to their task that, with their mustaches and beards which they had acquired in London, they successfully passed as Portuguese. But Inouye almost gave everything away when he reached for his sword to carve up a servant whom he overheard say to another: "This stingy, hairy devil wants a mosquito net, an unjustifiable luxury. Let us give him a net with holes to punish him for his cheek." Fortunately Inouye had no sword, and with more presence of mind Ito led him away to allow Inouye's samurai blood to cool and avert discovery.

Two or three days later, a messenger from the British Legation came at night to call them into conference. At the Legation they were told that the Powers had consented to allow these two young and scarcely identified men to be entrusted with the mission of rushing down to Prince Mori and attempting to bring him to reason before the allied fleet should set out from Yokohama.

As they started, the Minister asked the two Japanese youths whether they wanted to return to England for study if their mission failed.

"No," was the prompt reply of Inouye. "In that case, we shall probably be among the first to fall with drawn swords fighting against you."

The English man-of-war took them to the nearest safe port, and landed them so that Inouye and Ito could make their way by themselves into the Choshu Province. They found, as soon as they landed, that popular frenzy for expelling the foreigners had reached such a height that even the women were carrying dirks in their sashes for personal frays with the "hairy barbarians." Natives told the returning clansmen they would never get as far as their own province in European clothes, and supplied them with samurai garments and the customary two swords so they could continue their way without exciting suspicion.

Their arrival at the Choshu capital created a sensation. They had no difficulty in getting early hearing from the clan elders, and made lengthy speeches to Prince Mori on the futility of trying to stem the foreign tide. The Prince summoned Inouye alone for several private hearings on what the young observer had seen in England, and Inouye used his utmost eloquence to convey to the Prince the wealth and power of foreign nations.

Inouye and Ito spent five days arguing and pleading with their clansmen; but on June 29, 1864, Prince Mori summoned them and told them that although he recognized the force and validity of Inouye's arguments, and though he appreciated the patriotism which impelled them to take such a

stand at the risk of their lives, he regretted that he was unable
to brave popular opinion in the clan and he could not agree
to the memoranda submitted by the Powers.

A day later, a Choshu proclamation called on all samurai
to be prepared for the expected clash with the Powers. Meanwhile Inouye and Ito were ordered to return to the English
warship waiting for them, and attempt to bargain for further
delay. Negotiations aboard the warship failed and Inouye and
Ito returned, resigned to the fate not only of their own principality but of Japan. When the clan elders asked them if they
wanted to return to England to continue their studies Inouye
replied: —

"What use is there in a man's acquired knowledge when
the country he seeks to serve may in the meanwhile be wiped
out of existence? If the execution of us two can in any way
regenerate the spirit of the samurai class at this moment, why
not kill us and appease this clamor?"

Inouye and Ito remained in the hornets' nest still pleading
for rationality among the Choshu until both had very narrow
escapes from death. One group of samurai hotheads waylaid
Inouye at night. While one man tackled him around the legs
another swung his long sword as Inouye fell. He had a miraculous escape. As he went down his own sword pushed itself
through his belt so that it lay along his spinal column. His
would-be assassin's blade struck steel against steel and failed
to cut through Inouye's body. Inouye sprang up, drew his
sword that had saved him from death and fought until he
was cut down with abdomen wounds and left for dead.
Through the rest of his life he bore twenty large and small
scars from that encounter. Of such metal was Mitsuis' "front
man" at the beginning of the Meiji Era.

Ito had a more romantic escape from reactionaries of his

clan. Fleeing from a band he took refuge in a tearoom and was hidden under the floor by a girl, who later became Mrs. Ito.

So Ito was saved for Japan — only to be shot down by an assassin in Manchuria in 1909 — and Inouye was saved for Mitsui.

The two then stood to one side and let the Choshus learn their lesson from the allied fleet, which wasn't long coming. The five nations moved on the Choshu stronghold September 5, 1864, and before the day was over had blasted all fight out of the Japanese gamecocks.

Incidentally, America was able to spare only one ship for the enterprise, due to some war business of her own at the time, the Civil War. Consequently, when the allies figured up indemnity to be demanded of the Choshus, America was cut in for only $785,000 of the total $3,000,000. The cl 1 promptly refused to pay; but the Shogunate, by now the "Happy Hooligan" of Japan, anxious to keep the good will of foreigners, dutifully took over the debt and began installment payments. When the Shogunate fell, the Imperial Government in good faith continued the payments until they were completed in 1875. Thereupon, America, in a burst of altruism, returned the entire sum with a note of thanks. Japan took the sum and according to one authority used it to build the present breakwater at Yokohama where today the Water Police board incoming steamers to ask Americans please to state their business on coming to Japan.

Chapter *IX*

THE MITSUIS MODERNIZE

~~~ WITH THE RESTORA-
tion an accomplished fact in 1868, the Imperial Government
rewarded the Choshu clan for its support with the appointment of two clansmen as the heads of departments in the new
Government. They were Inouye and Ito, by now the two ablest
statesmen of their clan whose abilities and prophecies in considerable measure had come to be recognized.

Fortunately for the Mitsuis, Inouye became Finance Minister. In those early, haphazard days of the Meiji Government,
when the element of opportunism was not missing, politicians
were as anxious for financial support as financial houses were
for political aid. They were essential concomitants for success
in the El Dorado of government and finance that came to
light in Japan.

The union of Mitsui and Inouye under the circumstances
was a "natural," productive of much wedded bliss in later
years. Inouye himself was quite frank about it. Inouye's
biographers explain it succinctly: —

The Mitsuis were one of the oldest financial households in the
Empire. Their financial contributions to the cause of the Restoration were immense, and since the Restoration their willing-
ness to sacrifice any amount for the welfare of the new Government was impressive. It hardly needs to be pointed out that
Inouye gave support to the Mitsuis because he was able fully

to recognize their national importance and because he could well estimate the *knowledge of the political advantages the Meiji government could reap by utilizing the Mitsuis'* financial power.

As told in the previous chapter, one of the first concessions given to the Mitsuis was the work of transacting the exchequer business of the Government, in conjunction with the *Ono-Gumi* and the *Shimada-Gumi*, mainly because only these firms seemed able to work out the puzzle of grab-bag type of currency then in circulation.

When the bureau of specie and currency and the bureau of commercial law were established by the Government, Inouye saw to it that a Mitsui man was appointed *todori*, or governor, of each.

When the Imperial Government decided to transfer its seat from Kyoto to the more centrally located city of Yedo, the old Tokugawa capital, as further impressive sign that the Emperor had come out of his Eastern seclusion, the Mitsuis were given the task of raising funds for the expensive and ostentatious journey. Yedo was renamed "Tokyo," or "Eastern Capital," in preparation for the historic event; and with lavish display the young Emperor Meiji traveled by palanquin the 400 miles from Kyoto to Tokyo to establish his rule in the old castle of the Tokugawas in the heart of the city.

The Mitsuis were called upon by the Government to provide 50,000 ryo in bullion as expenses for the Imperial journey. It was another great strain on the Mitsui finances, but there were recompenses, not the least of which was the privilege accorded Takaaki Mitsui, head of the House, of walking near the palanquin of the Emperor as it moved along the historic

Tokaido highway between Kyoto and Tokyo. A notable portrait of the procession done by a contemporary artist shows the head of the House of Mitsui, with his characteristically thin, patrician face, well in the foreground of the array of notables. It was a deserved honor, for Takaaki Mitsui was attending his ruler to the new seat of Government as Treasurer.

In 1871, when the Government built and opened a mint with modern equipment at Osaka, with the expressed hope of unifying the currency of the country, it appointed Mitsui-Gumi as fiscal agent of the mint with the specified task of exchanging new coins for old and also for collecting and forwarding gold and silver bullion to various parts of the realm. Offices of the Mitsui agency were established in Kyoto, Osaka, Tokyo, Yokohama, Kobe and Hakodate. Again Mitsui efficiency and long training in co-ordinating of branches profitably were put at the disposal of the Government and the sacrifice did not go amiss.

Mitsui efforts, in fact, were neither unappreciated by the Government nor unnoticed by the general public. The financial prestige of the House was becoming so widely known that it came to be said commonly that the Government's financial department was in Suruga-cho, Tokyo headquarters of the Mitsui offices. During this period there naturally sprang up rumors and unsubstantiated reports that the Mitsuis were manipulating Government money to their own advantage. But there can be no doubt that the Mitsuis were risking the family fortunes and three hundred years of steady business growth on a new and untried Government by no means certain of permanence.

*   *   *

On the other hand, there was a significant change in the firm's business policy about this time. The Mitsuis' weather-vane extended a little higher and apparently was catching the shifting breezes more quickly than their rivals'.

The Mitsuis, it may be remembered, were still in the cloth-goods business and their store, *Echigo-ya*, in Tokyo, had been a profitable concern. A great boom was experienced, in fact, when it became known that the Imperial Government was coming to Tokyo. When blasé Tokyo, despite uncertainties of the times, bestirred itself to dress up for the event, its dignitaries and notables went to Mitsui's store for their apparel requirements. A print still preserved by the Mitsuis depicts crowds flocking into *Echigo-ya* to buy their clothes for the coming of the Emperor.

The Mitsuis had had a virtual monopoly on supplying the Shogunate's cloth needs, and its textile store was the largest in Tokyo, with a staff of more than two hundred clerks and employees.

In spite of this, Rizaemon Minomura, Mitsui director who had functioned so well during the decline of the Shogunate days and still was one of the guiding geniuses of the firm, began urging the Mitsuis to give up the shopkeeping end of the concern. Family members rebelled at the thought, but during those days Minomura frequently was seen passing through the gates of the Inouye residence and most likely had been "tipped off" that there was more money to be made for the Mitsuis in the field of finance than in textiles.

Recalling that Minomura had saved the firm during the Shogunate days, the Mitsui family finally gave in and permitted their managing director to divorce the textile branch, which up to 1870 had been predominant. To Minomura, the textile business was merely excess baggage in the Mitsui march to riches along the financial highway opened by the Government.

As a further indication of this maneuver the Mitsuis changed the crest of their *Echigo-ya*, or drygoods shop, from the familiar three bars and a diamond. The Chinese character for "*echi*" also can be read "*koshi*." The new crest adopted was merely this "*echi*" or "*koshi*" in heavy script; but the Mitsuis added "*mitsu*" to the "*koshi*," making it the famous *Mitsukoshi* store, which continues to the present day, and with the same crest, in Tokyo. It was not until 1904, however, that the Mitsuis completely disposed of this store, which had been under their management for more than two centuries. By then, the Mitsuis were completely assured of the wisdom of Minomura's advice and it was no longer efficient or profitable enough to compete with small shopkeepers. They parted with their entire store holdings and the business was taken over and incorporated as a separate company under the name of *Mitsukoshi*. It still occupies the original site of the old *Echigo-ya* in Suruga-cho, and together with its newly opened branches on the Ginza and in Shinjuku is well known to visitors to Japan as the largest and most remarkable department store anywhere in the Orient.

The Mitsuis helped the new Government open its mint. Finance Minister Inouye suggested to *Mitsui-Gumi* that they might like to open modern banks modeled on the European or American systems, in Tokyo and other centers. The Mitsuis were quick to seize upon the idea, and shortly thereafter formally petitioned the Government for the privilege of issuing convertible notes and submitting with their petition a plan for such a bank.

The Mitsui firm's own phrasing of this activity is suavely rendered in this fashion: —

The *Mitsui-Gumi*, ever ready and indefatigable in assisting the Government's economic and financial policies, were strongly impressed with the timeliness of the suggestion and at once set about planning the formation of a note-issuing bank, with power to put into circulation 1,500,000 to 2,000,000 yen in paper money, which should pass as a legal tender side by side with the Government fiat money, providing that they would hold a specie reserve amounting to 75 per cent of the total issue. [The modern term "yen" had by this time been substituted for *ryo* to represent the unit of currency.]

As soon as a plan was decided upon, they sent in a petition, the first of the kind in the country, for permission to establish a bank. The petition which was addressed to the Department of Finance in July, 1871, said in part: "We members of the Mitsui family have been convinced of the desirability of establishing modern banks in Tokyo and other open ports, and of engaging in the banking business in the most sound and trustworthy way, modeled after the tried methods obtaining in Europe and America, thereby to facilitate the financial transactions of the country. We pray that the Government grant us the privilege of issuing convertible notes, and beg to submit herewith the plan of the proposed bank and the method of issuing notes for stated amounts."

The Mitsui petition addressed to the Department of Finance was guided through Cabinet approval by Inouye, and in August, 1871, the Mitsuis were notified that the Government would have the necessary banknotes printed in America and that they would be turned over to the Mitsuis for issuance. This plan, however, abruptly was dropped as the Government decided in favor of adopting a national bank system along the lines of America's. The sanction granted to *Mitsui-Gumi* for issue of convertible notes through its own bank was canceled but the firm was given the task of issuing, for the Government, 6,800,000 yen in Treasury convertible notes and 2,500,000 yen in "colonization convertible notes."

The Mitsuis did not lose hope of establishing their own modern bank and went ahead with full preparations by putting in order and consolidating the interests of Mitsui holdings which at that time consisted of the exchange firm and the textile firm in Tokyo, with branches of both in Kyoto, Osaka and Yokohama, and of the same trading establishment at Nagasaki that had initiated Mitsui's first foreign commerce with the Dutch at Nagasaki.

Inouye, recalling his own trip abroad and the accrued benefits, at this time advised the Mitsuis to send some of their own family to America to study the American banking system and industrial developments. The Mitsuis promptly accepted the advice.

Five young Mitsuis, between the ages of fifteen and seventeen, were picked to go. This was the first trip away from Japan for any Mitsui. Among those picked to go was Choshiro, later Baron Hachiroemon, tenth in direct descent from the Founder of the business House, and heir apparent of the main family. Hachiroemon is the only one of the group that went to America who is still alive. He retired as head of all the Mitsui interests in 1933.

The others were Takenosuke, Yonosuke, Saburosuke and Teijiro Mitsui, three of whom afterward were to rise high in the Mitsui firm and head branches of the family.

The young Mitsuis left Japan in 1872 and spent two years in America. At first they were enrolled in a preparatory school at New Brunswick, New Jersey, planning later to enter Rutgers University. Two of the boys, however, passed up Rutgers for a year's study in the textile mills of Lowell, Massachusetts.

The Mitsui library, repository for family memorabilia for ages but with little of it in English, preserves only the hotel bill of the Mitsui brood on their arrival in New York. The Mitsuis stopped at the then imposing St. Nicholas Hotel on Broadway for one day, August 28, 1872, and were charged thirty-six dollars for four rooms. "Hack to depot" was an extra four dollars. Another hotel bill bespoke a week-end excursion to Walton, New York, where the Mitsuis had five rooms at "the Catskill Mt. House" for "3¾ days" for "$186."

Thirty-five years later, Baron Hachiroemon Mitsui — he received his title in 1896 for aid to the Government in the first Sino-Japanese War — revisited New York with the Baroness, a daughter and a retinue of a dozen servants. They were on a nine months' tour of the world. This time the Mitsuis put up at the Plaza Hotel, and the bill was not preserved. The Baron gave out numerous interviews, saying: "Americans are the most tactful, accurate and reliable businessmen in the world. I prefer to deal with them above all others." An American-Japanese war was "impossible," he said. Baroness Mitsui was asked her opinion about the hobble skirt, which had arrived in New York in 1910. "The Japanese women," she replied, "have worn hobble skirts for centuries. Our kimono are cut just like your hobble skirts. I would suggest that if your women are going to keep hobble skirts they learn to walk like Japanese."

The Baron had little time for sightseeing in New York then, spending his days in the financial district.

Even before the Mitsuis had left for America in 1872, the family was so certain of starting its own modern bank with Government sanction that it began construction of a new building in Tokyo to house the prospective enterprise. When

THE MITSUI BUILDING BEFORE THE
EARTHQUAKE OF 1923

THE PRESENT MITSUI BUILDING, GOMEI KAISHA
ENTRANCE

the Government gave the Mitsuis a setback by initiating plans for a central bank, the family kept on with their building. It was completed in June, 1872 — a squarely built, three-story foreign-style edifice, not only the finest commercial structure in the capital then, but one of Tokyo's landmarks properly celebrated and preserved in woodcuts of the era.

As a concession to the Kyoto influence in the House of Mitsui, the building was surmounted by a huge, fantastic green dolphin. The dolphin is an ancient charm against fire in Japan. Previously the dolphin had been used chiefly on castles, but the Mitsuis were first to adorn an office building with the charm.

The dolphin protected the building for thirty years, until the structure was razed to make way for larger quarters. The newer building was in the more modern German style of architecture then reaching Japan, and the Mitsuis, caught up in the spirit of modernism, considered the dolphin too old-fashioned to adorn the edifice. The fire and earthquake of 1923 leveled the new and undolphined building, and the Mitsuis felt quite bad about it, privately pointing out among themselves that if the dolphin had been riding the ridgepole the building might have escaped. So the beloved dolphin was retired in landscaped splendor in a prominent spot in the baronial grounds of Hachiroemon's residence in Tokyo, where it is still preserved. There was no need for him when the latest Mitsui Bank building was completed in 1929, the finest bank building in the Far East. Modern science took care of the fire-proofing and the dolphin was allowed to remain in retirement.

In the Mitsui campaign for a modern bank of its own, early in the Meiji era, it is interesting to note that the term "bank" written in *kana* characters was employed for the first time in

Japan when the Mitsuis addressed their petition to the Government. The definition of the word had reached Japan only a few years before through Yukichi Fukuzawa, the famous educator and founder of Keio University, which became the Educational Ministry of the Mitsui kingdom. Fukuzawa had returned from an earlier mission to America with the word and a proper understanding of it, but the Japanese word equivalent had yet to be coined. The English word "bank" derives from "bench." The process of banking in Europe, just as it did in Japan, grew from an exchange business carried on by merchants from benches in the streets of Florence, Italy. When the Florentine merchants failed, they broke up their benches in the street, which gave rise to the word "bankruptcy," or "broken bench."

The Mitsuis had the idea but no word for it, so they were forced to use the word "bank" literally, in making known their desires to the Government.

Meanwhile the Government promulgated a National Bank Act and called upon the Mitsui-Gumi and Ono-Gumi to establish the First National Bank of Japan as a joint enterprise. The Mitsuis had no great desire to join Ono-Gumi in this project but they were leaving no stone unturned in their campaign to get in on the ground floor of modern national banking. The petition presented to the Government for the joint enterprise, signed by three Mitsuis, — Hachiroemon, Jiroemon and Saburosuke, — together with three members of the Ono family (whose given names always began with Z) read as follows: —

The two houses are agreed in their desire to establish, as their joint undertaking, a bank with a capital of two million yen. It is assumed that there will be others later who wish to join in the business, and it is their intention to increase the capital of the proposed bank to five million yen in due course. They understand that the Government has already carried out investigations as to rules and regulations. These the promoters undertake to obey strictly and never to deviate from them in any detail. They pray that they be granted permission to proceed with their enterprise.

Permission promptly was granted and the First National Bank was established on June 11, 1873, with a capital of 3,000,000 yen, of which *Mitsui-Gumi* and *Ono-Gumi* subscribed 1,000,000 each. The bank opened for business July 20 in the building that had been erected by the Mitsuis.

Still campaigning for their own bank, the Mitsuis set out on another course. As a preliminary step, they carried out a house-cleaning known in Mitsui history as the "great reform of 1873." Head-clerk Minomura swung the axe freely on Mitsui personnel, gathered in loose ends of the organization, and initiated a number of reforms — including the divorcement of the textile retail business from the exchange house that already has been described. Then, under Minomura's guidance, the Mitsuis founded a new private bank, the *Kawase Bank Mitsui-Gumi*. (The English word "bank" had by this time been converted into a Japanese word, "*ginko*," but the National Bank Act of 1872 prohibited the use of *ginko* by any but national banks.)

In using the word *Bank* in their title the Mitsuis admittedly were "catering to the popular partiality for English words" then in vogue in Japan. At the same time, the word *Bank* enabled the Mitsuis to evade the proscription in the National Bank Act against use of its equivalent, *ginko*.

Meanwhile the Government was going through a severe financial crisis that brought for Mitsui the most trying period in the history of the House up to that time. As soon as the new Government was out of its swaddling clothes its modern-minded leaders saw the necessity of getting rid of the feudal, landowning aristocracy. As long as the daimio held their lands as minor sovereigns, there was always danger that another warrior might emerge from the system and set up a new dynasty of usurpers. A series of regulations issued over a period of two years brought pressure upon the clans and the daimio. They were ordinances typical of Oriental psychology in meeting such an issue. One, for example, required an Imperial official to be named in every fief — named, it is true, by the daimio; but the idea was significant.

Government leaders who were clansmen were pulling the wires in their own constituencies where their more conservative elders were in direct charge of the clans, until finally the four great clans of Choshu, Satsuma, Tosa and Hizen — who stood the best chance of profiting politically by the move — acted voluntarily to turn in their landholdings, presenting a memorial saying: "We reverently offer up all our feudal possessions with the prayer that the Imperial Court will enact laws . . . so that a uniform rule may prevail throughout the Empire." It was a powerful example, backed by the knowledge that these four clans had the military power to deal with recalcitrants. The rest of the daimio followed the lead, and only 17 out of 276 refused to act voluntarily. In the end there was no open protest to the agrarian hara-kiri of the landowning nobility.

In return for this magnanimity by the feudal chiefs, the Government pledged itself to support them, at least until conditions were more stabilized, with an elaborate pension system. This almost proved the financial undoing of the new Government. The magnitude of the bonus plan, comparable to the American bonus system initiated after the World War, is evident from the number of people taken on the public payroll by the Government. About 400,000 samurai households and nearly 300 large daimio establishments were judged entitled to receive support, the Government pledging to maintain some 2,000,000 persons in a style to which they had been accustomed out of state revenues, in return for repossession of the feudal lands. The Government generously offered to pay each daimio half of his former average revenue, an offer no daimio was likely to turn down, for it was a secured income while previously their revenues were subject to the vagaries of the rice harvest and other uncertainties. A diplomat resident in Japan at the time gave this example: A daimio with the nominal revenue of 100,000 *koku* of rice, which was computed at about £64,000, would receive under the pension plan 50,000 *koku*, or about £32,000. Moreover, he no longer would be required to support his landless samurai, the Government taking over that task too on a similar proportionate basis. Under the circumstances there was little wonder that feudalism was abolished in Japan so easily, but there are still writers fond of dwelling on the idea that Japan accomplished in a few months what required centuries in Europe.

Difficulties began when the Government sought to convert revenue from taxation into currency. It was not so simple as regarding one *koku* (4.96 bushels) as being worth so many yen. Besides the rice taxes, there were other forms of levies which the Tokugawas had devised to reach every taxable person. Generally these came under two headings, labor service required of the peasants and farming class, and money payments demanded of artisans, merchants and middlemen. All these taxes under the new regime were to be poured into the national treasury. This was further hampered by the lack of uniformity in currency. Silver and gold, mostly debased, were both legal tender at a ration of about seven to one, and then to complicate the situation even more various fiefs had their own paper money, some of it issued by Mitsui and circulating among several neighboring fiefs. On top of all this there was the comparatively simple matter of balancing the budget, which Japan tried to do almost from the inception of the Meiji Government.

It would not be correct to say that the difficulties were too great for Finance Minister Inouye, but there were too many elements of unsound finance in the arrangement; so, in exasperation, he resigned and was ready to devote his talents to the Mitsuis.

In the circumstances in which the Japanese Finance Department found itself, [McLaren wrote of Inouye] it is not difficult to imagine that even the most capable and industrious Minister would have enough worries to overwhelm him. The problem of commuting the rice and labor taxes into terms of money occupied no little time, and was solved only after an immense amount of negotiation with the agricultural classes. Furthermore, after the revenues had at last been estimated in terms of yen, the two men who were at the head of the Department of Finance became convinced that the Government was bankrupt, or about to become so, and resigned their posts, having prepared a statement of their views on the matter which was immediately published.*

The man who succeeded Inouye as Finance Minister was Shigenobu Okuma (later Marquis), with whom the Mitsubishi interests already had allied themselves. That marked the beginning of the Mitsui-Mitsubishi politico-financial tug-of-

* A Political History of Japan During the Meiji Era, by W. W. McLaren. Allen and Unwin, London.

war. It was a truism of the period in the early days that it was not only necessary for businessmen to acquire political backing but that it was equally necessary for politicians to have financial backing. That was before the plums had begun to fall.

Years later, when the Mitsuis were patronizing Keio University and were sending their young men to Keio, Okuma founded Waseda University which became the Mitsubishi school, thereby sending the Mitsui-Mitsubishi rivalry into another field. Keio and Waseda today are the two greatest non-Imperial universities in Japan, and their rivalry is no less keen than that of their original backers.

A nationwide panic occurred in 1874 and 1875. Mitsui-Gumi, Ono-Gumi and Shimada-Gumi, as has been said, were entrusted with the exchequer business of the Government soon after the Restoration was accomplished. At first the business was rather simple, consisting mainly of managing the affairs of the Imperial family newly coming into affluence. Then as the clans surrendered their lands, the national funds were expanded; and in time their service was extended from the Central to Prefectural Governments, so that by 1873 these three houses were rendering a treasurer's service on their own responsibility for seventy-five local governments in addition to the National Treasury. At first they were not required to furnish any security regardless of the amount of official money passing through their hands.

This proved a bonanza for all three houses and inaugurated a period of feverish business rivalry among them. Ono-Gumi with its new wealth in hand branched out into all kinds of business, including mining and trading in raw silk and various cereals. Ono-Gumi's participation in the founding of the First National Bank was sufficient evidence of its new prosperity.

The Mitsui version of the partnership arrangement is that Ono-Gumi was slightly on the irresponsible side and the more conservative influence of Mitsui was needed to balance things. But it is apparent that the real reason was that neither Mitsui nor Ono-Gumi trusted each other. This system of balanced responsibility is a time-honored one in Japan.

As the amounts in the hands of Mitsui-Gumi, Ono-Gumi and Shimada-Gumi grew larger, the Government began to demand securities at the rate of one-third or one-quarter of the amount held in trust. Then came an unexpected blow that wiped out Ono-Gumi and Shimada-Gumi, leaving Mitsui alone in the field and going strong — under the unofficial guidance of Inouye.

Paper money, the value of which had steadily depreciated, was flooding the country and severely hampering trade. The Finance Ministry decided the proper way to restore its value was to put out an issue which would replace all outstanding issues and which would have full face value. National banks were called on to help, the Government ordering them to invest sixty per cent of their capital in the Government's bond issues, paying for the bonds in the old depreciated paper money. The balance of forty per cent was to form a specie reserve.

When the value of the new paper money issued by the National Banks also began to fall, a wide public demand arose for specie. The burden grew more onerous on the banks as they were put in the position of having to pay high prices in paper for specie.

At one time the Government resorted to threats of severe punishment in its attempt to make specie and its new paper money circulate at the same rate. This had the usual effect of turning the public against paper money. After several exemplary drastic punishments, for transactions in which wealthy merchants attempted to evade regulations, they began to resort to a secret code. Takekoshi cites as a typical instance the following letter of a merchant who wanted to buy specie with paper money: —

Dear Sir:

In regard to the marriage of your daughter, Miss Omasa, of which you talked to me yesterday, her age is just right if she is eighteen years old as you say; and I have in mind a very good young man whom I can recommend as a suitable fiancé to your daughter. The union, if realized, would be a very good match. I suggest you give consideration to the matter.

Awaiting an early answer from you, I am

Yours, etc.

"Miss Omasa" was code, of course, for specie; and the merchant was offering a deal if the price of specie was ten against eighteen of paper money. Such letters ostensibly regarding the matchmaking of a marriageable daughter were common in Japanese business circles and might well escape suspicion of any prying officials.

When a report got around that Ono-Gumi was having difficulties, the Government grew anxious about the large deposits it had in that company's vaults. There was a hurried conference in the Finance Ministry, at the end of which the three favored depositories, Ono-Gumi, Shimada-Gumi and Mitsui-Gumi, were ordered on short notice to refund the Government's deposits, or put up the equivalent in specie. This unprecedented, unheard-of demand bore all the earmarks of a behind-the-scenes plot to leave someone holding the bag — and it was not the Mitsuis.

Ono-Gumi and Shimada-Gumi could not meet the demand. The Government deposits were taken from these two houses, and they promptly went into bankruptcy. The Mitsuis had the money on the barrel-head; but admittedly every last coin and ounce of metal in the vaults and tills of the main office and various branches, as well as land deeds, bonds and other securities, had to be scraped-up to furnish the required sum. The amount that had to be raised, according to Mitsui records, was 4,249,950 yen. Ono-Gumi was compelled to close its doors in November, 1874, and Shimada-Gumi in February, 1875, at the height of the nation-wide panic.

How the Mitsuis escaped the consequences of the Government's drastic ruling which overcame their competitors properly may be the subject of some speculation. It is known that Minomura, managing director of the House of Mitsui at the time, was on intimate terms with Inouye. There is no suggestion that the ruling itself was designed to ruin the competing houses. It may have been warranted by an honest apprehension of Inouye's successor in the Finance post. Very likely Okuma was anxious to ascertain whether any of the houses had been playing fast and loose with Government money, and instituted the National Bank call to dispel his fears. Whether or not there was an advance tip from Inouye to Minomura cannot be substantiated, but the important consideration is that the Mitsuis had the money to show, and escaped the axe.

Was it a twinge of conscience that caused the Mitsuis to record that they "had not the heart" to stand by and see Ono-Gumi, with which they had been associated in exchange business for over a century, go down deserted? The Mitsuis wrote to the then Minister of Finance, Shigenobu, afterward Marquis Okuma, pleading for the Ono-Gumi and proposing at the same time a way to liquidate their indebtedness. They had the satisfaction of seeing the Government slacken its pressure and allow the *Ono-Gumi* to remain as a going concern. The public gave the *Mitsui-Gumi* credit for this friendly act in helping their old associate."

Meanwhile the Mitsuis, continuing policies laid down in the "great reform of 1873," began the development of their *Kawase Bank Mitsui-Gumi* into a financial institution modeled after the French *Société Anonyme*. There being no statutes of any kind to regulate purely private banks, six members of the Mitsui family and one non-member petitioned the Prefectural Governor of Tokyo for establishment of a "nonnational" bank.

The petition, dated July 7, 1875, still preserved by the Mitsui library, is typical of a Japanese approach with mellifluous expressions of humility and self-effacement. It submitted that a half-dozen of the best financial brains of the country were "ignorant and uninformed, and not possessed of enough self-confidence to draw up anything like perfect regulations themselves" to regulate the ordinary banking business they wished to establish. However, they "ventured to submit a draft of all their papers relating to the establishment of the proposed bank" and hoped the Governor of Tokyo Prefecture would see fit to forward it to the Finance Department of the Government with his own endorsement.

The petition was pigeonholed while Okuma was still Finance Minister, but in 1876 a shift in Cabinet politics in favor of the Choshu clan brought Inouye back into the Cabinet as Finance Minister. Consequently, there was no great surprise when the Finance Ministry almost immediately saw fit to sanction establishment of a bank by the "ignorant and uninformed" Mitsuis. A proviso was added, however, that pending the enactment of a general law on banking, the Mitsui

Bank should be conducted as an act of private understanding among all parties concerned, including depositors. The Mitsuis thereupon altered the liability provision in their articles of association, making the shareholders' liabilities unlimited, instead of limited as in the original draft.

Thus the Mitsui Bank, the first private bank ever established in Japan, was organized with unlimited liability in the form of a French *Société Anonyme*.

A statement drafted by Rizaemon Minomura, the guiding genius of the House at the time the new bank was started, read, according to Mitsui translations: —

Many are the commercial houses known for their great wealth from the days of the Tokugawa Shogunate which have become of late painfully reduced in circumstances or have even gone out of business altogether. This lamentable fate has overtaken them because they have erred in their aims or blundered in their policy. In view of the warnings they afford, we must not remain idle.

The way to avoid the false steps they have taken is to form a company. Companies are of various kinds, but the best is the *Société Anonyme*, in which the names of members do not appear, but it is named after the business it undertakes to conduct. Its policy and system are decided by majority votes and are carried out openly, thus insuring justice and fairness. Moreover, the articles of association and regulations are all subject to the approval of the Government and must be strictly observed, leaving room for deviation. Herein lies the excellence of such company formation.

In adopting this superior method of running our business we meet the requirements of our times. We henceforth abolish the name of *Mitsui-Gumi* and transfer the business to a private bank, to which we give the name of *Mitsui Ginko*. The new organization terminates the relationship of master and servant. We all become, equally, friends as members of the new society and hope to share and enjoy the benefits which it may bring by making our hearts as one and working together. This is the object of forming the present Société Anonyme.

It was a well-calculated statement that stood out in the forefront of the new sentiment of Western Democracy that was making itself felt in Japan with the introduction of a wide range of Western institutions. The confusion of the transition period, of prying Japan loose from feudalism to take up the ways of the West, was now at its height. The Mitsuis clearly were in the van of this new progress, and the prospectus of the bank was such that all classes of depositors might be attracted.

The capital of the new bank, fixed at 2,000,000 yen divided into 20,000 shares, was taken up half by "The Headquarters of the Mitsuis," the forerunner of the giant family holding company that was to be formed in later years; 5,000 shares by individual members of the family on their own private accounts; and the remaining 5,000 shares by employees and former servants of the House. Altogether the number of shareholders amounted to 383.

The bank opened for business July 1, 1876, in the old Mitsui-Gumi building in Suruga-cho, Tokyo, and took over the business of Mitsui-Gumi, consisting of 11,369,055 yen deposits and 9,911,347 yen loans and 1,580,544 yen cash. Almost immediately thirty-one branches and sub-branches were opened throughout the country. While a general banking business was carried on, its principal work at first was handling the official funds of the central and prefectural governments. The branches and sub-branches were located at points most convenient for transacting Government business.

This arrangement proved most satisfactory during the

period already mentioned, when the Government was changing its policy of collecting taxes in rice and other commodities to cash. In the midst of this tax transition period, nature played one of its usual tricks on Japan — but this time instead of crop failure it was abundance that brought difficulty. Unusually rich crops throughout the country caused the value of farm products to fall just when the Government was ordering the producers to convert their crops into money for paying the taxes.

The new Mitsui Bank, with its branches and sub-branches conveniently scattered through the country, was equipped to take care of just such a situation as this. Minomura sent out word from Tokyo for all branches to help the unfortunate farmers with their heavy crops by advancing money against rice with which they might pay their taxes. There seems to be no way of determining what interest the Mitsuis exacted from farmers, but apparently it was suitable to the farmers and danger of a serious agrarian crisis was averted on account of the already smooth working of the new Mitsui Bank.

Organization of the Bank from its inception was virtually the same as it is today. At the top stood the "Great Board of Management," comprising a president, two vice-presidents and three auditors, all of whom were elected usually from among the Family Heads. Ranging downward from the Great Board was a long string of officials and employees called "the staff," divided into fifteen grades.

Inouye's return to the Cabinet was the source of still another great contribution to the fortunes of the House of Mitsui. Between the time of his resignation over the issue of changing rice taxes into money taxes and 1876 he had been something of a free lance in the business world. He had made connections with practically all the financial cliques in the country, apparently on the lookout for what would be the most profitable connection. The lengthy authorized biography of Inouye mentions the fact that Inouye, a Marquis now, aided in this period "not only the Mitsuis" but also the Konoike, Furukawa, Kaijima, Tanaka, Fujita and other financial households. One whole chapter in Volume III of this biography in Japanese is devoted to Inouye's "contributions to the business world." These pages idealize Inouye's "many-sided" acts of assistance to dozens of business firms, listing especially the now-rising Mitsubishi shipping business destined to be Mitsui's greatest rival.

"To drown his discontent" when he quit his financial post Inouye had half-heartedly started the trading firm of *Senshu Kaisha*, the earliest trading company organized in Japan on modern lines. *Senshu Kaisha* means "First Profit Company."

The Mitsuis, at this time, were not active in the foreign field in spite of the Founder's instruction of three centuries before to trade with the foreigners at Nagasaki. When the country was opened to foreign trade in 1854, through the lack of knowledge of Japanese merchants and their hesitancy the import and export business of the country naturally fell into the hands of foreign firms, which quickly had established themselves in the treaty ports. The Mitsuis had opened a sort of exploratory branch office in Yokohama in 1859.* In 1875

---

* First records of Mitsui trade with Americans appear in the permanent ledger of the Mitsui Kyoto store that year. On July 15, 1859, an American and a Russian visited the Yokohama branch of the Kyoto store and purchased several varieties of brocade. On the next day two Americans came in and placed such a large order that the Mitsuis had to call on the main store at Kyoto. The names of the Americans were too difficult to render into Japanese but subsequently an "Honorable Mr. Bubble of England" called and bought some silk. The Yokohama store also functioned as a general reporting agency on the strange

they opened, also in Yokohama, a company known as the *Kokusan Kata* (roughly, "the National Products Group") which dealt principally in the sale of staple goods in the Izu Islands and in an overland transportation business between Tokyo and Yokohama.

The Inouye trading company quickly outdistanced the Mitsuis in Yokohama, but then Inouye was recalled to the Cabinet. Choosing carefully from his wide field of connections, Inouye decided to turn over his company to the Mitsuis. Moreover, one of Inouye's own protégés, Takashi Masuda, went with the company, an important acquisition for Mitsuis when the *Senshu Kaisha* became amalgamated with the *Kokusan Kata*. This marked the birth of the modern *Mitsui Bussan Kaisha*, Mitsui's great international trading company, and according to Mitsui's own account "laying of the first stone for the vast pyramid of the Mitsui's vast modern combine."

The *Mitsui Bussan Kaisha* thus was inaugurated in July, 1876, "to export overseas surplus products of the Imperial Land, to import from overseas products needed at home, and thereby to engage in intercourse with the Ten-thousand [many] countries within the Universe." Takenosuke Mitsui and Yonosuke Mitsui were the principal directors and Masuda the company president. The new Mitsui Bank had the modest but important rôle of supplying capital for the new trading company.

For several years the Company's business was small, probably because of its lack of experience in the new field and doings of foreigners in the port city. A funeral excited lengthy comment, including careful pen-and-ink drawings where words failed. The paper used in these Mitsui ledgers, a handmade product called *nishi-no-uchi*, is marvelously preserved.

partly because Japanese industry was entirely undeveloped. This was a matter to which the Mitsuis soon were to give their attention.

With Inouye back in the Cabinet and the Mitsuis in close touch with him the Government was persuaded to undertake to raise a loan of 12,500,000 yen to encourage industrial enterprises. This was the first time the Government had issued a loan of this nature for public subscription with the proposition entirely foreign to the people. Naturally the Mitsui Bank was given the greater part of the task and with the collaboration of the First National Bank, and the Mitsui Bank and its thirty-one branches, worked strenuously to float the loan. The difficulty lay in convincing the public that it was a measure of self-betterment rather than one representing forced contributions to the Government exchequer similar to the flotations which the Mitsuis had put over early in the Meiji reign.

Again the Mitsuis were pre-eminently successful, the loan being heavily oversubscribed by the closing day for the subscription list, the Mitsui Bank itself securing subscriptions to the amount of 12,470,000 yen. So, again, the Mitsui financial reputation was entrenched.

The Mitsuis had another small flyer in wartime financing in the Satsuma Rebellion of 1877. The Imperial Government was compelled to send an army into the field against 40,000 well-drilled, well-armed Satsuma men in a campaign that lasted from January until September. While the Satsuma men wasted time besieging an unimportant castle, the Government had time to collect its own forces — not forgetting to call in the Mitsuis as army paymasters — and send an expedition into Kyushu, with disastrous results for the Satsuma men. For the Government it demonstrated conclusively that an army recruited from all classes was an institution on which the State could depend and that fighting ability was not the sole monopoly of the samurai.

Gaining confidence on every side, the Government in 1880 set up a bureau with the idea of gaining complete control of Government funds, which heretofore had been farmed out, principally to the Mitsuis. This marked the beginning of a business recession leading to a serious situation in the Mitsui firm. Mitsui Bank deposits, which at the end of 1877 stood at 7,623,183 yen, fell to 6,157,280 yen at the end of 1881, while loans decreased from 6,606,015 yen to 5,124,627 yen. In June, 1882, the Government established the Bank of Japan, which took over the work of the new bureau and the whole fiscal business of the treasury, wiping out in one stroke the chief business of the Mitsui Bank.

Meanwhile Mitsuis' great director-general, Rizaemon Minomura, had died in 1877, in his fifty-seventh year. Before his death he apparently saw difficulties confronting the Mitsuis, for it is commonly said that he wrote a passage in his will advising, somewhat superfluously, his fellow executives and Mitsui Family Heads to call in Inouye when the firm needed help.

In losing the fiscal business of the Treasury the Mitsuis now received a staggering blow, but for the time being they wanted to try out their own reform. Meeting in January, 1885, the shareholders elected Saburosuke Mitsui President of the Bank in place of Hachiroemon Mitsui and a month later circularized all branches and sub-branches inviting all officers and employees to send in their written opinion in sealed envelopes on the necessary course to meet the situation and reform the Bank's business. This was typical of the Mitsui policy always to exhaust every resource within the firm before calling on outside help in solving a problem. The following April, the head of the Bank drew up a program of reform consisting of ten clauses, based on suggestions from the three hundred or more officers and employees who contributed them, and immediately put the program into force. The effect was a steady increase in business. Deposits had gone up to 15,525,540 yen by 1893 and loans to 11,354,529 yen, the business almost doubling since 1881 when the recession set in for the Mitsuis.

When the Bank of Japan was established, the Mitsui branches scattered throughout the country were appointed to act as the Bank's local agents in transferring tax revenue from the provinces to the central Treasury. This was a business lucrative enough for the Mitsuis, but in 1890 the Government abolished the system of remitting prefectural tax income and again the Mitsuis suffered a setback. On the surface, there was no indication that the Mitsui Bank was suffering any adverse circumstances; but deep below there were disturbing elements. Another nation-wide depression had set in before 1890, occasioned by extensive crop failures, unfavorable trade balances, and loss of currency abroad. In 1882 capital invested in business amounted to 51,000,000 yen; but by 1890 it had dropped to 17,000,000 yen. The farm debt had increased to 233,000,000 yen, while some 300,000 landowners sold their ancestral holdings to raise funds. Many banks and business firms collapsed, some with which Mitsui had close connections.

While the chaotic conditions were at their height a sensational article appeared in the newspaper *Kokkai Shimbun*, purporting to reveal that the Mitsui Bank was about to go under. This caused an immediate run on the Kyoto branch, but money was rushed there in time to save the bank. Then the effects of the Kyoto run spread to the Tokyo main office, and the Mitsui firm seemed to be in its gravest peril.

It was then that the Mitsuis bethought themselves of the passage in Minomura's will and called on Inouye to come to their aid.

In addition to his long friendship with Minomura, Inouye was motivated by a knowledge that there would be serious repercussions throughout the financial world if the Mitsuis collapsed. The hard-headed, scar-faced old warrior did not hesitate. Quickly surveying the situation, Inouye sent a personal note to Governor Kawada of the Bank of Japan asking him to put the national bank's financial reserves behind the Mitsuis temporarily until he succeeded in easing the situation.

But before Inouye agreed to take off his coat and plunge into the affairs of Mitsui he demanded and ascertained from the family and executives their implicit trust and co-operation. The Mitsuis immediately drew up a memorandum promising that no objections would be raised, then or later, to whatever reforms and adjustments Inouye might find necessary to save their firm from collapse. Equipped with these powers Inouye took the helm of the Mitsui ship in the winter of 1890.

In coming to Mitsui's rescue Inouye immediately proposed two drastic innovations. The first was that he should rewrite the ancient family Constitution to bind the eleven branches of the family more closely together, and the second was enforcement of a rigid economy to tide the family over the crisis. The basis of his economy program was the moral teachings of the famous Sontoku Ninomiya, renowned agricultural reformer and sage, who lived from 1787 to 1857.

"Crazy Sontoku" Ninomiya (page 105) was founder of the first rural credit associations in Japan, an early equivalent of modern co-operative societies. Some of them still exist in Japan, more than one hundred years old, an additional bit of evidence that there isn't very much new under the Rising Sun. Inasmuch as Ninomiya's principles of frugality, carried out through Inouye, had much to do with saving the Mitsui family fortune, and since his credit associations played an important part in the social and economic life of the people, something about Ninomiya may be told here.

He was born of peasant parents in the poorest possible circumstances. From the age of fourteen when his father died he took over the responsibilities of a large family. He gathered hay and wood and sold them in neighboring towns, and spent his evenings twisting rope, but managed to find time to learn to read and write.

When a parsimonious relative upbraided him for wasting oil in his midnight studies, he determined to provide his own oil. He sowed a field of rape seed, and exchanged the crop for oil and returned to his studies. Eventually he won local fame for the frugal management that had put him into ownership of a profitable farm. When a neighboring daimio fell into financial straits, Ninomiya was given a trial at managing the estate and he began his reform system that made him famous. It consisted primarily of cutting-down expenses, abolishing all luxury, and instituting his system of *Bundo Ho* — that is, saving from the income of each year a certain percentage to be added to productive enterprises. He carefully audited debts, summoned creditors, and won their agreement to a moratorium — and in five years had the estate clear and a balance in the treasury. This brought him more engagements in rehabilitating large estates, until his reputation was almost nation-wide.

Ninomiya's *magnum opus* was the restoration of the once-rich Soma daimiate to prosperity. Ninomiya made a careful study of the domain, and then wrote a lengthy report going into the details of the history of the district; he analyzed the income and expenditures, made extensive recommendations as to the treatment of waste land and so forth, and finally laid down, not a Five-Year Plan, but a Sixty-Year Plan which was followed completely; with the result that at the time of the opening of Japan to foreigners, the Soma domain was one of the most prosperous in Japan. He was the early Kemmerer, Hoover and Cooper of Japan, all in one.

Finally taken in tow by the Tokugawa Government, he was used somewhat as a Red Cross disaster-relief director, being sent to all parts of the nation, suddenly impoverished by flood or famine or by slow decay, to install his reform system. Between disasters he lived quietly in Yedo, teaching his principles to a few disciples. He originated the household formula: "If you are in debt, you must paste up the amount in front of the kamidana [god shelf] so that you may see it every morning before you go out."

He was Japan's first conservationist. Said Ninomiya in 1850: "If we rely upon Nature, we need have no fear for the recovery of our country, for Nature constantly heals and repairs. We must look to Nature not as an idle boy looks to his father, but as an industrious boy looks to his parent, kind, yet severe in punishment and eager to recognize the boy's merits. Nature will give no benefit without labor."

He organized the Hotoku Society, with branches widely scattered throughout the rural areas. These were essentially co-operative credit institutions with the professed object of advancing the well-being of the farming class, especially by inculcating frugality and industry and by helping its members with loans to be used solely in productive work. The societies took charge of individual savings as deposits, and from them loans were made to members who for various reasons had failed to accumulate anything during the year. The loans were on personal security, for only persons who were well known to all other members of the society were admitted. Claims of misfortune were recognized by a board, but no loans were advanced to the lazy spendthrifts or disloyal members. A just distribution of wealth among the members of each society was the principle aimed at by Ninomiya.

The 1850 formula of the great physiocratic economist, with certain adaptations, was applied by Inouye to the Mitsui family in this period of crisis in 1890.

The Mitsuis had had the framework of their family Constitution, drawn up by their ancestors, as well as other similar documents and treatises, stored away in the family vaults. Inouye ordered them all assembled from their scattered repositories, and after lengthy study found them antiquated and entirely inadequate for application to the current crisis, especially for a family which by now was at the head of an already complicated system of banks, exchange firms, trading and business concerns of various kinds.

The Mitsuis, naturally, are not inclined to give any too much credit to Inouye; but there is every evidence that it was Inouye who first visualized the importance of keeping the Mitsuis in an economic family-unit to take its place in the vanguard of progressing Japan.

It was Inouye who first realized the need of legally isolating the family's property and holdings from those of the Mitsui companies. This he proposed to accomplish both for the purpose of safeguarding the family's position and of better consolidating Mitsui's business holdings. He proposed, in short, to make two big water-tight compartments of the structure.

To this end, Inouye first sought the advice of a Frenchman, Gustave Boisonard, who was a legal adviser of the Government at the time. Boisonard was asked to furnish examples of the family Constitutions of well-known financial households in European countries, and to draw up a legal formula constituting the structure he had in mind. Boisonard's report was disappointing to Inouye. The French lawyer thought it would be impossible to satisfy Inouye's hopes, inasmuch as no similar document could be found in the legal records of France and other European countries.

Inouye then turned to a German adviser to the Government, Roesler, who had assisted in compilation of the new Commercial Code. Inouye and Roesler had several personal meetings, and Roesler finally gave it as his opinion that although it would be difficult to draft a family Constitution with the legal binding powers that Inouye desired, some German families had had success with Constitutions traditionally observed more by established custom than by law. Examples were furnished, and with these in mind Inouye set to work on redrafting the Mitsui family Constitution, which in its modern form already has been detailed.*

* Page 17.

Chapter X

TALENT SCOUT AND MONOPOLIST

~~~ KAORU INOUYE GAVE
to the Mitsuis their second great *banto*, or "head clerk." He
was Hikojiro Nakamigawa, one of the outstanding business
leaders of the incredible expansion era that began in Japan
shortly before the turn of the Nineteenth Century.

It is still a subject of speculation among the student-cadets
and their preceptors in the Mitsui organization as to who
contributed most to the great business success of the Mitsuis,
Hikojiro Nakamigawa or Rizaemon Minomura.

With the usual reliance on fanciful metaphor, one Mitsui
archivist puts it this way: "Due to Minomura's efforts, the
House of Mitsui rose like a phœnix from the dead ashes of
the Tokugawa period. But it was Nakamigawa who gave the
phœnix wings with which to fly." Over them both, of course,
towered Inouye, who was never more than an "adviser" receiving pay that defies accurate calculation and other benefits
that can only be appraised.

A nephew of Yukichi Fukuzawa, founder of Keio University, Nakamigawa had much to do with making that great
seat of Japanese learning, in later years something of a Mitsui
seminary. Keio graduates had been filtering into the firm of
the new and fast-rising Mitsubishis, chief rival of the Mitsuis,
until the aggressive Nakamigawa intellectually muscled-in on
Keio for the Mitsuis. There was nothing left for Mitsubishi

to do but to go over to another side of town and start their own university, Waseda, while the Government chipped in with Imperial University as its own fountain of talent. Those three are still the leading universities of Japan today.

Nakamigawa was born on the island of Kyushu and started an intense study of the Chinese classics in a school at Nakatsu. Early in boyhood he became an admirer of his uncle, Yukichi Fukuzawa. Stories of his uncle's courage in shipping to America as the body servant of the captain of the first Japanese warship to cross the Pacific, and of his later return to America in an important mission, had penetrated Kyushu. Nakamigawa begged his parents to allow him to go to Tokyo to study in the school Fukuzawa had founded, but his parents and clan were afraid of letting Nakamigawa get into contact with foreign ideas. Instead, the youth at the age of sixteen, in 1869, was shipped off to Osaka to enter a school of modern gunnery.

Arriving at Osaka, the determined Nakamigawa never left the waterfront until he had bargained with the skipper of an American ship for passage to Tokyo. At the capital he went immediately to his uncle's school, where he was welcomed and promptly enrolled in *Keio Gijuku*. He showed a ready adaptability not only to study but to the Fukuzawa ideals of independence and liberal thought.

He graduated in 1873 and was named a teacher in the Uwajima Foreign School in Shikoku at the age of twenty-two. He took up his duties with a Webster's Dictionary as the sole source of his foreign knowledge. Within a year an opportunity came for him to go to England with Shinkichi Koizumi, father of the present president of Keio University, Dr. Shinzo Koizumi.

Inouye, out of the Cabinet then, was, by his own accounts, undertaking a private business trip to London to "rest and recuperate." When Japanese met Japanese abroad in those days they usually started at least a lasting friendship, and Nakamigawa and Inouye were no exception. The elderly statesman was greatly impressed with the perspicacity and progressive outlook of the young Keio graduate.

Nakamigawa returned to Japan in 1877, leaning a little to the intellectual side and showing no signs of going into finance or industry. He was taken on as a teacher at Keio and spent his leisure writing articles for magazines on his impressions of England and the great future for Japan now that Western industrialization was getting a full sweep.

The Sat-cho see-saw took another tilt and the Choshu clan's fortunes rose. Inouye returned in 1878 from London to become Minister of Industry and then Foreign Minister. He immediately bethought himself of Nakamigawa, and invited him to join the Foreign Office as head of the new Telegraph Bureau. Nakamigawa accepted, and had a two-year tour of duty in that governmental department.

Meanwhile the independent Fukuzawa, Keio head, who refused to be drawn into clan politics, was starting a personal movement which produced a brief three-cornered struggle. Several of Fukuzawa's disciples had found places in governmental posts and were declaiming against the despotic manifestations of clan rule. The Satsumas and Choshus stopped fighting each other for a while to turn on this new threat, and in a combined movement ousted the Fukuzawa disciples from their posts. Nakamigawa's sympathies were with his uncle and he resigned from the Foreign Office — probably before the sweep quite reached him.

Soon after he quit the Foreign Office, Nakamigawa was appointed president of the *Jiji Shimpo*, a promising new Tokyo paper owned by Fukuzawa. He wrote editorials upholding Fukuzawa's ideals of liberalism and independence from clan and governmental politics. He started a small but brilliant stream of Keio talent from the University to the *Jiji*. Within three years, Nakamigawa had made a brilliant success of the *Jiji*, adopting the slogan "*Nippon-ichi*," or "Best in Japan."

While he was head of the *Jiji*, he retained his strong friendship with Inouye. When Inouye was in office, he was the source of a good deal of reliable information, which consistently seemed to appear first in the *Jiji*. When he was out of office, the direction was reversed and the enterprising staff of the *Jiji*, through Nakamigawa, kept Inouye informed of quick-changing developments in the political world.

Nakamigawa's success with the *Jiji* tempted him to try his hand at business for the first time in 1887. He attempted to organize an import and export business — no very original idea at the time, for in that fast-moving era even the children in port cities were playing foreign-trade games. Nakamigawa promptly failed through lack of resources. He then spotted a new enterprise in the south of Japan, the building of the Sanyo Railway, one of the first in the country. His patron Inouye "knew the right man," and Nakamigawa was inducted as president, in 1888.

Two years later came the Mitsui distress-call to Inouye. Inouye had some large general ideas for a Mitsui reorganization, including application of the Ninomiya thrift system and rewriting the family Constitution, but he wanted a reliable lieutenant or finger-man directly in the organization, and chose Nakamigawa.

Inouye explained the situation of 1891 to his protégé, painting the rosy prospects of a connection with the Mitsui firm. Nakamigawa promptly refused the offer. He said the Mitsuis

were too bound up with tradition and slow-moving for the
new era that was opening up in Japan.

"That's why you are the very man for the job," Inouye told
Nakamigawa.

"But will they let me have my way?" Nakamigawa asked.

"I'll see that they do," said Inouye.

Nakamigawa started in as a director of the Mitsui Bank
August 19, 1891. For the first six months, independently of
Inouye's own survey, he made an intensive study of the Mitsui's actual financial position, remedies for defects and plans
for building-up the various Mitsui concerns. Nakamigawa
wrote out a lengthy prospectus, showed it to the Mitsuis in
passing, and in February, 1892, as Vice-President and Acting
President of the Mitsui Bank, he took control of the Mitsuis.
From that date on, the eleven Mitsui families had little to do
save nod their heads, make a few suggestions on philanthropy,
and sit back to let the dividends fall in their laps.

At the time Nakamigawa took control he was thirty-seven
years old. Takayasu Mitsui, President of the Bank, was only
forty-two. The youth régime was in the saddle.

Nakamigawa immediately began infusing new and young
blood into the Mitsuis. Nakamigawa had the conviction, if
not illusion, common to American industrialists of a later period, that if the energy and the enterprise of bright young
newspaper men could be diverted into the channels of commerce, some remarkable results might be achieved. To this
end he began raiding the *Jiji*. Moreover, he had his observers
reporting on the best boys at Keio, and like a football coach
before the big game "scouted" Mitsubishi, Mitsui's growing
rival, for young talent.

Sanji Muto, who had just returned from abroad and was a
reporter on the *Japan Gazette*, English-language newspaper in

Yokohama, was drawn into the Mitsui firm by Nakamigawa. At the age of twenty-eight Muto was put in charge of Mitsui's Kanegafuchi spinning mill at Kobe and Toyoji Wada, who had returned from abroad with Muto, and was only two years older, was named head of the Tokyo offices of Kanegafuchi. Muto in his biography speaks wonderingly of the trust the Mitsuis reposed in him and in Wada at their ages.

Yoshio Takahashi, twenty-five-year-old *Jiji* reporter, was snatched off the paper to take charge of the Mitsui textile department. Others whose ages ranged from twenty-four taken on at this time by the ever-questing Nakamigawa were: Ginjiro Fujihara, Shogoro Hatano, Umeshiro Suzuki, Seihin Ikeda, Toyotaro Isomura, Seishu Iwashita, Umekichi Yoneyama,* Satoshi Hiraga, and Osuke Hibi. All of them became important figures in the Mitsui organization.

Still another *Jiji* reporter made into the Mitsui type of businessman was Raita Fujiyama who headed the mortgage department of the Mitsui Bank. Fujiyama acted as chief muscleman for Nakamigawa in many a deal, most notably when Nakamigawa took over the Oji Paper Company, destined to be the foundation of one of the greatest trusts in Japan. Mitsui even reached out and pulled in Mitsubishi's star, Eiji Asabuki, a leader of Keio alumni, to make it easier for Mitsui to spot the best talent in the University. Little wonder that Mitsubishi, copying Mitsui methods, turned to Waseda in an effort to grow its own talent. (Japan's annual "world series" in baseball is played by Waseda and Keio teams, and Mitsui men usually are heavy backers of their traditional team.)

In picking his Mitsui talent Nakamigawa made use of an-

---

* Yoneyama, veteran Mitsui executive known as the "Father of Rotary" in Japan, is President of Japan's New York World's Fair Commission.

other method not unfamiliar to Western business leaders. He spent much of his time traveling about the country inspecting various Mitsui interests. He made it a point to take a promising young Mitsui man with him on each trip. Nakamigawa frequently asserted the qualities of a man most quickly were discovered by traveling with him. It was something of a tradition that a Mitsui employee, if he were so fortunate as to be chosen to travel with Nakamigawa, was catalogued for life in the Mitsui concern as a result of the trip.

Mitsui salaries up to the time when Nakamigawa joined the firm had been comparatively low and had caused some dissatisfaction in all branches. Nakamigawa was quick to take note of this, and a new wage-scale to meet the increasing cost of living was adopted. He introduced a merit promotion plan and encouraged prompt discussion and settlement of any grievances.

Having laid this groundwork within the short space of a year or so, Nakamigawa promptly set about restoring the ailing health of the Mitsui Bank. He adopted the simple formula that business is business and Mitsui had no friends in business. At times his methods seemed ruthless, as he cut every unsound connection between the bank and friends and relatives of the Mitsuis who had been receiving favors for sentimental reasons.

Notable was the brusque treatment Nakamigawa dealt out to the hitherto inviolable Higashi Hongan temple in Kyoto of the Shinshu sect, one of the largest divisions of Buddhism. The temple had borrowed upward of a million yen from the Mitsui Bank with no more security than its name. For several years prior to the advent of Nakamigawa the temple had paid no interest whatever.

Nakamigawa, on finding this in the Mitsui books, stormed

out of the bank, caught a train to Kyoto and told the temple authorities the very first thing they would have to do would be to register the palatial residence of the chief abbot as security on their loan. Moreover, the cold-blooded Mitsui manager hinted darkly that if back interest was not paid promptly the Mitsuis would think nothing of seizing the residence.

The threat threw such a scare into the chief abbot or "living Buddha" that he sent out all priests on a nation-wide pilgrimage to collect money to pay the temple's debts. The priests entered the drive with such fervor that they not only collected money enough to pay off the whole debt but had enough left over to make important repairs to the temple.

Some time later when Nakamigawa visited the temple he ironically remarked that there should be a statue of himself in the compound for the incidental service he did to the sect in kicking it on its feet. Nakamigawa's biography remarks that the priests laughed in appreciation of the joke but the hard-boiled Mitsui director gave them a banker's smile.

At another time Nakamigawa, in his banking cleaning-up, brought suit against Finance Minister Katsura which led to actual attachment of the Katsura mansion which the Mitsuis held until Katsura paid his debt. It is even of record that Nakamigawa refused to grant a loan to the great Prince Ito, the Constitution maker and old clansman friend of Inouye, Nakamigawa's mentor. Inouye shook his head over this and remonstrated that Nakamigawa was going a little too far, but the latter replied that he wasn't running the Mitsui Bank on a friendship basis and he wasn't sure that Ito was good for the loan.

By such ruthless methods, Nakamigawa in the couse of a few years succeeded in restoring the Bank to a sound and healthy condition. Then he began application of important

TAKASUME MITSUI (center) WITH HIS FAMILY

He is the youngest son of Baron Hachiroemon Mitsui

broader policies. Burning with the old Fukuzawa ideals of independence and aloofness from officialdom, Nakamigawa sought to divorce the Mitsuis from all Government connections and turn the firm's resources into the straight functions of private industrial capitalism.

It was a stimulus in a direction never before approached by the Mitsuis, who for so many years had been relying on close working with the Government. Doubtless it was all very well for the Mitsuis to have this propulsion at this time, but the divorce was not to be forever. Nakamigawa died at the early age of forty-seven, and while he had brought to the Mitsuis a needful spirit of independence, he left the Mitsui interests so large and unified that close connections with a capitalistic Government could not be avoided.

It was, in short, Nakamigawa who in 1891 gave the Mitsuis their place in the forefront of the march of capitalism started by the policies of the Meiji Government. Times were changing fast. Railway construction was pushed, postal and telegraph services extended, a strong mercantile marine was started, harbors improved, and the Government was transferring to private hands many Western enterprises it had started in the 1870–1880 period. As the young industries moved from Government to private hands, due provision was made for various kinds of protection and encouragement, a policy that has continued to this day in the form of a benevolent paternalism.

A Constitution had been given to the country February 11, 1889, and a commercial code promulgated. The commercial code was essentially German, and the Prussian model was used in drafting the Constitution. Western methods had to be invoked to regulate Japan's increased industrialism. Nakamigawa had gone so far as to serve notice on the Government that the Mitsuis, particularly the Bank, were detaching themselves from Government patronage wherever possible. The Mitsui Bank, since the Government had organized the Bank of Japan, had done little more than turn over its branches throughout the country as collection and forwarding agencies for the Bank of Japan. Nakamigawa found the profit percentage very low in spite of the prestige of the function, and he immediately suspended this service. There was another shake-up and reform in the Bank, and the head office issued instructions to all its branches strictly enjoining them to discontinue the use of discriminatory terms hitherto employed — such as "the people's deposit," "the people's money," "the Government money," and so on.

Nakamigawa's next step was the reorganization of the Mitsui Bank into a partnership. This was done by buying up all the shares held by non-Mitsui shareholders and limiting the partners to five members of the Mitsui family, Hachiroemon Mitsui, Takayasu Mitsui, Morinosuke Mitsui, Gennosuke Mitsui and Hachirojiro Mitsui. The partnership plan was effected mainly to get rid of the unlimited liability feature of the Bank in its *Société Anonyme* period. The reorganized bank was capitalized at 2,000,000 yen as before, but it took the name of *Gomei Kaisha Mitsui Ginko*, or Mitsui Partnership Bank. The new bank opened for business July 1, 1893, with Nakamigawa as managing director.

The Bank now was ready to expand its field of activity in the general commercial banking sphere, no longer to be slowed down by a petty fiscal connection with the Government. Within a few years eleven branches that had dealt almost exclusively with the collection and forwarding of Government money were closed down.

*   *   *

Having prepared the Bank to carry out his business ideals, Nakamigawa began to point all the other Mitsui interests in that direction. This was perhaps the most important change of policy in Mitsui history. Like Minomura, his predecessor, Nakamigawa strongly believed in lifting Mitsui out of competition with little firms and little men, both in the retail textile business and small-term loan banking; he believed in turning Mitsui capital into larger industrial fields as a more proper and remunerative outlet. Nakamigawa in other words saw the folly of killing rabbits with an elephant gun, and went for larger game. Within a few years, under his direction, the Mitsuis acquired a hold in its present extensive activities, notably spinning, with the Kanegafuchi Spinning Company, the largest in the world; paper-making, in the Oji Company, the biggest in the Far East; and mining, in the Mitsui Coal Mining Company, the biggest in Japan.

The Kanegafuchi Company, or its forerunner, The Tokyo Cotton Trading Company, was incorporated in November, 1886, with its principal plant in Sumida, Tokyo Prefecture. The Mitsui textile firm and other leading dealers in cotton cloth were its principal shareholders. Through poor management, the firm dragged along inefficiently until the Mitsuis called the attention of trouble-shooter Nakamigawa to the spectacle. Nakamigawa stepped in on the basis of Mitsui shareholdings, had himself appointed president, and named Asabuki, whom he had snagged away from Mitsubishi, as managing director. Sanji Muto, as has been told, was sent to Kobe to take over the plant there and told specially to get ready to tap the great China market, which presented the utmost potentialities. Muto also was given *carte blanche* to raid all contemporaries and rivals for the best talent in the technical end of spinning and to institute an unprecedented system of good treatment for labor and high wages. The Kobe branch soon had so monopolized equipment and laborers that the rest of the spinning firms in Japan organized and lost a drive against Kanegafuchi. The controversy was settled satisfactorily by arbitration of the Bank of Japan governor and, strangely enough, the Mitsubishis.

Mitsui Bussan Kaisha began importing Indian cotton in such large quantities for the Kanegafuchi Spinning Company that they opened an office in Bombay in 1893. It is noteworthy that a Japanese consulate and a shipping line followed Mitsui into India.

At about this time Nakamigawa acquired from the Government the model silk-weaving mill established with the aid of French experts in 1872 at Tomioka, Gumma Prefecture. This mill had an interesting history. When the Government began its operations, it issued a circular to all samurai inviting them to send their daughters to be trained in silk-weaving. This was one of Japan's first and somewhat typical attempts to solve an unemployment problem. The rights and privileges of samurai had just been abolished and the Government was perplexed about their support. Silk-reeling seemed to open possibilities, and the Government ministers believed if the samurais' daughters could be trained into industry they might be able to support their fathers.

In answer to the circular a large number of aristocratic young ladies, accompanied by maids and retainers, showed up for work. The French experts, who were still around to see that the mill got started, became so excited over this influx of feminine beauty that they soon had the proverbial "one-armed paperhanger" looking like a slow-motion picture.

Nakamigawa also took over factories at Miike and Nagoya

and Shinmachi, Gumma Prefecture, with Mitsui Bank capital, instituted the Mitsui speed-up method and soon had a thriving young industry, thereby laying the foundations for Mitsui's present position in silk exporting.

Acquisition of the Oji Paper Company was by similar methods. In 1872 the Meiji Government had induced Mitsui and the small Shimada Company to put up 125,000 yen apiece to organize a paper company, erecting a mill in the village of Oji which today is included in one of the wards of the northern part of Greater Tokyo. Equipment arrived from England in 1874 and the Oji Company produced the first machine-made paper in Japan. Viscount Eiichi Shibusawa, one of Inouye's protégés in the Finance Ministry and an on-and-off co-worker of the Mitsuis, was made president of the company. When, in 1892, Nakamigawa saw the possibilities in the Oji Company, he sent two of his lieutenants, Fujiyama and Seishu Iwashita, the boys from Keio, into Oji as managing directors. The Shimada Company was soon out of the picture, and then Nakamigawa sent still another lieutenant, Ginjiro Fujihara, over to Oji "to adjust the company's affairs."

The adjustment made it a Mitsui concern. Ginjiro Fujihara, president of the company, in 1936 wrote: * —

In America some paper companies are larger in capital investment, but I hardly think that any of them can beat us in profit-making. When a large corporation is formed with watered stock by merging many plants, it is natural that the new organization should be financially weak. The consequence would be failure to pay a dividend, the business eventually passing into the hands of receivers or bankers. In the paper industry, at least, the Japanese need not be ashamed of their country as poorer and weaker.

* From *The Spirit of Japanese Industry*, by Ginjiro Fujihara, Hokuseido Press, Tokyo, 1936.

Nakamigawa also was responsible for shaking-up and putting on a paying basis the Shibaura Engineering Works, another Mitsui holding that had lain more or less dormant since its acquisition from the Government but was destined in later years to become an important industry of Japan. Samples of modern machinery first were purchased by the Government at the International Exposition in Vienna in 1874. Four years later, the Government tried its hand at building European machinery, principally cotton-spinning machines, but the experiment ended in temporary failure. In 1875, the Tanaka Machine Works, reorganized later as the Shibaura Engineering Works by the Mitsuis, was started with six hundred workmen, principally to supply engines for naval ships.

To supply a need of the Kanegafuchi Company, the Shibaura Works was ordered to build a horizontal steam engine of 1,300 horsepower. It was the greatest feat attempted by Japanese engineers up to that time. The company required three years to build it. Foreign observers held their sides at the thought of the "clumsy" Japanese trying to master the intricacies of the monster machine and predicted it would break down within three months if ever it started at all.

But when the engine started, it ran day and night without a halt for thirty-two years in the Kobe mill of the Kanegafuchi Company. When, in 1928, the mill was electrified, the old steam engine was preserved in state as a tribute to early Japanese engineering. Reportedly no steam engine of this size for use on land ever again was built in Japan.

Thus Nakamigawa's renovation and industrialization policies ran the entire gamut of all the existing Mitsui enterprises at the time and came to permeate the entire structure. Conservative elements in the family occasionally tried to block him, but he silenced them with his boldness and plowed ahead. Even his old patron Inouye, exponent of sound finance methods, came near an open break with Nakamigawa, criticizing his methods as overaggressive; but the Mitsui-builder could not be stopped until his death at the age of forty-seven on October 7, 1901.

Thereafter, the Mitsuis drifted back into their old policies. It probably wouldn't have made much difference in the long run for the Mitsuis if Nakamigawa had lived on for another twenty years, but one of his great admirers told this writer that if Nakamigawa's efforts to keep the Mitsuis in the highest forms of industrialization, leaving the small businessmen alone, had been carried on, his later successor, Baron Takuma Dan, might never have been shot to death by a malcontent in 1932.

The direct successor of Nakamigawa as directing genius of the Mitsui interests was Takashi Masuda, the trader.

Therein lies the open secret of the amazingly well-rounded development of Mitsui. It was chance, perhaps, but the whole course could not have been laid out better with blueprints. It ran like this: Minomura pulled the Mitsuis out of the chaos that came with the overthrow of the Tokugawas and made a family organization a business organization. Nakamigawa made a business organization an industrial one and opened new vistas of banking and investment. Masuda, the merchant, built up the foreign trading end. There was no lopsidedness. Over the latter two stood the omnipresent Inouye, for more than a quarter of a century Mitsui's guiding light in the Government. And then when the machine was assembled, along came Takuma Dan, mining man and esthete, who took his place at the control board like an accomplished organist and played a symphony in finance.

Masuda had not the aggressiveness and heavy finance visions of Nakamigawa, but he was a realist, and pertinacious as a Tosa dog. It is clear enough that had their times been reversed, had Masuda preceded Nakamigawa, the Mitsuis would have been left far behind in the capitalistic race that started with the "Enlightened Era" of Meiji. Masuda never could have achieved the organizational reforms of Mitsui that Nakamigawa accomplished. But after the latter's death, he was the right man to carry on steadily and surely while developing his own specialty for the House, that of foreign trading, for Masuda was a merchant to the marrow.

Masuda once served as houseboy for Townsend Harris, the American who followed Perry to Japan and succeeded in effecting workable trade treaties to replace the ambiguous provisions in the 1854 treaty concluded by Perry.

The early contacts Masuda had with Harris made a deep impression on the thirteen-year-old Japanese boy. Eugene H. Dooman, foremost authority on the life of Harris, points out that the first American diplomat in Japan was primarily a merchant who had been engaged in business for many years in various parts of the Pacific. "His attitude toward international questions," Mr. Dooman writes, "was the attitude of the merchant. He was not interested in dynastic quarrels. His only concern was to prepare an environment within which it would be possible for merchants to trade profitably." *

Masuda was born in 1848 on the small island of Sado in the

* From a paper prepared by Mr. Dooman on the occasion of a memorial meeting for Townsend Harris held at Zempuku Temple, Tokyo, in 1931.

Japan Sea where his father was engaged in working the gold mines as an official of the Tokugawa Shogunate. Little Sado Island still boasts of its two chief contributions to modern Japan — its gold mines and Masuda. In 1856, the family moved to Yedo, where the father gained a more important governmental post.

The first foreign legations were beginning to arrive at the Shogunate capital. In each case Buddhist temples were allocated to the new foreign representations as quarters. Harris came up from Shimoda in 1859, and was assigned to the historic temple of Zempuku in the heart of Yedo. Anxious to have his son learn English, the elder Masuda arranged for him to take lessons privately from one of the Foreign Office interpreters who had been assigned to Townsend Harris.

In 1931 Phi Beta Kappa in Japan held a memorial service at Zempuku-ji not only to recall the association of Harris' residence there but to make the picturesque Buddhist temple better known to American residents of Tokyo.

The Phi Beta Kappa committeemen cast about for suitable speakers on the occasion and had a perfunctory program laid out when happily it was recalled that Baron Masuda, retired, white-bearded patriarch of the House of Mitsui, once worked in the temple for Townsend Harris. He was the one man in all Japan still living who could recall personal memories of Harris. The committee called on Baron Masuda at his villa at Odawara and were surprised to find him at eighty-four still active and vigorous both in body and mind, interested in flower-growing, the tea ceremony, antiques and motoring.*

Baron Masuda readily consented to speak, but asked that his address be in Japanese. But then, as he prepared his memoirs recalling boyhood days of seventy years before, his Eng-

* Baron Masuda died December 23, 1938.

lish came back to him. He decided to speak in English and on the day of the memorial the words of a language he had learned in the shadow of the temple flowed from him with vigor.

The speaker recalled that in 1861 he had walked ten miles a day wearing straw sandals to the Harris quarters to learn English. After a time Masuda was taken on by the Foreign Office with "office-boy rank." He was assigned to the temple quarters of Harris. In his speech, he said: —

"According to the feudal custom of those days, boys of the samurai class attained majority at the age of fourteen and then became eligible for Government positions. In 1861 I was really thirteen but made a false declaration in order to receive the appointment. My principal work at Zempuku-ji was to serve tea when officials appeared. Later my position was raised to that of junior interpreter, but my English vocabulary was very poor."

Masuda recalled the danger Harris underwent at the height of antiforeign agitation in favor of expelling "Western barbarians." After a band of patriots attacked the British legation in 1862, Harris was warned and his bodyguard and entire staff took positions for a last stand. The thirteen-year-old Masuda girded up the sleeves of his kimono and loosened the blade of his samurai sword in its sheath ready to help defend the lone American in any melee. But no attack occurred.

Masuda told of Harris' fondness for roast beef, a rarity in Japan, and how the juniors slipped in at night to carve out experimental pieces from a quarter of beef suspended from the kitchen ceiling. When they were detected Harris called them to account, not for taking the beef but for cutting it the wrong way.

"Owing to my good fortune in having come in contact

with Americans in my boyhood days," concluded the Mitsui patriarch, "I am pleased to state that I understand the American mentality better than some people, and my confidence in the American people has been helpful in business. When I went to America in 1907 I was successful in arrangements for American-Japanese co-operation in business. Our [Mitsui's] agreement was concluded with President Coffin of the General Electric Company for the international operation of the Shibaura Engineering Works which has been successful ever since."

But to return to the varied early career of Masuda: When he was seventeen or eighteen, on leaving Townsend Harris, he was permitted to accompany a Tokugawa mission to America and Europe. In France where young Masuda, together with other members of the mission, was received by Napoleon III, the youth received permission to remain behind for a short course in military training. When he returned to Japan he was commissioned to help train the Shogunate's army in French military methods.

When the Shogunate fell, Masuda lost his job, but relying on his sparse knowledge of French, found a connection with a foreign trading company in Yokohama. Then he had the good fortune to meet Kaoru Inouye at a time when Inouye was taking under his wing — and later Mitsui's — almost every young Japanese who had a foreign-style suit of clothes. Inouye found a place for Masuda in the Finance Ministry, and then when he quit he took Masuda with him into the trading company which was established at Yokohama.

Reference already has been made to the merger of Inouye's trading company and the small venture started in Yokohama by the Mitsuis before 1876. When the merger was effected, Masuda became president of *Mitsui Bussan Kaisha*. Masuda afterward continued his close relations with Inouye, providing another string between the statesman and the Mitsuis. At first the *Mitsui Bussan Kaisha* was greatly handicapped in competition with foreign firms already planted in Yokohama, but it was Masuda who was able to foresee that the time would come when the foreigners' business would fall into the hands of the Japanese. His determination and persuasive arguments with Nakamigawa kept the young trading firm going, for Masuda was able to call on the resources of Mitsui Bank.

Mitsui Bussan Kaisha was founded on a loan of 50,000 yen, from the Mitsui Bank, but in the space of sixty years had an authorized and paid-in capital of 100,000,000 yen, and was doing a business of more than 1,500,000,000 yen a year. Of this, about 300,000,000 yen in trade was done in goods that never touched the shores of Japan, for Mitsui's foreign branches handled anything anywhere just so there was a profit to be made. The Mitsui branch in New York for example became one of the largest dealers in the New York rubber market.

When *Mitsui Bussan* was established it had only ten employees, but among them were youths who became leading businessmen in Japan twenty-five to fifty years later. There was, for example, the famous Kyohei Magoshi, who put Mitsuis into beer and himself became the beer king of Japan. Still later there was Jotaro Yamamoto, who became active in Seiyukai politics, figured in a notorious bribery case, and still later became president of the South Manchuria Railway. There was Kenzo Uyehara, known to New York as "Silk Uyehara," who had more to do with encasing American legs in silk stockings than most Paris authorities. Still another was Yunosuke Yasukawa, acknowledged to be the greatest trading genius *Mitsui Bussan* ever had, under whom the present chief managing director of the Mitsui interests, Kaneo Nanjo, polished off the finer points of his business training.

Masuda introduced to the Mitsuis the art of getting and the efficacy of dealing in monopolies. With Inouye's help he became the sole purchasing agent for the Government Mining Bureau. When later Mitsui acquired from the Government the rich coal mines in Miike in Kyushu, he began exporting coal abroad. Mitsui Bussan's first trading connection with Britain, as early as 1876, was in coal trading. Then as the Powers began to establish factories at Shanghai Mitsui had a coal agent at that city several years ahead of Japanese consular representation, and started to build up a vast China market. A little later Masuda opened Mitsui branches in Paris, London and Hongkong. When Mitsui's big cotton spinning interests, Kanegafuchi, started the factory wheels going and called for raw cotton, Masuda in 1883 established first foreign connections in India and in China for importing to Japan raw cotton to be turned over to Kanegafuchi. He secured a monopoly on cotton spinning and silk-reeling machinery from a Manchester, England, company and to the later consternation of Western Powers very soon demonstrated that raw cotton could be brought to Japan, made up into cloth, reexported and sold in foreign markets more cheaply than it could be processed at home.

To spur the business of Mitsui silk mills Masuda imported silkworm eggs from Italy, distributed them freely among cocoon-raisers, and hired itinerant experts to go about the country giving free demonstrations to the farmers on more advanced technique of an ancient Japanese art. Within twenty-five years Japan was producing seventy per cent of the world's raw silk supply.

Masuda saw the steady growth of railway construction in Japan and obtained from Andrew Carnegie a monopoly to sell in Japan Carnegie steel and rail equipment. When the Sino-Japanese war of 1894 broke out, Masuda was first in the field with munitions deals abroad and gained a virtual monopoly on supplying governmental needs. Choshu clansmen were in the saddle and particularly were dominating the army when this war began and the Mitsuis were almost overloaded with army contracts.

In the boom period following the 1894 war *Mitsui Bussan* rode high. There seemed to be no end to the list of commodities and goods which Masuda found that Japan could use, and he started importing them with large profits.

Meanwhile the Mitsui Bank was keeping pace with the fast-changing times. In November, 1898, the Bank increased its capital to five million yen and admitted six new Mitsuis to the partnership. They were Geneyemon Mitsui, Fukutaro Mitsui, Yonosuke Mitsui, Saburosuke Mitsui, Takenosuke Mitsui and Tokuyemon Mitsui. Coincidentally came frequent changes in rules and organization, laying the foundation for the system generally in force today. Constant efforts were made at high selectivity in personnel and the encouragement of the most efficient service by the staff. Still another new scale of higher salaries was fixed and a pension system established for old and faithful employees.

The Bank extended even more widely Nakamigawa's system of taking into service college and university men while the rest of the business world of Japan still clung to the traditional family custom of relying almost exclusively on shop-bred clerks and apprentices. Nakamigawa's business experience was proving a signal success. Among other innovations introduced was the system of "deposit at notice" and "call loans" which had been totally unknown to banking circles of Japan. Moreover, the Bank also set a precedent by abolishing the old practice of counting money down to the thousandth part of the yen. They made a rule to drop all fractions under the sen, or hundredth part of the yen. Other banks were soon following their example.

In July, 1899, the Bank added to its regular business that of warehousing, a lucrative enterprise under trade conditions in Japan. Mitsui started with two storehouses, one in Kobe and the other in Tokyo, but eventually the business became too large to be managed by the Bank and in 1909 it was reorganized as the *Toshin Soko Kabushiki-Kaisha*, a subsidiary company. The original capital of two million yen was increased in 1918 to 5,000,000 yen and in 1923 to 15,000,000 yen.

In both the Sino-Japanese war and the Russo-Japanese war ten years later, the Bank was at the forefront in raising war funds, and in the prosperous years that followed the conflicts, it reaped a proportionate reward. Deposits rose from 16,775,-547 yen in 1893 to 37,729,086 yen in 1903. Loans likewise doubled to a total of 26,663,648 yen and profits reached 484,-220 yen in 1899. The Bank moved into the first steel and brick structure ever built in Japan at Suruga-cho, Tokyo, on November 17, 1902.

After the 1904 war increase in business of the Bank and a 229.7 per cent increase in profits were reflected in these figures: —

	Deposits	Loans	Profits
1904	41,710,308 Yen	30,227,667 Yen	395,383 Yen
1907	70,338,956 Yen	55,070,179 Yen	2,007,505 Yen
1909	78,319,898 Yen	64,872,992 Yen	1,220,190 Yen

The Bank established another precedent by tapping the Western money market when the city of Kyoto, through the Mitsuis, floated a municipal loan of 45,000,000 francs in Paris. This widened the field of the Bank's operations and brought about another change in organization. A joint stock company now was formed after the models of American and European business corporations at the Mitsui Bank, Ltd., in October, 1909.

The old "partnership bank" was dissolved, at that time, handing over its banking and warehouse business to the new company. The capital of the new bank was divided into 200,-000 shares, of which ten members of the Mitsui family, who had acted as its promoters, took 38,000 shares and the rest was spread among other connections of the Mitsui interests. Baron Takayasu Mitsui became president, and among the managing directors was the rising star Seihin Ikeda. Among the directors was Takuma Dan, later to become Chief Managing Director of the Mitsui interests.

Until 1909 the Mitsui banks had used systems of auditing and inspecting that dated back to the old Mitsui exchange house of the 1700's. The old ledgers, used for two centuries, written by hand on a quality of paper remarkable for its state of preservation, are still retained, without a single break in sequence, in the reinforced concrete fireproof Mitsui library in Ebara Ward, Tokyo, today. The library is not open to the public and visitors are rarely admitted, but the writer was taken through the vaults and shown at great length the orderly rows of Mitsui Bank ledgers.

When the new joint-stock-company bank was formed in 1909, a new system of inspection and auditing was instituted to keep a closer supervision on the Bank's business. It featured, primarily, a double system of checking. The head office in Tokyo sent out examiners without notice to all branches, which in turn were required to do their own auditing and inspecting at least once every six months.

In 1906, to meet the growing needs of the country's foreign trade under the aggressive tactics of Masuda, the Mitsui Bank made Barclay and Company of London its first foreign correspondent. Soon afterward connections were made with leading financial houses in the money capitals of the world. As Japan established close relations between its own money markets and those abroad, the Mitsui Bank in 1911 revised its Articles of Association to include in its regular business transactions issuing and underwriting public loans, company bonds and stocks, acceptances and guaranties and trusteeship for collateral bonds.

The World War brought extraordinary commercial and industrial prosperity to Japan, due to tremendous excess of exports over imports, changing the role of Japan from a debtor nation to that of a creditor nation. The Mitsui Bank overlooked nothing in this period, underwriting Government bonds, subscribing to the loans of Allied Powers, and importing more foreign capital to Japan. The Bank's business spurted in this fashion:

	Deposits	Loans	Profits
1909	86,162,862 Yen	72,828,814 Yen	875,241 Yen
1912	85,350,722 Yen	77,892,400 Yen	1,320,050 Yen
1915	114,810,144 Yen	94,959,317 Yen	738,105 Yen
1919	306,571,664 Yen	260,805,085 Yen	3,483,494 Yen

In 1919 capital was increased from 20,000,000 yen to 100,-000,000 yen, and the shares increased from 200,000 to 1,000,-

ooo. The *Mitsui Gomei Kaisha*, the giant holding company, which had been formed to draw off the profits of all the Mitsui concerns, took 500,000 of the new shares for the Mitsui family members. The remaining 300,000 new shares at a premium of forty-five yen a share were offered for public subscription and were sold out in three hours. The first call on the new shares at 50 yen each was made and paid in together with the premium on September 1 of that year. This put the paid-up capital of the bank at 16,000,000 yen, and the premiums in excess of the face value of shares were turned into a reserve fund for the next term, making it total 22,073,745 yen. The Mitsui Bank with its 300,000 shares held by the public thus became a public company in name and fact, ending a role stretching over two centuries as a private company.

In 1926 the Bank celebrated its semi-centenary of modern existence. Deposits had increased from 11,369,055 yen to 475,857,350, and capital from 2,000,000 to 100,000,000 yen. The country had waged three wars, and gone through the shattering ordeal of the 1923 earthquake and all stages of economic vicissitudes, but the Mitsui Bank emerged from each with unimpaired credit and always increasing prosperity. From a tiny exchange house set in the back end of a dry-goods store with little more equipment than a pair of gold scales, it had grown in 1926 to nineteen offices in Japan and five banks abroad, including Shanghai, Surabaya, Bombay, London and New York.

Today, the vast Mitsui enterprises radiate from the Mitsui Main Building in Suruga-cho, Tokyo, one of the outstanding business structures in the Far East. It is the nerve center of the Mitsui organization. The $10,000,000, five-story Mitsui building is on the identical site where the first Mitsui banking and drapery house was opened in Tokyo nearly three hundred years ago. The present building replaces the headquarters which were damaged by the great earthquake and fire that almost leveled Tokyo in 1923. The exterior is a modern adaptation of the Roman classical style and is finished in Inada (Japanese) granite. Fifty-three-foot Corinthian columns adorn the outside. New York architects and engineers carried out the specifications of the Mitsuis in emphasizing unity, mass and endurance. Extreme modernism was avoided, but the fifth floor is a setback in the New York manner. On completion the Mitsuis, with elaborate Shinto rites, dedicated the building as "an everlasting monument" to the Founder and the present House of Mitsui.

Chapter XI

FROM COAL TO SCANDAL

STORE, BANK, TRAD-
ing company — and then mining. That was the orderly development of the Mitsui Kingdom. Minomura, Nakamigawa,
Masuda — and then Dan. That was the succession of Mitsui
geniuses behind the expansion.

The president of one of Mitsui's subsidiary companies, a
tweed-suited, poker-playing Japanese who spent fifteen years
in New York, sat talking to the writer in the American Club
in Tokyo. He lighted a Corona Corona cigar and pondered
briefly the question: What was the secret of Mitsui's growth?

"It's simple," he said. "They got the Miike mines. And
they not only struck pay dirt in the Miike mines, but they
found Takuma Dan there. That was all they needed. It was
the turning point in Mitsui history. If Mitsubishi had got the
mines and Takuma Dan, the Mitsuis today probably would
have been just another wealthy family."

The Miike coal fields, ninety miles south of Moji on the
island of Kyushu, had been worked wastefully and incompe-
tently for three hundred years. There are nine seams of coal in
the field of 102,000 acres, seams from twenty to twenty-five
feet in thickness. The Tokugawa Shogunate worked the rich
colliery on a small scale, never suspecting its possibilities until
Perry's ships arrived belching black coal smoke out of their
ungainly stacks. When the Meiji Government took over from
the Shogunate, the mines were in the kitty, and as industrialism spurted forward the mines took their proper place.

Back in the days when the Meiji Government was handing out largesse to persons and firms who had been helpful in overthrowing the Tokugawas, several groups were trying to get the Miike mines. The Mitsubishi firm, and Mitsui's other competitors of the period, *Ono-Gumi* and the Asanos, were pulling their own strings for the mines. Masuda, the trading genius who had built *Mitsui Bussan*, got wind of the bargain-counter rush.

There was one obstacle. Finance Minister Matsukata held the unorthodox opinion that the Government ought to keep the mines. But when pressure became strong from his colleagues, he told a Cabinet meeting that he would consent to an auction with the stipulation that they should not be sold for less than 4,500,000 yen. That made it a matter of "face" with the Minister. If they were sold at a lower price, he would have to resign, leading very probably to a Cabinet upset. To Matsukata the 4,500,000 yen seemed high enough to insure Government retention.

But Masuda had the usual Mitsui ace up a sleeve. He called on Kaoru Inouye and, with some subsequent negotiation by two Mitsui bank directors, it was suddenly announced in 1888 that the bid of "Mr. Hachiro Sasaki" for 4,550,000 yen had won the mines. Sasaki of course was a representative of the Mitsuis. And Sasaki, by a strange coincidence, was the name of the family the Mitsuis once took unto themselves in their early formative period. The Mitsuis paid 1,000,000 yen in cash for the mines and the rest in fifteen annual installments.

Within a year the Mitsuis not only had recovered the 4,550,000 yen but made a handsome profit. One conservative estimate is that the mine has averaged 3,000,000 tons a year at ten yen a ton for fifty years. On a basis of thirty per cent clear net profits, the Mitsuis in a half-century have realized 450,000,000 yen on a 4,500,000-yen investment.

But this is getting ahead of the story, for it was Takuma Dan who made the mine pay.

Dan was the third son of an impecunious samurai of the Fukuoka clan settled in the vicinity of the mine. As usual, the child was a bright boy — this is getting to be a monotonous aspect of the story of Mitsui — and at the age of eleven was adopted by the Dan family in the same clan. The head of the Dan family was the financial chief of the clan. A year later, in 1871, young Dan was taken to America by the head of the clan, who was going on an inspection tour. Dan and another youth about his age, Kentaro Kaneko, who later became one of Japan's great statesmen, were deposited in a Miss Arland's School in Boston to learn their A B C's.

After graduating from grammar school Kaneko, ambitious to become a politician, decided to study law. Dan at the time told him, "I do not like politicians." (While Dan studiously tried to keep his name out of politics all his life, ironically he was shot to death because of a country boy's dissatisfaction with politics.)

"I intend to study mining," Dan told Kaneko, "because in my province is the Miike coal mine and other rich mineral deposits. My ambition is to enrich my country by bringing these resources to the surface."

Dan entered the Massachusetts Institute of Technology and specialized in mining and metallurgy. After graduating, he returned to Japan at the age of twenty-four and rushed to Kyushu, hoping to find employment at the Miike mines, still in the hands of the Government. At the moment there was no place for the young engineer. He took a job as teacher of Eng-

MITSUI MINING COMPANY

MINERS' COTTAGES, WITH SPORTS GROUND
AND CLUBHOUSE

lish in a school at Osaka for a time, until he landed a job on the Government staff then administering the mines.

When Takuma Dan became a Government engineer at the Miike mines in 1884 his salary was $400 a year. When he was murdered in 1932, Mitsui reportedly was paying him $291,-000 a year, by far the highest salary ever paid in Japan.

Dan's ability won him rapid advancement at Miike. Within four years he moved up from engineer to foreman, to supervisor, works manager and superintendent. But there were problems at the mine which seemed all but insurmountable in the light of the engineering knowledge then available in Japan. The Miike coal seam is wet, one of the wettest in the world, and there seemed no chance of working its rich, lower drifts unless some method could be found to keep the flow of subterranean water in check or to pump it out. On his own recommendation, the young mining superintendent was relieved of his duties and sent by the Government to Europe and the United States to discover means of draining the mine. This was in 1888, when Takuma Dan was thirty years old.

While he was abroad the Mitsuis began negotiations with the Government for the mine. They asked who would run it if they took it over, inasmuch as they had no mining men in their personnel. The Government replied that the young superintendent, a very capable man, would be thrown in with the deal. So, when the Mitsuis bought the mine, Takuma Dan came with it.

Dan was leaving England for the United States when the news came that he was working for Mitsui, but that he would be accorded a free hand. Dan returned in 1889 with a huge suction pump and supervised its installation together with other up-to-date machinery, and soon had the mine clear of water. Application of his engineering knowledge at Miike became famous in mining circles abroad, and foreign engineers who came to Japan made pilgrimages to Miike to see the heaviest colliery pumping plant then in existence.

Besides putting the mine on an immensely profitable basis, Dan by a fortunate circumstance was laying another valuable nest-egg for the Mitsuis.

At about the time the young engineer was working almost night and day clearing the mine of water and débris a good-looking country lad from the near-by village of Omuta was visiting the mine daily. He volunteered to help Dan without pay and the engineer accepted. Physically strong, personable but silent, the youth, who gave his name as Utaro Noda, brought his own lunch and never asked for any more from the mine than a cup of tea at noon. He would run errands, lend a hand with the machinery or attempt anything at Dan's bidding.

One of the major problems confronting Dan as employment increased at the mine was relations between the mine officials and the local population. Dan was an engineer but no diplomat. As questions of wages, quarters and other relations arose between village and the mine, Dan found Noda was an invaluable assistant in negotiating with the local residents.

In time Noda was taken on as a sort of personnel man by Dan to maintain friendly liaison with the village. Noda exhibited such marked qualities as a politician that Dan encouraged him to stand for prefectural assemblyman. Dan of course suggested that Noda join the Seiyukai party, which was then coming into existence under the ægis of the Choshu clan members with whom Mitsui had been friendly.

Noda was elected to the prefectural assembly, later to the Diet, and became nationally known as Seiyukai leader.

In 1918, Noda became Minister of Communications in the Cabinet of Premier Hara, who was the first commoner to hold the Premiership. It was, notably, during the ministry of Premier Hara that the influence of businessmen began to supplant that of the clan leaders in politics. The practice of buying M.P.'s with money and influencing elections by the power of wealth had been inaugurated by the bureaucrats of an earlier day. The army, in fact, was the first great offender, and frequently used Government resources to buy election support for men it wanted in office.

Few party politicians [McLaren wrote in his *Political History of the Meiji Era*] have made as immense fortunes out of bribes as have the Cabinet Ministers. The foundations of the Inouye and Okuma fortunes were laid in very early days. Inouye during his incumbency of the Department of Public Works had charge of the building of all railroads. The construction expense per mile was cut in half after his resignation. Okuma, who while in the Finance Office was called upon to provide means for carrying on the campaign against Satsuma in 1877, adopted the expedient of an issue of paper money, and it is commonly reported in Japan that he carried off several cartloads of the scrip which remained in the Treasury after the rebellion had been suppressed. The official careers of both these men had ended about 1881, and from that time on they devoted their energies mainly to serving the interests of the great business houses of Mitsui and Iwasaki [Mitsubishi] respectively. The first issue of the *Japan Year Book* in 1905, in a section made up of short biographical sketches of the influential men of the country, refers to Inouye as the Mitsui representative in the Council of Elder Statesmen.

When Hara became head of the Seiyukai, he saw that the only way to break the power of bureaucracy was to build up a huge party fund from the businessmen and he stopped at nothing to obtain this fund.

The result was a series of unsavory scandals still fresh in the memory of Japanese today. Hara broke away from the incubus of bureaucracy, but by tapping business coffers he created a larger one. "The governmental paternalism which had extended help through subsidies, tariffs, and the transfer of well-fledged industries from official to private hands was beginning to see its creatures turn upon it in an effort at control," writes Professor Harold S. Quigley.

In 1920, when the forty-second Diet was dissolved and Hara began casting about for funds to swing the subsequent election, he reminded his Communications Minister, Noda, of his relationship with Dan of the Mitsuis. It is recorded in one biographical account of Dan that he willingly agreed to advance "a large sum" to repay his obligation to the former country boy, who had done so much to make his administration at Miike successful.

This is the first clearly defined incident of an important monetary contribution to the Seiyukai from the Mitsuis — but a Mitsui spokesman belittled its significance, characterizing the episode as a commendable example of lasting friendship. It was not long, however, until such editorials as this were to be found in the Japanese papers: —

Statesmen can hardly do anything nowadays without allying themselves with monetary magnates. Every influential statesman is backed up by some monetary interest and the connection between businessmen and statesmen is getting more intimate than ever. . . . The Mitsui Club, the Industrial Club and the like practically have power to control the Foreign Office and police [Yorodzu].

Hara was stabbed to death November 4, 1921, by a young railroad employee, who explained that he personally was fed up with corruption and degeneracy in politics.

It was Takuma Dan who was to lead the Mitsuis through tremendous and profitable expansion during the World War period. The success he achieved with the Miike mining had brought him quick advancement with the firm. In the fifteen years that followed his assumption of directorship of Mitsui mining activities, more and more responsibilities were placed on his shoulders and he became a director in one after another of Mitsui's companies.

Gradually, he was taken away from the details of mining technology and handed company administration. The mining business had been conducted by the *Mitsui Gomei Kaisha*, the holding company, until 1911 when it was separately organized as the Mitsui Mining Company with a capital of 20,-000,000 yen, subsequently increased to 100,000,000 yen.

In 1915, with the World War getting under way, Dan was made senior managing director of the *Mitsui Gomei Kaisha*, the highest post in the Mitsui organization, and thus became the lineal successor of such great Mitsui *banto* as Minomura, Nakamigawa and Masuda.

Making money out of Japan's wars was an old story with all the Mitsuis, but none of his predecessors covered so much ground as Takuma Dan. From the time they helped finance clan warfare before the Restoration and then became paymasters of the Imperial forces of the Central Government, the Mitsuis had been in the forefront of military industrialists.

The Satsuma Rebellion of 1877 had revealed to the new Imperial Government the necessity of protecting and encouraging the production of manufactured articles. The Government forthwith had adopted a policy of ordering crude or finished materials for arms, ammunition, clothing and other supplies from specially selected individuals or firms at standard prices but allowing a wide margin of profits.

The Mitsuis of course were pre-eminent among such favored concerns.

This [Government policy] amounted to an indirect subsidy [says Kobayashi] and factories were established in localities where army divisions were garrisoned for the purpose of manufacturing war materials, and soon became suppliers also for the general market. The factories thus established and remaining to this day laid then the foundations of their present well-to-do positions by selling their products largely to military factories. At the opening of the Sino-Japanese War [in 1894] war materials of great variety and amount had to be hastily provided and those which could not be produced at once in the military factories had to be made in private factories, the work of which was consequently increased very suddenly. Therefore the authorities gave every convenience they could to those factories, and by joint effort with the latter, worked in the direction of the development of these industries so that all the articles necessary for the war were fully supplied without hindrance.*

In the ten years between the Sino-Japanese War of 1894–1895 and the Russo-Japanese War, the paternalistic Government continued its subsidies and favors. By 1904, the Mitsuis owned some of the most flourishing of the industries on which the Government depended for manufactured articles, as well as for raw materials combed from the world markets through the trading branch of the Mitsui concern.

* *Military Industries of Japan*, by Ushisaburo Kobayashi. Oxford University Press.

The most effective means of protection [says Kobayashi] was [for the Government] to buy their products by free contract, or by limited tender, which allows only those persons who are appointed to bid for sale. The latter method, seemingly not so effective, worked in practice was well as a subsidy because war materials are sold in great quantities and comparatively high prices are paid for them, as there are not so many competitors in this case as there would be otherwise, and, moreover, the amount of demand is constant and the price seldom undergoes any sudden changes. The producers thus stand on a very solid basis. This system may have the evils attached to monopoly; but it was unavoidable as a means of protection for domestic industry when the economic condition of the country was not advanced. We can not exaggerate too much the past influence of military industry upon the economic world of Japan.

In the next ten-year interval between conflicts — that is, between the Russo-Japanese War and the World War — the rapidly expanding Mitsui firm, still working hand-in-hand with the military, formed an alliance with the great Vickers munitions interests of England. The Armstrong armament firm — prior to its merger with Vickers — already was exploiting the Far Eastern field. Sir William White of Armstrong had aided the Japanese in designing and constructing some of their early warships. While in the Orient he lost no opportunity of doing a little private business for his firm, playing off the Chinese against the Japanese. As his biographer* puts it so frankly: —

White was not unwilling to play the part of *honnête courtier* by pointing out the growth of the Japanese navy to his Chinese clients, or of the Chinese to their indomitable rivals. In doing so, he was careful to insist on the confidential nature of his de-

* *The Life of Sir William White*, by Frederic Manning (Dutton).

signs and the daily progress of our scientific knowledge. By such means he was able to increase the profits of the great company which employed him, to extend what is perhaps the most important of national industries, and to kindle in the hearts of two Asiatic peoples the flames of an enlightened and sacred patriotism.

In 1907, when the Government ordered the establishment of the Japan Steel Works with the assistance of the War and Navy Ministries, most of the shares were taken by the Mitsuis and Vickers. It was capitalized at 15,000,000 yen. Ten plants turned out gun barrels, ammunition hoists, steel castings, torpedo tubes, projectiles, gun carriages and a wide variety of other material. For twenty-five years it was the only private establishment in Japan which manufactured arms. It owed its origin and existence, as Kobayashi points out, entirely to the military industry.

At the start of the World War, the Mitsui-Vickers alliance gave rise to a national scandal that precipitated a Cabinet crisis and brought prison terms for some high Mitsui officials.

In June, 1910, officials of *Mitsui Bussan* learned through private connections with the Navy Ministry that a new battle-cruiser was to be ordered abroad. As agents for Vickers, the Mitsuis started pulling wires for the contract. They entrusted the task chiefly to Tsurutaro Matsuo, a naval constructor-general on the reserve list, technical adviser of the Mitsuis and head of the machinery department of the trading company. Matsuo, by fortunate chance, was a bosom friend of Admiral Matsumoto, director of the Naval Stores Department of the Navy Ministry.

Matsuo, as subsequent court proceedings revealed, consulted Kenzo Iwahara, one of the Mitsui directors, on the amount of bribe Mitsui and Vickers could afford to give to

Matsumoto for the contract. The figure was fixed at one third of the commission the Mitsuis were to receive from Vickers. The Mitsuis thereupon notified Vickers of this arrangement and asked for an increase in the commission. This was finally set at five per cent or 1,150,000 yen. The contract was signed, and Matsuo began making payments to his naval friend, depositing the money in two accounts in separate banks. Vickers went to work on the warship.

With the opening of the Diet session in January, 1914, a veteran member of the Lower House called attention to press reports of a blackmail trial in Berlin. An office employee of Siemens-Schückert, German munitions dealers, one Herr Richter, was accused of stealing documents and attempting to "shake down" his firm for a considerable amount over the alleged bribery of two high Japanese naval officers in connection with building a radio plant for the navy.

Unfortunately for the Mitsuis, the new battle cruiser *Kongo*, which had been built in England by Vickers, arrived in Japan almost simultaneously with reports of the bribe revelations in Berlin. Diet members, who had been stirred up by evidence of veniality among certain naval officers in the Richter affair, promptly turned the spotlight on the *Kongo* deal.

The Mitsuis had expected that. Minseito members of the Diet were always gunning for Mitsuis. The *Japan Weekly Chronicle* reported that, even before the *Kongo* was mentioned in the Diet, "It was decided in anticipation of judicial inquiries into the affairs of *Mitsui Bussan Kaisha* to alter the entries in the firm's books, and to do such other acts as were considered necessary or advisable in order to conceal all traces of what had been done."

But the Diet speeches continued, widening into open charges against the Mitsuis. They were sensationally reported in the press, and the public was quickly roused. Indignation meetings were held in Tokyo, Kobe, Osaka and other cities. On one occasion a crowd of 40,000 in Tokyo became so unruly troops had to be called out. Police boxes were upset, windows smashed and other depredations occurred. Responding to the public feeling, the Diet performed the highly unusual feat of paring the current naval budget. The Lower House shaved off some 30,000,000 yen and the Upper House 70,-000,000. When they failed to compromise on an intermediate sum, the Cabinet, headed by an admiral, resigned.

The next Premier was the aged Count Okuma, who had long been connected with the House of Mitsubishi, chief Mitsui competitors. Naturally, Okuma, who rarely overlooked an opportunity to blast the Mitsuis, saw to it that the Mitsuis received full publicity for their part in the shady *Kongo* deal. Trials came with a speed hitherto unheard-of in Japan, and Mitsui was pretty badly hit. Seven directors of the Mitsui trading company were found guilty of bribing navy officials and received prison sentences up to two years each. Admiral Matsumoto was sentenced to three years and required to refund to the Government some 400,000 yen which he had received as a bribe. Matsuo, the Mitsui technical adviser who acted as go-between in arranging the deal, received another two-year sentence.

On August 29, 1914, the *New York World* received a strange letter in typical Japanese-English containing a news item which, the writer said, "ought to find interest and publication anywhere under the sun." The letter contained the information that "Mitsui & Co., Japan's largest firm of exporters, accused of having paid 400,000 yen to Japanese prominent in naval circles in order to win for Vickers and Co., a contract for constructing the cruiser *Kongo*, has paid over to the Japanese Government 750,000 yen to be used for the education and care of convicts and ex-convicts. The amount represents the commission made by Mitsui & Co., minus the 400,000 yen alleged to have formed a corruption fund."

The letter was signed by K. Mochijuki, "proprietor of the Liberal News Agency of Japan." Mr. Mochijuki, clearly, was acting as an early press agent for the Mitsuis in America at a time when some unfavorable reports of the firm were on the trans-Pacific cables.

Mr. Mochijuki admitted that several "gentlemen" concerned in the bribing were convicted, but added: "The gentlemen could not see the justice of the verdict and appealed to the higher courts."

Although [Mr. Mochijuki continued] the case is yet pending and although the remainder of the commission, 750,000 yen, was honorably, honestly and properly earned as a result of commercial dealings, Messrs. Mitsui have been largely grievous that its traditional business uprightness was besmeared by such a suspicion and rumor and decided to contribute the money for the cause of charity.

Just why the Mitsui donation was made for benefit of "convicts" was not stated. The fact that seven of its directors were soon to enter that classification might have had something to do with it. The publicist went on to say that as a result of the Mitsui gift, the Japanese Government could extend its rehabilitation work among discharged convicts, and concluded: —

Statistics show that convicts receiving the benefits of a spiritual as well as practical training in most instances turn over the new leaf and do not again break a law.

A. Morgan Young of the *Kobe Chronicle* summarized more soberly: —

> The whole business was felt to be a public disgrace, since directors of the greatest mercantile firm in Japan and high officers of the navy, Japan's special pride, were involved. Commercial morality, it was generally recognized, was at a very low stage, but that the navy should be thus venial was a great shock to national confidence.

The Mitsui naval scandal received such wide attention in Japan that it was made the subject of a historical drama staged in a public theater at Kure, one of Japan's biggest naval ports, while the trials still were going on. This is in line with an old Japanese tradition. Before the Westernization that began with Emperor Meiji, there were no regular newspapers and such publications as did appear were strictly enjoined against publishing news of any important event involving either the Government or the Imperial Household. There were no such bans on plays accurately depicting the event of the moment. The play *Chushingura*, the story of the Forty-Seven Ronin, is the classical example of a Japanese drama that recorded public feeling over an event of national interest. When the forty-seven loyal retainers of a slain feudal lord were required to commit hara-kiri for avenging their master, the news was banned from publication but reached the public largely through the resulting stage play, which is still a popular drama throughout the country. This gave rise to the custom of dramatizing the most important of current events. And so strongly does the tradition persist in Japan that when the Mitsui naval scandal was enacted at Kure there was no thought of official retribution on the grounds of criminal libel or contempt of court.

The Mitsuis paid dearly in the esteem of the public for their part in this scandal. Indeed, the assassination of Baron Dan, in 1932, might be traced to a lingering public antipathy toward the Mitsuis, and it remained for his successor, Seihin Ikeda, to "humanize" the Mitsuis for a brief spell until the military clique took command and it no longer mattered whether a great Japanese industrial concern was "human" or not.

Mitsui's World War activities spread even to the United States, where the firm financed the Standard Aero Corporation and the Standard Aircraft Corporation in 1915. The president of Standard Aircraft was Harry B. Mingle, a New York lawyer who had formed a college friendship with a Japanese and afterward for a time acted as local attorney for Mitsui in New York. These facts were subsequently brought out in a Senate investigation.

Starting with a few small army and navy orders in 1916, Standard's business with the American Government jumped into the millions when the United States entered the war. A healthy "war baby," the Mitsui affiliate reportedly received a total of $14,000,000 for planes and parts during the war.

After the war, Government payments to Standard were among thirty-six cases of alleged aircraft fraud audited by the Finance Division of the Army Air Service. The specific amount of the Government claim was not fixed until 1926, when the United States Attorney in New York filed suit to recover $2,594,438.48, which he alleged had been wrongfully paid to the company.

The Standard case drew some sensational testimony before the Brookhart Committee in the Senate, which, in 1924, investigated charges against Attorney General Harry M. Daugherty. The case was mentioned as one of the alleged war frauds Daugherty failed to prosecute. However, the testimony concerning Mitsui was almost lost sight of, on account of the national interest in the Daugherty scandal, the activities and suicide of Jess Smith, and the "Ring" that met in "the little green house on K Street" in Washington.

The late Gaston B. Means, former agent of the Department of Justice and notorious hoaxer in the Lindbergh case, told the committee on March 14, 1924, that he had received a $100,000 bribe from "a Jap from Mitsui and Company," and that he had turned the money over to Jess Smith. At about the same time, he testified, the War Department withdrew from the Department of Justice the case it had worked up against the Standard Aircraft Corporation.

But it was difficult to take Means seriously, even in those days. He admitted, somewhat pridefully, that he had been charged with every known crime, but had been convicted of nothing more than a street fight. While testifying, he was under four indictments for a "shakedown" operation in New York.

Senator Burton K. Wheeler read into the record the report of another former Department of Justice agent, Captain H. L. Scaife, who had worked on the Standard case. The report said in part: —

The Standard Aircraft Corporation and the Standard Aero Company are enterprises of Mitsui & Co., Japanese bankers and fiscal agents of the Japanese Government. During the period of the war, the Standard companies were prominent members of the group of contractors which controlled American aviation.

This investigation has established the fact that agents of the Japanese Government are constantly collecting information of the most intimate character as to the industries, resources, harbors

and other information of a vital character concerning this country and that these agents work through Mitsui & Co. . . .
    Mitsui & Co. are indirectly exerting a powerful influence in this country, which extends to Congress and departments of the Government and they have on their payrolls attorneys and politicians who are attempting to run roughshod over this country to whom they owe their first allegiance.

When an investigation of the Standard contracts began, the law firm of Cadwalader, Wickersham & Taft notified the Chief of Finance of the air service that they had been retained by Mitsui & Co., Ltd. to represent their interests, and requested that certain accountants who had been in the employ of these interests be permitted to work with the Government's representatives during the audit of the books of the Standard Aircraft Corporation. Their request was refused unless Mitsui & Co. would admit its liability in the premises.

On April 2, Captain Scaife took the stand. He read a letter from George W. Wickersham, former Attorney General, prominent Republican leader and head of the law firm of Cadwalader, Wickersham and Taft, to Solicitor General James M. Beck. Emphasis was put on the fact that the message began "Dear Jim," although it merely requested Mr. Beck to remind the Supreme Court that it had consented to the advancement of "the Yamashita case." There was no connection with Mitsui and Company. Captain Scaife said he was reading it to show "the invisible Government" in operation.

The witness, aided by a series of leading questions from Senator Moses, declared he was trying to show that the law firm was counsel for "very extensive Japanese interests," that these interests were "acting in a way inimical to the United States," that the law firm was seeking special favors from the

Department of Justice for its clients, and that it had succeeded in blocking his investigation of the Standard Aircraft Corporation. He also claimed that access to the company's books had been denied him and the Army Air Service.

The following day, Thomas F. Lane, legal adviser to the finance division of the Air Service, who had been in charge of the aircraft fraud investigations, said that "about an automobile load of books and papers out of some New York office and some of Mingle's [president of Standard Aircraft] books" had been obtained with Means' assistance. The accounts between Mitsui and the Sloan Manufacturing Company* at Plainfield showed an item of $1,619,000 in the assets of Standard Aircraft, which, "as far as I could figure out from a close study and after years of study," represented a loss sustained in financing the old Sloan firm. By this bookkeeping, he claimed, "they" hoped to recover the money through various settlements with the United States Government.

"Mingle further told me that one of the Japanese who had been on the board of Standard Aircraft to help protect the interests of Mitsui and Company shortly after the Armistice had committed suicide," Lane went on. "He had his picture on the wall and pointed it out to me, saying, 'That poor devil got scared and committed suicide.'"

Mingle himself died mysteriously in New York the autumn before Lane testified before the committee.

The witness mentioned one other unsolved mystery in the case. The Government, claiming an overpayment of $978,000 to Standard Aircraft, agreed to take a quantity of raw materials and parts in compensation. About 122 carloads of this material left the plant at Elizabeth, New Jersey, and promptly disappeared.

"Where that property went, who receipted for it, what

* Predecessor of the Standard Aircraft Corporation.

became of it, so far as I know has never been determined,"
Lane complained.

To all this, Mitsui, through its New York manager, Mr.
Shigeji Tajima, on April 4 issued an unqualified denial. Standard Aero and Standard Aircraft, he stated, were devoted exclusively to the production of airplanes for the United States
Government. Mitsui financed the company and received only
6.7 per cent interest on its money and "no profits whatsoever,"
the manager insisted in a letter to the Senate committee.

Mitsui aided only in furnishing the capital because it
wanted to be of some assistance to the United States and
Allies in winning the war, the letter added.

The statement by Means that he had received from a Mitsui representative $100,000 to be turned over to Jess Smith
was denounced as untrue. No sum of money had been paid to
Means, the Department of Justice or any other branch of the
Government in connection with the Standard Aircraft transactions, it was stated, and the committee was informed that
it was free to examine the Mitsui books at any time.

Several other minor statements made by Captain Scaife
were held to be in error, while the allegation that the Standard
Aircraft assets had been raised $1,619,000 to include a loss
sustained by Mitsui in financing the Sloan Manufacturing
Company was called "wholly without foundation."

In the course of the letter, Mr. Tajima briefly outlined the
part Mitsui was playing in the American airplane industry: —

Mitsui & Co. held the preferred stock of the Standard Aircraft
Corporation, and that corporation was indebted to it for money
advanced to an amount of nearly $2,000,000. After a settlement
of pending contracts with the Government on June 24, 1919,
the corporation was dissolved and out of the moneys received
from the Government, Mitsui & Co. received from the corpora-

tion the par amount of the preferred stock, in addition to the amount of the indebtedness for the advances above referred to, with interest. The representatives of the Government asserted that, upon the establishment of the claim against the aircraft corporation, they proposed to procure reimbursement from Mitsui & Co. for the amounts so received. The claim against the aircraft corporation was first asserted through the Air Service Bureau of the War Department in June, 1921.

This situation made it necessary for Mitsui & Co. to see to it that a suitable defense was made to the claim of the Government.

To sum up the whole situation, we wish to call the attention of your committee to the fact that the Standard Aero and Aircraft Corporations were devoted exclusively to the production of airplanes for the United States Government and that they were financed by Mitsui & Co. out of their own resources, and that Mitsui furnished all the necessary working capital and received in return only the money which it had invested in and advanced to the corporations with 6 per cent interest and absolutely no profit whatsoever. This is not a case where any war profits were received. All production was under the strict supervision of the United States Government officials. The employees were all Americans, and Mitsui only aided in furnishing the capital because it wanted to be of some assistance to the United States and Allies in winning the war.

Back in Tokyo, Baron Dan called the whole case "laughable."

It was just a coincidence that within ten days after the Mitsui denial the United States Senate voted seventy-six to two to abrogate the so-called "Gentlemen's Agreement" under which Japan promised to refuse permission to laborers to migrate to the United States. Thus was enacted the "Exclusion Act" which caused so much feeling in Japan against the United States.

Chapter *XII*

DEATH TO THE DOLLAR=BUYERS

NINETEEN HUNDRED
and Thirty-two was "the Year of the Monkey" in Japan. Under the strange zodiac of the old lunar calendar, the Year of the Monkey comes every twelve years. A great many people in Japan still cling to the beliefs and usages of this zodiac, and to them the Monkey Year is the year of misfortune. The word for monkey is *saru*, which also means "leave" or "desert." Sometimes when the older country people hear the evil word *saru* they will murmur *tsuru-kame* instinctively, like the "God bless you!" after a sneeze. *Tsuru-kame* means "crane-turtle." The crane supposedly lives a thousand years and the turtle ten thousand. By that incantation, the sinister influence of the word "monkey" is neutralized.

The 1932 Year of the Monkey brought its share of misfortunes to the Mitsuis.

It opened with an optimistic statement by the new Premier, Tsuyoshi Inukai, leader of the Seiyukai, the political party the Mitsuis generally had supported. Within five months he was shot down.

Junnosuke Inouye, outgoing Finance Minister, had a New Year statement that was not so optimistic — since he was on the other side of the fence, a member of the Minseito party, the "outs." Inouye was shot down within a month.

Baron Takuma Dan, esthetic Chief Managing Director of the Mitsuis, spent the New Year holidays among his priceless art objects. He was not a politician, so he had no statement to make. But he survived only two months of the Year of the Monkey. A blank-faced peasant youth shot him to death.

Mr. Sanji Muto, head of the big Mitsui cotton spinning concern, the Kanegafuchi Company, said in his New Year statement: * "We [meaning the Mitsuis, it would seem] have fought for the replacement of the gold embargo for the past two and a half years, and our fight has resulted in victory. The nation must thank Kenzo Adachi."

If he had said "the Mitsuis" instead of "the nation" his statement would have gone into the nutshell category.

Japan had maintained the gold standard from 1897 until September, 1917, when the United States placed an embargo on gold exports. This cut off the principal source of gold imports for Japan, and Japan acted with a similar embargo to prevent Japanese losses of the metal. Return to the gold basis was delayed in Japan by a series of national misfortunes, including a commodity panic in 1920, the great earthquake of 1923 and further financial difficulties in 1926 and 1927.

In the summer of 1929 when prices were high and general world-wide prosperity prevailed, it was decided to return to the gold basis, but the actual step was not taken until in January, 1930, when the world price decline and depression were under way.

The costs of Japan's rapid industrialization and growth of finance capitalism had fallen mostly on the farmer. Some six million families, or forty-eight per cent of the nation, were still engaged in agriculture after the World War, and in 1930 the aggregate taxes paid by the farming population were more than double that of industry and commerce. From the time

* Mr. Muto, incidentally, was not assassinated until 1934.

of the Meiji Restoration, industry and commerce had benefited from Government favors, but not the farmer.

The farmer was not blind to the maladjustment of Japan's
capitalism, nor was the army. A study of social conditions had
been introduced in the military academy, and as the prospective officers came mostly from the soil themselves, the seeds
of a new social philosophy were falling on fertile ground.

The Minseito Cabinet, under Premier Hamaguchi, had
come into office in July, 1929, committed to economic re-
trenchment, disarmament and Sino-Japanese co-operation.
The liberal-minded Baron Shidehara, Minseito Foreign Minister, and son-in-law of Baron Iwasaki, of the Mitsubishis, had
sought by pacific means to open up foreign markets capable
of absorbing Japan's manufactured exports in quantities to
cover needed imports of food and raw materials.

But the Minseito program had received two staggering
blows between September 18 and 21, 1931. The Japanese
Army, acting on its own responsibility, began the occupation
of Manchuria, and England suspended gold payments in exchange for sterling. All attempts of Baron Shidehara to local-
ize the Manchurian conflict failed, and a serious anti-Japanese
boycott sprang up in China, coincident with the drop in price
of British goods on the Chinese market. Meanwhile the drain
of gold specie from Japan reached serious proportions, on account of depreciation suffered by Japan's sterling holdings in
London, which constituted the bulk of its foreign reserves.

The Seiyukai started clamoring for reimposition of the gold
embargo, and the stage was set for a *coup* of far-reaching consequences in Mitsui history.

Kenzo Adachi, chief secretary of the Minseito party, had
been credited with bringing about a landslide for his party in
the general elections of 1930. He was rewarded with the post

of Home Minister. But Adachi had hopes of becoming Premier. One of the earliest of the Fascist-minded Japanese, he saw an opportunity of bettering his career by joining the *Kokuhonsha*, a society propelled by the famous General Sadao Araki to preach the gospel of "the Imperial Way," uniting the nation to uphold the Emperor's leadership in morality and ethics, and to pursue an aggressive policy in China.

Adachi was no sooner in the Home Ministry than he began maneuvering for a coalition Cabinet. He failed to find supporters among members of his own party and was forced to resort to a bold maneuver. He refused to attend Cabinet meetings and at the same time refused to resign, alone. The Premier was powerless to remove him, because of his influence in the party, and failing to function without a Home Minister, the Minseito Cabinet was compelled to resign. Thus it may be said that Adachi single-handedly wrecked the Minseito Cabinet on December 11, 1931, at a time when the party held a large majority in the House of Representatives — illustrating the supine position of the Diet in the face of personal political maneuvering backed by money interests in that period.

Adachi's strength [wrote Professor Harold S. Quigley, in *Japanese Government and Politics* (D. Appleton-Century Company)] lay in his long experience, in his success as a campaign manager and in his affiliations with the military authorities who desired a more bellicose Cabinet, and with the great Mitsui trust, which, in company with other banking houses, desired to re-establish the embargo on gold. His ambition caused him to observe the rising leadership of Mr. Junnosuke Inouye, Finance Minister. . . . Adachi was by nature an imperialist to whom the cautious Shidehara (Minseito Foreign Minister) and the economically-minded Inouye appeared to be out of step with Japan's movements in China.

Japanese papers openly charged that Adachi received more than 2,000,000 yen, or nearly $1,000,000, for his successful coup which brought about the downfall of the Minseito and facilitated departure from the gold standard.

The Seiyukai, the Mitsui-backed party, formed a Cabinet December 13, 1931, and immediately re-established the gold embargo. The Seiyukai had always stood for the principle of Government aid for industry and, since the autumn before, industry had been complaining of British competition in the East after Britain went off gold.

The suspension of the gold standard, said Heisaburo Okawa, a leading industrialist of the time, was "as welcome as rain after a drought."

It certainly was to the Mitsuis, who had been buying dollars — America was still on the gold standard — seemingly on a speculative basis.

The Mitsuis were reported to have profited by about 50,-000,000 yen overnight through their dollar holdings when Japan went off gold. Other bankers of course benefited. Altogether, it was estimated that about $200,000,000 was held speculatively by the big financial interests. The principal holders, according to one estimate, were Mitsui, with $50,000,000; Sumitomo with $20,000,000; and Mitsubishi with $10,-000,000.

Mitsui spokesmen today explain the whole affair as being no more than good business. They maintain Mitsui was simply recouping losses suffered by the depreciation of some 50,-000,000 yen in sterling holdings in London when England went off gold. The interests of the firm chiefly were industrial and would benefit by the stimulus of a depreciated yen, especially in the Orient, in competition with the depreciated pound. Moreover, as long as the Minseito maintained the high value of the yen, the Mitsuis were gambling heavily on their dollar-buying.

The simple way, of course, would have been to buy up a lot more dollars and then get rid of the Minseito, but no one in authority in the Mitsuis knows anything of any deal with Adachi to wreck his own Cabinet.

The Mitsuis point out that the Mitsubishis, who were connected with the Minseito and whose interests were largely financial rather than industrial, would have benefited if the Minseito had stayed in power and kept the yen up. It is also pointed out that Finance Minister Inouye had been identified with the First National Bank, controlled by the Shibusawa interests, and had several birds himself to kill with one stone.

And so the Mitsuis, with a little stronger hand, simply had beaten their rivals at their own game of politics.

Nevertheless, there had been bitter talk and charges in the press. Somewhat unfavorable publicity was given to a certain boisterous party in Osaka in the midst of soaring prices that struck hard at the public. While the people were paying for the high-stake game between Mitsui and Mitsubishi, with food costs spurting upward by thirty to forty per cent, the Japan Cotton Spinners' Association threw a party with a host of Osaka's "most beautiful geisha and floods of sake." The cotton spinners' group in a single night had profited by 17,-500,000 yen from the twenty-five per cent increase in the value of their raw cotton holdings. The president of the association was head of the Kinka Cotton Spinning Company, a Mitsui subsidiary.

The widespread condemnation had increased when it was revealed that the private financiers' gain was the Government's loss, since the hurried restoration of the gold ban had left the Yokohama Specie Bank with foreign obligations amounting to some 170,000,000 gold yen which had to be paid in depreciated yen.

So there was a question whether Mr. Sanji Muto meant that the Mitsuis or the nation should "thank Kenzo Adachi" for replacing the gold embargo.

As the Year of the Monkey opened, an article in the Japanese magazine *Fujin Koron* said: —

The northeastern districts of Japan are suffering from the poorest fall crops on record since 1869. Last year the farmers suffered from a bumper crop with an accompanying fall in the price of rice. Even then they had no rice to feed themselves when they paid for fertilizers, taxes and other necessities.

Today they are eating roots. They have sent out their daughters to become prostitutes in the bigger towns and their young sons to Manchuria to protect the vested interests there. Part of the money which they got in exchange for the liberty of their daughters has gone toward payment of taxes and tenant fees. Without money and food, they face six idle months now.

Due to the absence of means of sustenance families are being dissolved, husbands parted from wives, children from parents. Thieving is reported here and there, some of the poorest preferring imprisonment to starvation.

The northern provinces are noted for their pretty girls. From Akita and Yamagata prefectures come the largest number of girls who engage in licensed prostitution throughout the country. Until about a year or so ago the number of girls who went into prostitution for one reason or another did not surpass 700 a year from these two provinces. Last year the number was doubled and there is no doubt that the number has been increased enormously in the current year. Villages of these two provinces today have practically no girls of a marriageable age left.

In an independent investigation the magazine found that in one typical village "ten girls a month for the past several months have been sold into prostitution by needy fathers." Another incident cited was that of a farmer who had a son serving in the army. When the regiment was ordered to Manchuria, he posted a letter informing his father of the move. He failed to put on a postage stamp, and the father could not find the four sen necessary to receive the letter. A month later he was informed officially that his son had been killed in Manchuria.

Meantime, eighty-six industrial concerns, half of them Mitsui enterprises, or affiliates in one sense or another, benefiting by the replacement of the gold embargo, raised dividends, some of them to as high as seventeen and eighteen per cent.

Frazier Hunt, American newspaper writer, sat down at dinner with four Japanese students of a Tokyo University, all from middle-class families, and heard some curiously prophetic words. "What do you fellows want?" he asked. "We want a government that will not belong to any party," one of them answered. "We want our politics to be separated from big business and favoritism. We think that, some way or other, a new scheme of government and social life can be worked out here in Japan."

"You mean some sort of state socialism?"

"Yes, something like that. We want equal sharing in the benefits of the important industries and we want debts to be reduced. Party governments have been unable to attempt all this; it must be done by some strong and powerful force backed by the genuine will of the people."

"A sort of Fascism?"

"Well — you understand," he hesitated, "somehow or

other we want to form a new machine that will take care
of our peculiar Japanese aspirations, both international and
within our own country."

As unrest spread, a Korean threw a bomb at the Emperor's
procession. The Seiyukai Cabinet, according to custom, resigned, as taking the responsibility, but was allowed to remain
in office until January 22 when dissolution of the Diet was decreed for the February 20 elections.

The reason for the Diet dissolution was obvious. The Seiyukai Cabinet faced a Minseito majority in the Lower House
and had no desire to withstand interpellations on the current
situation. The party was anxious to sweep in a majority by
capitalizing on the war fever and a positive policy toward
Manchuria. Junnosuke Inouye was ready with his pointed
questions and severe criticism of the Seiyukai for reapplying
the gold embargo, and on certain other financial policies
which Mitsubishi thought were beneficial to Mitsui.

Inouye already was condemning the "Dollar-Buyers," a
term that was widely taken up in a subsequent election campaign with dire effects for the Mitsuis. "From long experience
we know that some speculators will not stop at anything. In
extreme terms, they don't care even for the national interest,"
wrote Inouye in the leading Tokyo paper, the Asahi. Those
were heady words to feed a populace more frequently given
to brooding over political wrongs than most.

The Seiyukai Cabinet then went before the country
pledged to establish an "independent," that is, "aggressive"
foreign policy, and "pursuance of a thoroughgoing program
for the development of industry."

The election campaign became a battle of slogans. Some of
the Minseito slogans were bitter. One was "Inukai and Doru-

kai." Dorukai means dollar-buyers. Some more were: "Dollar-Buyers sacrifice the State. Friends of Dollar-Buyers are Enemies of the Masses. One cannot feed upon a fictitious boom. Rising prices and declining loyalty."

The Seiyukai retaliated with "Better times or Depression. Honest Inukai and False Wakatsuki. Takahashi (Seiyukai Finance Minister) brings Fortune; Inouye brings Misfortune. Defend the Specie and Defeat Inouye. Hegemony over Asia or Slavery to Europe and America?"

Meanwhile, the military, paying little attention to the political campaign, started their occupation of Shanghai, which only served to inflame the war fever.

As the election campaign continued, Inouye took a leading part, making stinging speeches against the Seiyukai.

On the night of February 9 Inouye was getting out of a car to address a public meeting for a Minseito candidate when a twenty-four-year-old member of a reactionary society stepped up and shot him three times in the heart. The assassin surrendered and explained simply that he hated the financial policies of Mr. Inouye and blamed him for the current hardships of the agricultural population. The assassination removed no mere politician, but the outstanding financial figure in public life in Japan. Time and again he had built a strong financial foundation for the country only to have Cabinet overthrows and wars level it.

Inouye's death was a severe blow to the Minseito in view of the forthcoming election, but Minseito defeat had been anticipated. It is an axiom of Japanese politics that the Government party never loses an election. There were the usual charges of police interference and extensive buying of votes by the Seiyukai, but the results weren't changed. The Seiyukai won 304 seats, the Minseito 147 and laborites 5.

The aggressive, imperialist Seiyukai was now in the saddle with a formidable line-up. General Araki was the Seiyukai's War Minister, leader of the reactionary Society of Patriots and of the younger officers of the General Staff who were inspired by Shanghai and Manchurian successes to take things in their own hand at home. Some Japanese writers began referring to the Inukai Cabinet as "the Araki Cabinet."

Another friend of the Mitsuis whose star was rising was Yosuke Matsuoka, now head of what remained of the old Choshu clan. Matsuoka was being sent to Shanghai as a personal representative of Premier Inukai to negotiate peace after Japan had occupied the city, but later he was to be better known as the Japanese delegate who walked out of the League of Nations and became president of the South Manchuria Railway, in which Mitsui was heaviest private investor.

The Mitsuis, with their strong political alignments, clearly were poised for another great surge forward. Everything had been taken care of but the public.

But the slogans of the recent political campaign still rang in the ears of the people. The Mitsuis were Dollar-Buyers and against the interests of the State, according to Minseito-Mitsubishi charges.

The forty-fifth general meeting of the shareholders of the Mitsui Bank was held March 2, 1932. This was the day the Lindbergh baby was kidnaped in the United States, and subsequent developments in Japan, including the peace of Shanghai, received little prominence.

At the bank meeting the net loss for the term was revealed

at 12,297,026 yen. Out of the bank's special reserve fund of 14,500,000 yen, 12,500,000 yen was taken to make up the loss. From the regular reserve fund of 30,700,000 yen, 2,400,-000 was taken for dividends and another 323,311 yen for retirement bonuses.

The elegant Seihin Ikeda, senior managing director of the Bank, rose at the shareholders' meeting and gravely reported: —

Deposits during the past six months have gone off 72,570,000 yen, through withdrawals by large depositors. On the other hand, loans outstanding at the end of the last term totaled 542,040,000, gaining 7,520,000 yen over the term before. [The yen was then approximately 33 cents.] The Mitsui Bank realized fairly good results in the general banking business, but, because of the drop of market prices of securities, had to write off 9,460,000 yen. Moreover, the bank incurred a large loss by the decline of pound holdings.

Then, for public consumption, Mr. Ikeda earnestly added: —

Criticisms have been leveled against the Mitsui Bank in the last election campaign for having bought dollars after the suspension of the gold standard by England. It must be explained that during the first half-yearly term of 1931 the Bank invested in short-term debentures in England on arbitrage through New York, with the object of using part of its superfluous funds, and at the same time the Bank entered into contract for selling dollar futures for the commitment. However, because of the suspension of the gold standard by England, the movement of gold between England and America was deadlocked and arbitrage became extremely difficult. This forced the Bank to buy dollars necessary to cover the commitment of future dollar selling. The Bank also

purchased dollars to pay interest on debentures for electric light
and power companies and to fix up import contracts for traders.
These were all ordinary commercial transactions.
I may add that any criticism for having carried on speculative
buying of the dollar is unjustifiable.

The day after this speech was made the so-called Araki
Government sought an emergency measure to issue 22,000,-
000 yen in bonds to cover expenses of sending more troops to
Shanghai. Businessmen informed Premier Inukai that it
couldn't be done.

It was commonly reported that it was Baron Takuma Dan,
managing director of all the Mitsui interests, who was prevailed upon to bear the sad news to the Premier. This cannot
be substantiated, but is most plausible — for now the large
industrialists were becoming alarmed at world reaction against
the Shanghai and Manchurian adventures.

The tempo was being quickened in Japan. The Lytton
Commission of Inquiry had just arrived at the behest of the
League of Nations to ascertain whether Japan had seized
Manchuria. Foreign Minister Yoshizawa, at a dinner in honor
of the Lytton inquirers, said: "Remember, gentlemen, the
word 'Manchuria' is indelibly engraved in the memory of the
Japanese nation as the battleground of two costly wars, where
fell her brave sons by tens of thousands.' " Henry Pu-yi, remnant of the last imperial dynasty in China, was on his way
to Mukden to become head of the new State which Japan
named Manchukuo. The Lytton Commission was paying its
respects at the Meiji Shrine and was being entertained at
dinner by Prince Chichibu, brother of the Emperor. Dr. Inazo
Nitobe, widely known liberal and publicist, had been almost
literally kidnaped from St. Luke's Hospital in Tokyo by a

group of army reservists, forced to go to the Army Club and humiliatingly apologize in person for a remark made against the Japanese Army. (Dr. Nitobe had said the army clique was injurious to the nation.)

Officials of the Home Ministry were organizing to send representatives around to the homes of all soldiers then in Shanghai and Manchuria to ascertain if their families were in need of financial assistance. The Oki Electric Works, leading telephone manufacturers, was allowing half-pay to each of the workmen called to service. The Nippon Electric Company was allowing one-third pay.

The nation was bowing before the army clique. By now, the Mitsuis were alarmed, wondering how far the military group would go, demurring against further backing, yet afraid to resist. In Tokyo it was reported that Washington had influenced J. P. Morgan and Company to bring pressure on Japanese financial interests, seeking to stop the headlong dash of the army in China.

March 5 was a dark day for the Mitsuis.

The night before, Baron Takuma Dan, now called the "Prime Minister of the Mitsui kingdom," attended a banquet given in honor of the Lytton Commission by leading businessmen at the Industrial Club. As he sat at the table, anticipating that he would be called on for a brief speech, he scribbled his message on a piece of paper. It ended with this sentence: "Any questions you may feel inclined to make we are pleased to answer frankly." Baron Dan reread the message carefully, and scratched out the word "frankly." It was the last message he ever wrote — and his last editing; but his great perspicacity and evaluation of the times, as well as his honesty, must have compelled him to delete the word "frankly." The script is still preserved by the family.

The next morning the Baron rose at eight o'clock and breakfasted with the Baroness. After breakfast, as was his custom, he read the Japanese papers and the *Japan Advertiser*, the leading English-language newspaper of Tokyo. In the Japanese papers he saw some caricatures of himself as a Dollar-Buyer, and laughed at them. He left home at eleven o'clock with his bodyguard, for the Mitsui Bank.

Usually the Baron entered the imposing Mitsui Building by a side entrance, but that morning he chose another entrance, opposite the Mitsukoshi department store.

As he emerged from the car, the aforementioned expressionless youth stepped up and, holding a revolver close, fired once. He dropped the revolver and stood back waiting to be overpowered by the bodyguard. Baron Dan crumpled on the sidewalk. He was removed to a dispensary room on the fifth floor of the Bank Building, and leading doctors were summoned from Mitsui's own hospital; but he was beyond medical aid. He died at 12:20 o'clock.

The assassin was a peasant youth from one of the villages that had been hard hit by the recent depression. Moreover, he was a member of the Blood Brotherhood, a reactionary society headed by a forty-seven-year-old Nichiren priest, Nissho Inouye, a former army secret agent. The priest planned wholesale assassinations in furtherance of a nebulous plan to "purify" the nation and its politics.

Countless such patriotic societies exist in Japan, deriving subsistence for the most part from outright blackmail. They are allowed to flourish openly because political parties use them. The public fears them, and no official body has the temerity to put them down because they carry out their crimes with the avowal that they are acting in the name of the Emperor. Every thinking Japanese condemns them, but none dares attack them for fear of the consequences. They gather for membership an unclassifiable group of impressionable youths, mentally aberrated malcontents, and a sprinkling of smart muscle-men.

Assassinations are not uncommon in Japan. In the racial character itself is a curious strain of violence and fatalism which overpowers many minds in times of excitement. The country seems to possess more than its normal share of men who brood over public wrongs, real or imaginary. The public, in turn, with tastes influenced by the bloodthirsty romances of Japanese chivalry, bestows a sentimental sympathy on anyone who risks his life to avenge an apprehended wrong.

The fact that the assassins of both the Minseito Junnosuke Inouye and Seiyukai Dan were members of the same Blood Brotherhood indicates its confusion of thought, and the vagueness in the mind of the leader. That he had absorbed some of the Fascist ideology of Germany, just then reaching Japan, was evident, however, in his testimony at the trial of fourteen members of the band in July, 1933.

"How do you feel about the assassination plot?" asked the judge.

"There is nothing to think about it," the priest Inouye replied. "I will strive to attain our objective for social reforms as long as I live."

"What social reforms are you actually hoping for?"

"Party politics in Japan disregard the Constitution. Party politics are privileged politics. Politics of the Right Wing in Germany is politics of God. Political parties are to be blamed for the high-handed manner in which matters are carried out by the privileged class. All matters should be left to the Emperor's decision."

"What kind of society do you contemplate?"

"I am thinking about it, but I know nothing about the future. Moreover, I am unable to decide on such an important matter alone."

Chapter XIII

JAPAN'S "MANIFEST DESTINY"

IN THE PHENOMENAL growth of Japanese foreign trade from 1932 to 1935, leading to world-wide charges of Japanese "dumping," the Mitsuis took a commanding lead. During that period, the powerful trading organization of *Mitsui Bussan Kaisha* handled from 40 to 50 per cent of Japan's exports and imports, and from 60 to 70 per cent of the total trade of Japan's new state, Manchukuo.

Mitsui's (that is Japan's) competitive power in the world markets, ability to undersell foreign manufacturers, brought a general outcry against the Japanese in England, America and other Western nations. Numerous articles on "the Japanese trade menace" began to appear in the Occidental press. In the United States, following a considerable increase of imports from Japan noticed in 1935, complaints from American manufacturers were voiced in Congress. Senators Walsh of Massachusetts and George of Georgia sought a "limited embargo" involving the imposition of a quota restriction on Japanese imports by Presidential action.

There were the usual charges of dumping, unfair trade practices and export subsidies, but emphasis most frequently was placed on the low costs of Japanese labor, which, with currency depreciation, permitted Japan to flood the markets with her cheap manufactured goods. We have previously discussed the Mitsuis' part in the political drive to devalue the yen, and now its effect was beginning to be felt. For example, the Mitsuis before devaluation could make a shipment to

America and receive, say, $5,000. In pre-devaluation Japanese currency, this would be the equivalent of 10,000 yen. But afterward, even though the dollar itself had been lowered in value, the $5,000 could be converted into 15,000 yen.

But the low prices of Japanese goods brought much more vituperation against living standards and wages in Japan than against currency depreciation.

While Japan's exported goods were handled largely by the Mitsuis, with their advantage of interlocking association of banker, exporter and shipper, about 65 per cent of these products thrown on the world markets came from small factories and workshops with less than 100 employees each. Of Japan's industrial working population of some 6,000,000, almost three quarters are employed in such small factories and enterprises. Fully half of that number are employed in the still smaller enterprises with five or less workers which are not affected by Japanese factory legislation.

The Japanese answered charges of "cheap labor" with the admission that, computed in terms of foreign currencies, wages were low; but they were certainly adequate for the Japanese standard of living. In food, for example, instead of meat, wheat and dairy products that the Western worker demands, the Japanese subsist adequately on fish and rice. In the Western countries, meat, milk and flour are comparatively costly because their production requires larger outlays, while Japan is plentifully supplied with fish. Unlike wheat, which as a world commodity is subject to wide fluctuation in price, rice is an internally produced commodity for the Japanese, not greatly affected by outside influences. While the yen was losing 60 per cent of its gold value, the Japanese worker lost less than 10 per cent of his purchasing power as far as foodstuffs were concerned, it was pointed out.

In this, the editorial economists of *Fortune*, who made a detailed survey of Japan in 1936, concurred.

Elsewhere in the world [they observed] the industrial revolution has meant a general rise in the standard of living which has meant in turn a general increase in wage scales which has meant higher costs which have meant eventually a competitive drubbing at the hands of more recently industrialized countries. . . . In Japan the industrial revolution has not meant a general rise in the standard of living. The agricultural half of the population, always too numerous to live fatly upon Japan's limited farmlands, has long been habituated to an existence of extreme frugality and has long possessed a communal life making that frugality endurable. Partly by government policy, partly by social habit, and partly by the sheer weight of its own numbers, it has been held not far above the level it knew three or four hundred years before the revolution. . . . The consequence is that Japan, outwardly industrialized, maintains inwardly the life of a simple agrarian country. The further consequence is that her industrialization is an industrialization which must sell its goods abroad since her domestic market is incapable of buying her industrial products. The industrial workers of Japan live on one economic level while their goods sell on another.

In these small workshops and factories that account for so much of Japan's production, especially for export trade, virtual sweatshop conditions are found. An observer of the Geneva International Labor Office recently estimated that the Japanese work week even in the larger factories is about sixty hours, but in the small local plants there is no limit short of physical exhaustion for men, women and children.

The Mitsuis have thousands of these small shops on the string as well as their own large industrial plants. There is, in fact, hardly a marketable commodity made in Japan, whether in the humblest homes or greatest factories, that is not handled in the export markets by the Mitsui trading organization. Mitsui not only buys and sells for its own direct subsidiaries but for its competitors, for export associations, and for the Government as well.

The State [Freda Utley found in her 1936 economic study of Japan] forces all the small producers and traders to unite in guilds and associations under Government supervision and a very large number of them have Mitsui or Mitsubishi men at their head. Out of 212 guilds of small manufacturers, 114 are thus connected with Mitsui and 68 with Mitsubishi. These guilds and associations force their members to have their goods inspected, to buy raw materials jointly and to adopt the same specifications, thus facilitating marketing, especially export, for the big merchant firms, in particular Mitsui.

Sweatshop pay under the Mitsui system is necessarily low because the profits of the small factory are low, and the smaller the factory the more difficult it is to make a profit when the product goes into export trade. The little "capitalists" cannot afford nor do they have the facilities to export directly, and that is where the Mitsui organization steps in. But between the little manufacturer and the *Mitsui Bussan Kaisha* are agents, middlemen and the "associations" under the control of Mitsui. As a result the little manufacturer is hardly more than a hard-working employee himself, supervising the twelve-to-sixteen-hour day of his fellows, including women and children. His pay ordinarily would compare unfavorably with that of eight-hour-a-day minor clerks in Western countries.

*   *   *

But while the profits of the little men were small, no such rule held with the highly organized, interlocking Mitsui companies during Japan's trade boom of 1932–1935 while other countries were at the depth of world depression. In 1934, the Mitsui organization compiled statistics of profits made by 1,250 joint stock companies of all branches of industry during the first six months of that year. The average annual yield was 9.8 per cent for all companies, but the Mitsui companies ran far in excess. In banking, for example, the Mitsui Bank's profit was 19.1 per cent; the Mitsui Trust Company had a profit of 30.1 per cent, and the Mitsui Trading Company with its innumerable foreign branches and agencies, some of them trading in commodities that never saw Japan, reported a profit of 13.3 per cent.

Notable among the Mitsui concerns reporting that year was the Kanegafuchi Cotton Company, which piled up a profit of 40.3 per cent.

About this time the spotlight was thrown on Japan's commerce with India. For some years back England's great cotton textile center, Lancashire, had been growing apprehensive over the fact that Indian cotton could be transported to Japan in Japanese ships, manufactured, re-exported in Japanese ships to India and sold there at prices lower than those of either Indian or Lancashire manufacture. The British Parliament was pressed to alter tariffs in favor of India and Lancashire, but the Japanese still were able to undersell on the Indian market. By 1932 Japan's sales to India were far outdistancing India's sales to Japan, and the British earnestly began to look into the situation.

They found, among other complex factors, that Japan had been doing considerable propaganda spadework in India, pointing out the advantages of Japanese friendship. Among the organizations behind this movement was the Great Asia Association, liberally but indirectly supported by the Mitsui organizations. One of its leaders was General Iwane Mitsui, who later was to achieve a measure of fame as commander of the Japanese forces in the capture of Nanking in 1937. The Great Asia Association was spreading the doctrine of Asia for the Asiatics (meaning Japan, of course) with this pronouncement of its aims: "To bring order and reconstruction to the present chaotic condition of Asia is a duty that rests mostly on the shoulders of Japan. . . . She has been asked to put to work all her forces, cultural, political, economic, and if need be, military, in order to bring about unity and wholesale reconstruction in Asia."

The appeal for Asiatic hegemony had little effect outside Japan, politically, but Indian trade with Japan continued to mount, reaching such proportions and transparency that Mahatma Gandhi was moved to warn that economically Japan was a greater menace to India than Britain — in spite of broad hints from Tokyo that Japan might lend a hand in the emancipation of India. When eventually the outcry in England over the reversal of trade balance of India led to the adoption of a quota system and denunciation of India's trade treaty with Japan, the Japanese bitterly assailed England and retaliated with a boycott on imports from India.

One highly nationalistic party in Japan in a resolution bitterly condemned Britain "for squeezing 300,000,000 inhabitants of India in order to keep the superannuated Lancashire industry alive." Japanese publicists meanwhile were busy explaining that Japan's boycott of India was vastly different from the Chinese boycotts on Japan which had been given as the excuse for the Japanese invasion of Shanghai in 1932. The Great Asia Association of General Mitsui loudly appealed to the people of India for support against Britain's malicious trade maneuvers. One daily newspaper in Tokyo suggested that Japan boycott not only Indian cotton but Australian wool, Canadian wheat and British machinery. A naval officer's monograph, *England and Japan Must Fight*, went into its forty-fifth edition. His thesis was: "England is already on the downgrade; Japan has started on the upgrade. The two come into collision because England is trying to hold on to what she has, while Japan must perforce expand."

Meanwhile exports of Japan's cotton goods, as compared with Britain's, had grown at this pace (in millions of yards) : —

	BRITAIN	JAPAN
1928	3,866	1,419
1932	2,198	2,032
1934	1,995	2,568

With the boycott in effect, Japan was buying more cotton in America and exporting the manufactured goods to India, but eventually, with the higher American prices, a point of diminishing returns set in, affecting the raw material supply for small manufacturers. Then Japan consented to an economic disarmament conference at Simla.

During the course of this conference, in the traditional manner, one of Mitsui's versatile business stars wrote a remarkably revealing play setting forth Japan's position in that typical artistic way by which the Japanese mingle economics with esthetics. He was Sanji Muto, who had just retired from the presidency of the great Kanegafuchi Spinning Company.

The play was *Sangyo Nihon Koshi Kyoku* ("The March

of Industrial Japan"). A paraphrase of the first act, as given by A. Morgan Young,* follows: —

We begin with a scene in a farmhouse in May, 1858. There are handlooms lying idle and the family is obviously in the depths of despair. Shimadzu, the Daimio of Kagoshima, has started a cotton mill, and there is no longer any profit in handloom weaving. The dutiful daughters propose that their father should repair the family finances by selling them into a brothel. The father objects. A caller says that hands are wanted at the cotton mill. Again the father objects. The girls run away, and we see them next in the mill, on a day when the Lord Shimadzu is showing some officers of the Shogun's new warship round. He explains how cotton spinning is in its way as patriotic a work as creating a navy, and how he has ordered a lot of machinery from Platt Brothers [in England]. Just then there is a crash, the machinery stops working, and in the midst of a confused struggle a young man is dragged in whom the girls recognize as their brother.

He has just put the motive power (water wheels) out of action with a boulder. Seeing his sisters, he curses them. They should die of hunger rather than work for their enemy. Shimadzu calmly asks the young man what he means, and the youth thereupon tells him of the distress into which hand-spinning and weaving have fallen. Shimadzu is so distressed that he has a good mind to abandon the enterprise. Even now local supplies of raw cotton are insufficient, and it will impoverish the country to buy from abroad. But stay! Why not export the surplus manufacture and enrich the country? Yes, that is the idea!

And it was. Mr. Muto's play was more than prophetic. Never thereafter was the handloom in competition with "big

* *Imperial Japan*, by A. Morgan Young. (Allen & Unwin Ltd.)

business." Britain's cotton goods exports went back to the figures of 1858 while Japan, in a generation of hard-working small entrepreneurs under the propulsion of entrenched, monopolistic capital of the Mitsui type, spurted far ahead. An interesting footnote of the Muto drama was that Muto himself was mysteriously assassinated in 1934. On retiring from Kanegafuchi four years before, he became president of the *Jiji Shimpo,* Tokyo daily with which so many other Mitsui men at one time or another had been connected. It was reported that he had planned to expose in the *Jiji* the close connection between "big business" and successive governments. The *Jiji* openly charged that the assassination was instigated by "hidden persons." There was a police investigation but it was found conveniently that Mr. Muto's last words were that the killer shot him "because of the crematory." The assassin was an advocate of municipally owned crematories and had sought unsuccessfully to interest Mr. Muto and the *Jiji* in the project. It was a palpably weak motive for assassination, but nothing more came of the investigation. Rumors grew, however, until at least one writer devoted a magazine article to a denial that either the Mitsuis or Mitsubishis had anything to do with the assassination.

The Japan-India dispute over cotton finally was settled after two months' negotiations at Simla and Delhi. A compromise was effected. Japan, sorely in need of India's raw cotton, consented to call off the boycott and buy 1,500,000 bales of cotton a year in return for which India would purchase 400,000,-000 yards of piece-goods and lower the tariff. By 1934, Japan-India trade was back on a normal basis and the hullabaloo died down. Thereafter Japan bought increasingly more from India than she sold.

It would be wearisome to recite all the cheap manufactured

MOTORSHIP "AZUMASAN MARU," BUILT IN TAMA YARD IN 1933

articles sent into the world markets by the *Mitsui Bussan Kaisha* during the period of Japan's greatest trade expansion. Such varied articles as Swiss watches, lumber, garters, and Mexican curios were bought up in wholesale quantities abroad, shipped to Japan and then processed or put together for retail sales and subsequently sold, sometimes as non-Japanese products, in foreign fields. Japan's lower labor costs and the energetic co-operation of subsidized Japanese shipping lines made possible the two extra shipments.

So recently as February, 1939, a bill was introduced in the United States Senate by Senator Holman of Oregon to limit the exports of Douglas fir and cedar logs to protect the American lumber manufacturers from Japanese competition. According to the Senator, Japanese manufacturers can buy American logs, transship them in Japanese freighters, process them into various products and resell them, in either America or other foreign markets, at less than half the cost to the American producer. Domestic pine plywood, he cited as an example, sells at $137.50 per 1,000 board feet on the West Coast of America, compared with the Japanese price of $56.50 delivered in Baltimore.

The secretary of the British Hosiery Manufacturers' Association complained a few years ago that the British manufacturer could not meet Japanese hosiery prices "even if he got his material for nothing." William Henry Chamberlin* found that a Japanese ship touring the ports of West Africa with samples was offering automobiles for $275, bicycles for $5, typewriters for $12.50 and bicycle tires for seven cents. For a while, the *Mitsui Bussan* had on the market in India a spring automobile which sold for less than $100. The motive power was a strong coil spring, good for fifty miles without

* *Japan Over Asia.* (Little, Brown and Company.)

rewinding, and it was proposed to establish winding stations all over the country. Chamberlin also found, on one tour in South China, that American apples and radio sets were meeting severe competition from Japanese products sold at one-third of the American prices.

The phenomenal advance of Japan's merchant marine went hand-in-hand with the trade expansion of 1931 to 1936. Not only was the wide distribution of Japanese goods facilitated by the fast and efficient Japanese shipping lines touching all parts of the world, but net receipts from the shipping business were a continuously favorable item in the balance sheet of international payments. According to official returns compiled by the Finance Ministry, the nation's net receipts from the mercantile marine more than doubled during the period from 1932 to 1936. The Finance Ministry observed that had such a rapid expansion been maintained, the 200,000,000 or 300,-000,000 yen adverse balance in trade brought about by imports in preparation for war would have been written off completely. On the basis of the situation in 1937 before the outbreak of the last China war, it was predicted that the nation's shipping revenue for the year would reach 400,000,000 yen producing a net revenue of 250,000,000 yen.

During that period the Mitsui mercantile fleet, operating throughout the world and featuring a fast express service from Yokohama to New York, was taking in 30 per cent of its total revenues in foreign currency. When the war and resultant boycotts in democratic Western countries cut in on foreign shipping in Japanese bottoms the suggestion went out from high quarters in Japan that "it would be a good idea for private Japanese interests to register some of their ships in some friendly countries and operate them under the foreign flags on the high seas."

The close connection of the mercantile marine with Japan's machinery for expanding foreign trade was one of the most important factors of Japan's success in throwing her goods on the world markets. The Mitsuis not only had their own fleet but large blocks of shares in other lines. The Mitsubishis controlled the huge N.Y.K. line with its big passenger ships, and several smaller services. At the depth of the world depression, when more than 6,000,000 tons of international shipping was laid up, Japan had only 16,000 tons out of service. By August, 1936, Japan had 4,247,000 tons of shipping under registry and a year later another million tons was under construction in the country's shipyards.

How the interlocking system of banks, export associations, commercial houses and shipping concerns co-operate to fill the last inch of space in Japanese holds is aptly illustrated by Hessell Tiltman.* A Japanese freighter bound for South African ports has fifty tons of cargo space unfilled a week before the sailing date. An American ship might sail with this space empty, but in Japan the shipping line notifies the local Chamber of Commerce. An operative there runs through the list of members and finds an umbrella exporter and phones him.

"Do you export umbrellas to South Africa?" the firm is asked.

"We do not," is the reply. "When the cost of freight is added to the cost of manufacture, we could not sell there at a price which would compete with other sources of supply."

"Could you sell at a profit if there were no freight charges to pay?" would be the next question.

* *The Far East Comes Nearer.* (J. B. Lippincott Co., Philadelphia, London.)

"Certainly, and make ten per cent profit," might come the answer.

"Then send fifty tons of umbrellas to S.S. —— before such and such a date," states the Chamber of Commerce gentleman. "There will be no bill for freight."

But that is not the end. Sometime later, the umbrella-maker may apply to the Chamber of Commerce for space to South America. "What profit are you getting in South America?" asks the Chamber expert. Twenty to twenty-five per cent, is the reply.

"Well," the exporter is told, "some time ago we fixed you up with free space to South Africa. This time you will pay two-and-a-half times the usual rate to South America and be satisfied with ten per cent profits. That should square accounts."

And so it is rare that a Japanese ship ever leaves its home port without her holds filled to the hatch covers.

The results? Well, reduced to percentages, Japanese trade with Latin America, for example, increased 153 per cent in value between 1932 and 1933, another 123 per cent between 1933 and 1934, and reached a gain of 155 per cent in 1935 over the figures of 1934.

One of the most sensational items in the expansion of Japanese trade in the Western Hemisphere appeared in the case of Brazil, in which the Mitsuis had an outstanding hand. Japanese imports from Brazil, mostly cotton, jumped from 4,000,-000 yen in 1935 to 47,000,000 yen in 1936, which was more than the total value of Japanese imports from all South America in 1935.

As early as 1928, the Mitsuis became interested in moves to send Japanese colonists to Brazil and invested heavily in a company which extended monetary and other aid to Japanese desirous of settling in Brazil. Brazil at that time needed cheap labor for its coffee plantations and welcomed the efforts of Japanese industrial concerns to send well-organized, substantially subsidized groups to South America. By 1934, there were 173,500 Japanese living in Brazil, the largest group of Japanese in any foreign country except the new puppet state of Manchukuo.

During that year a large delegation of Japanese cotton spinners, including several high officials of *Mitsui Bussan* and the Mitsui textile interests, visited Brazil and offered to buy all of Brazil's cotton crop, trading Japanese manufactured cotton goods in return. They pointed out that by using Japanese ships they could handle the transportation costs both ways, meet Brazilian duties on manufactured goods, and still undersell Brazilian manufacturers. Previously only 3 per cent of Brazil's cotton crop had gone to Japan, and 55 per cent to England.

But under instructions from the homeland, the Japanese colonists had taken to cotton-growing in Brazil, chiefly in the state of São Paulo. On leaving Japan, the settlers had contracted to work on coffee plantations for one or two years; but when their terms expired they uniformly became Brazilian cotton-growers on the land set apart for them. In five years, São Paulo had almost doubled its cotton production through the industrious cultivation of new lands and by relinquishing coffee lands to the new crops. By 1937 it was estimated that at least 40 per cent of the cotton crop grown in São Paulo was the product of Japanese immigrants. The Japanese owned more farms in the state than any foreign nationality, except the Italians. One report said of the Japanese: "They are recognized as excellent workers and as good cotton farmers."

Brazil became alarmed at the influx of Japanese immigrants

and clamped down quota provisions, reducing immigration from 20,000 yearly to less than 3,000. Moreover, the Brazilian Senate annulled a land grant of 2,500,000 acres in the State of Amazonas which was to have been exploited by a Japanese company. Nearly a half million dollars already had been invested by the Japanese in the territory and about 200 families had settled there. The Japanese company, in which Mitsui was considerably interested, naturally had access to sizable capital resources, advanced through the Mitsui Bank and others, and was industriously going at the business of establishing a Japanese State within Brazil.

There were widespread Brazilian complaints that the new settlers refused to be assimilated in any way, retaining their own language and customs and building up large typically Japanese communities with evidences of attempting to wield political influence.

Tokyo had been working hard for relaxation of all such restrictions against her immigrants in Brazil. She sent friendly missions to Brazil, a floating sample fair of Japanese products, formed Japanese-Brazilian cultural associations in various cities, and put out considerable propaganda in Portuguese calling attention to the excellent qualities of the Japanese immigrants, that they were carefully recruited, had to be in good health, had experience in farming before they went to Brazil; that they would not send money back home, and would settle permanently in Brazil, providing an ample reservoir of cheap labor. A "brides' school" was established in Tokyo to train young women to be the wives of Japanese colonists in Brazil.

Whatever may be the outcome of the political-and-trade-wooing game, the Japanese are in Brazil to stay, and they remain Japanese. The Tokyo War Office recently took note of the fact that four Japanese newspapers in São Paulo had raised more than 500,000 yen as a contribution to the war in China. Four thousand Japanese settlers in Argentina collected sufficient funds to have a warplane built for the navy, christened *Argentina*, and 23,000 residents in Peru were to add another plane for China fighting.

These are only a few concrete examples of the spread of Japanese commercialism and politics abroad. No one has summarized the spirit of Japonism better than that mighty man of Mitsui, Ginjiro Fujihara, who was to have been president of Japan's World Fair in 1940. This veteran of thirty-five years' experience as a Mitsui executive wrote in his book, *The Spirit of Japanese Industry:* —

Our enterprising traders of the present day find their way to the remotest corner of the world. No matter how trying the climate may be, these modern pioneers go wherever they can sell Japanese goods. No region is inaccessible to them, if articles made in Japan can be introduced there.

[The Nairobi, West Africa, correspondent of the London *Times* once reported that "Medical officers in Tanganyika declare that the purchase of Japanese rubber shoes has done more to prevent hookworm disease than all the efforts of the health department." And the Osaka *Mainichi* commented on the report of a Japanese export expedition into darkest Africa: "To enable these naked people to put on clothes, and to enable them to replace coconut tableware with enamelled ware and porcelain ware made in Japan may perhaps be a responsibility to be shouldered by the Japanese."]

Even our own people are surprised at the extent of Japanese penetration, which no nation of the world seems able to thwart. Had such war lords as Hideyoshi and Nobunaga or the Tokugawa authorities backed the activities of Japanese pirates (in the 1600's) by adopting a more positive policy, the Japanese would have been able to accomplish something in India before the Dutch and British came there. The world today might have a map quite different from that which we have now.

The best way to feed our increasing population is to develop our industries and sell the products abroad. This is a national policy which I ardently hope the whole Japanese nation will endeavor to carry out. No matter what form of government may eventually be adopted, Japan under any ministry should take measures to provide employment for the people whose number keeps increasing.

I am far from recommending the use of armed forces for economic expansion in an aggressive way, but I rely on the army and navy for the protection which our foreign trade needs. No nation in the world can curb the progress of Japan's foreign trade if it is supported by the nation. We have a splendid opportunity to expand abroad; *it is the manifest destiny of the Japanese nation.*

Chapter XIV
PROFITS FOR EVERYBODY

APPROXIMATELY one hundred thousand Japanese receive their pay directly or indirectly from the Mitsui interests. The proportion of manual laborers to the white-collar personnel is about five to three.

American businessmen long resident in Japan, as well as other observers, repeatedly have been impressed with the loyalty of Mitsui employees to their organization. Such loyalty and devotion is a little difficult for Western comprehension. It is anomalous and intangible.

I asked a minor clerk in *Mitsui Bussan Kaisha* about his feelings for his employers.

"Do you like Baron Mitsui?"

"I do not know," he replied. "I saw him only once. That was when I won a race at an athletic meet for Mitsui employees. But whether I like him or not makes no difference."

"Well, how do you feel about working for the great Mitsuis, whose name is known all over the world?"

"We do not feel that we are working for Baron Mitsui, himself. We feel, first, that we are working for the advancement of Japanese industry. Then, we are proud to think that the Mitsuis are doing more to advance Japanese industry than any others. Next, I think we feel a great sense of satisfaction in the security of our jobs. In the end I imagine most of us feel that we are working for ourselves, that our job is the only way we have of earning our living. And we know that with reasonable application and industry our jobs with Mitsui will always be safe."

From the other side of the fence came still another explanation of the curious business idealism that pervades the Mitsui organization. When I asked a high official of *Mitsui Gomei Kaisha* for an interpretation of the spirit that unifies Mitsui employers and employees he thought for a few moments, then pushed a button on his desk. He spoke to his secretary in Japanese. The secretary brought a copy of *Asia* magazine for October, 1924. Marked off in red ink was this passage from an article by George Marvin, a writer who had discussed this subject with a Mitsui executive in America: —

" 'Kyoson' — that is the Japanese word, but how to do it in English? When two have the same thing, the same advantage — when on both sides the same interest holds together. How do you say that?"

"Co-ordination? Mutual benefit? Mutuality, perhaps?"

"No," interposes Mr. Hirata, supervising director of all the Mitsui interests in America, "not that exactly, though it is mutual . . . Well, the literal translation of 'kyoson' is 'mutual existence.' Yes, that is the closest English I can think of for this Japanese word. And this mutual existence, you must understand, is the fundamental principle of the House of Mitsui in its relations with its associates and employees and even with what you call the consumer, the buying public. This is the keynote of our organization.

"You cannot exist alone. You have got to exist with others. What is good for one must be believed good for the others. Not so hard to believe, perhaps, but much harder to keep always in practice. *Kyoson* is the Japanese word for what we mean and what we, or rather the family of Mitsui, have been trying to keep in practice for many, many years — you may say for centuries."

The trade union movement is practically nonexistent in Japan. What little progress the labor groups made in politics prior to 1931 was completely nullified when the militarists seized control. Since then strikes have been infrequent because of severe restrictions clamped on by the army. Collective bargaining is permitted in theory, but such labor unions as are left are under surveillance so strict that few of them dare risk a walkout. Few national unions retain any strength, many of their local units having been transformed under pressure into company unions.

The outbreak of war in China in 1937 and the swing to totalitarianism in Japan had the effect of depriving labor of its most outspoken leadership. The Left Wing Social Mass Party, which had started as a coalition of mildly radical groups, abandoned its ideology completely and reappeared as a militant Fascist organization. The idea of class struggle — as repugnant to the sensibilities of Japanese capitalists as to any other — was dropped in favor of "Japonism." Such pet projects as the nationalization of key industries, autonomy for laborers and completion of the existing social insurance system were denounced as obsolete and "incompatible with the new guiding spirit of national life." In addition to calling for the organization of a "whole-nation political party" on the Nazi model, Social Mass leaders endorsed the policy of setting up a "League of East Asiatic Races."

Even before the start of the war, the army took the precaution of applying drastic restrictions on workers in private munition firms, as well as civilian employees in arsenals and naval yards. The great Yawata iron works in Northern Kyushu, already turning out munitions at a capacity rate, summarily disbanded all labor organizations and put its employees under the guidance of a "personnel leader." The first sign of agitation for better conditions in other private war industry plants brought immediate "mediation" by the army.

Throughout Japan, workers were persuaded, as a "patriotic" gesture, to drop their demands for better pay and improved working conditions. A final blow was dealt to trade unionism in December, 1937, when police seized and imprisoned more than four hundred liberals, labor organizers and others suspected of harboring "dangerous thoughts."

The conscription of nearly 1,000,000 men for war service and the stepping-up of munitions production in 1938 brought an acute labor shortage. Workers found themselves in a superior bargaining position, but they had no voice. Instead, the Government stepped in to "adjust" labor into the key industries.

In February, 1939, the nation had an actual shortage of some 100,000 men, including common laborers. The 15,000 graduates of technical schools could choose from an average of six jobs apiece. Employment in the machine production industry was up 220 per cent from 1936.

Although male operatives are being replaced by women in some cases [wrote Eisaburo Saito in an industrial magazine] the only other way to cope with such a dearth of labor is to increase efficiency. Actually, working conditions on the whole have become worse since the outbreak of the China war. Working hours are generally longer, the Bank of Japan index shows. Even more discouraging is the increase in factory accidents, which have always been conspicuous.

To man their machines, the war industries offered successive wage increases; and by the spring of 1939 skilled workers were earning more money than Cabinet Ministers. With bonuses, these men were receiving up to 10,000 yen ($2,700) a year, as compared with the ministerial salaries of 6,720 yen.

Postal savings, the best indication of the small man's earnings, reached an all-time high, with 2,034,125 new depositors in a single month.

Under the General Mobilization Law, 5,000,000 laborers in 136 fields were registered by the Government, presumably in preparation for the day when they would be assigned to specific factories in "adjustment" to the wartime economy. During the next three years, approximately 3,800,000 workers are to undergo "vocational ability examinations."

Such Fascist regimentation has not brought an entirely new element into the life of the Japanese proletarian. The tendency toward a tightly knit, rigidly controlled economy has come down through the ages in Japan.

By tradition, the attitude of the employer toward labor has always been paternal. The Mitsui slogan of *kyoson* goes to an idealistic extreme, but the basic concept still governs the nation's industrial life.

I visited Mitsui's industrial center, Miike, last year, when the China warfare was a year old, and saw at first hand and at home 27,000 men who work for Mitsui. Over the rooftops of the miners' cottages floated dozens of service flags indicating that sons had died in China; prices were going up, various national assessments were eating into wages; food and clothing substitutes were coming into evidence, and there were many who said openly and frankly they hoped the war would end soon — but there was no unrest in Miike.

The Mitsui Miike industries are in and adjoining the city of Omuta on Shimabara Bay, island of Kyushu, about ninety miles south of Moji. Omuta has a population of about 100,-000. More than half the population of the town is supported by Mitsui industries.

Entering the town from the north, by train, I found it very

much resembles a smaller Osaka, with tall stacks pouring out thick black smoke on every side. Most of these stacks represent some Mitsui industry. The town certainly is Mitsui-conscious — even the non-employees regard the firm with a closer perspective than they do the Government, and much in the same light: as a big, inanimate force which goes on and on without obvious means of propulsion.

At Omuta I was met by two executives, one of whom spoke German and the other Esperanto. Mitsui officials evidently thought these two would take care of all the language barriers. As an afterthought they added a man who spoke English, but I had my own translator.

The first afternoon I visited the Manda mine, one of the newer shafts tapping the ancient Miike coal seam. There are 3,700 men working at Manda — and no women. The men work in three eight-hour shifts, except for a few hundred who work ten and twelve hours a day at tasks other than actual mining.

Among the features at this mine is a huge violet-ray tank capable of treating fifteen miners at a time. The ray treatments are given free to make up for what sunshine they fail to get. An airy, clean central bathroom with showers and pool, a safety-first schoolroom, a clean locker-room and a shrine just outside the door of the main assembly-room completed the picture. The miners habitually make their obeisances at the shrine before entering the shafts for their daily shifts.

Except for the usual bleached look of underground workers, the men appeared healthy and in good spirits.

Alive to the benefits of a settled and contented labor force, the Mitsui Mining Company has systematically developed a wide-range policy for raising the standard of comfort among its employees. Philanthropic experiments in Western countries have been studied and adapted to local circumstances until a broad program of welfare work has been instituted.

Across the road from the Manda mining premises is a twenty-acre park set aside for the employees. A focal point in the park is the commissary, or co-operative store, where employees may buy at low cost every necessity from sake to shoes. Suits of clothes sell for as low as eight yen, or about $2.50. Work shoes were five and six yen a pair.

In the main assembly hall a staff of three dieticians were teaching a class of forty or more miners' wives how to cook and prepare a balanced diet. Most of the pupils were brides. Some very appetizing Japanese dishes were in sight, in various stages of preparation and odor. There were several varieties of green salads and dishes with larger portions of meat than ordinarily may be seen in Japanese fare. The commissary has its own butchers which forage in the Kyushu countryside for beef and pork.

The assembly hall seats about four hundred and is equipped with facilities for free sound movies which are shown three times a week. Large club quarters near by provided billiards, a library, lounge rooms and others for various Japanese games. The grounds also boast a large concrete wading pool for children, an oversize swimming pool for adults complete with bleachers and a primary school for miners' children. Other facilities included a crèche, a meeting hall for the Young Men's Association, a wrestling ring and a large athletic field equipped for the usual field sports, including night baseball. A Shinto temple is at the top of the small hill in the park.

The next mine visited was the old Miyanohara pit where Baron Takuma Dan installed the turbine pump that started the Mitsuis on the road to mining riches. The famous engine, put in before Emperor Meiji reached middle age, was still turning over in 1938. The Miyanohara mine is all but abandoned now. It is worked only one month a year, but for the rest of the time they keep pumping out the water. The annual tonnage of the water drawn up is ten times the amount of coal produced there, but the coal is so rich and black that it is still profitable to keep the mine going for one month a year.

The Mitsui Technical School, built and presented to the town by the former Baron Hachiroemon Mitsui, is one of the prides of the community. The school, while privately supported, is open to anyone who can pass the entrance examinations, up to an enrollment of 240. The school primarily was intended to train competent foremen and technical workers for the Mitsuis, but graduates are not compelled to join the firm. Only the most promising are taken on. The tuition is fifty cents a month. A modest statue of Baron Hachiroemon Mitsui stands in the yard near the entrance of the white-stone structure, and there is a picture of him in the principal's office, but there are few other reminders that it is a Mitsui institution.

The Mitsui Mining Company has altogether five mines in operation at Omuta. The Yotsuyama, employing 4,029, is the largest and most productive. I spent a half-day 1,600 feet underground in the Yotsuyama mine and saw some of the thousands of men at work. The passages extend far out under Shimabara Bay. There was no sign of intolerable working conditions. The men were going at an easy, unhurried pace.

Afterward we walked down the rows of workers' houses in the Yotsuyama village. The houses are about fifteen years old. All are two-story and each has a small garden. There are outside toilets at the end of each row. All the houses are furnished with free electricity. Those at Yotsuyama are rented at one yen, or about thirty cents, a month. At Manda where the houses are older, the rental is from forty to sixty sen a month, and at still another village, where the houses are more than thirty years old, they are rent-free to the workers. Mitsui officials said one of their housing problems at the moment was putting up new cottages for workers taken on to replace those who had been conscripted. Families of the conscripts remained, of course, in their Mitsui-supplied homes although no members of the family might be on the Mitsui payrolls.

The Mitsuis provide a savings bank system for their miners, the company guaranteeing four per cent interest. Still another facility is a co-operative society for each village, to which the firm contributes an amount equal to the payments of the workers. Benefits are paid out on the occasion of sickness, accident, deaths, marriage or maternity. The society, besides running the co-operative stores, makes low-interest loans to members and safeguards their finances, keeping the miners out of the clutches of pawnbrokers and professional moneylenders.

Retirement allowances in proportion to the length of their service with the Mitsuis are granted to the miners. A worker who has been with the company twenty-five years on retiring is given enough money to build or buy a house outside the mining villages, if he cares to leave.

At each mine the company maintains well-equipped clinical rooms where patients are treated free, or at a nominal charge. In addition, there is the Mitsui hospital of one hundred and thirty-four beds with a staff of forty-two doctors and ninety-three nurses for more serious illnesses. Medical examinations are given at periodical intervals and frequent educational campaigns are put on aimed at insanitary customs or pests that might infect a village. The village superintendents and their staffs require periodic housecleaning, airing of bedding and general cleaning of the premises.

The spring and autumn festivals of the Mine God are religiously observed. On those occasions the company provides the expense of merry-making and feasting in which the whole community takes part for two or three days. Besides the usual intramural sports, the spirit of competition has been extended to flower-growing, a beloved Japanese pastime, and the Mitsui flower shows at Omuta are an institution. The miners display their prized chrysanthemums, dahlias and geraniums carefully cultivated on their small plots.

I spent three days at Omuta and saw all the Mitsui industries there at close range, with the exception of the dyestuff and chemical plant, and the machinery works, both of which have been virtually taken over by the Japanese military. Since the China war started an outsider can enter these plants only with a pass issued by the War Office in Tokyo. The dyestuff and chemical works, utilizing coal-tar by-products, employs 5,273 men. The machine works uses 2,535. A zinc refinery has another 1,982 employees.

Not the least of the industries at Omuta is the Mitsui harbor works. The harbor and coal-loading facilities comprise a model plant. Beginning construction in 1902, the Mitsuis ran two long breakwaters out into the bay, funneled them down to a bottleneck with sluice gates and then dredged out the channel and a basin with room enough to dock three ten-thousand-ton ships at one time. By closing the sluice gates and letting in more water the harbor's depth can be increased fifteen feet, enough to dock the Queen Mary if she ever turns up at Miike. A pier three hundred feet long has been opened for general use, and on this dockside Mitsui Bussan has its offices.

The firm went to Omuta mainly to act as sales agents for Mitsui products of the vicinity, but quickly branched out into handling anything and everything it could rake in from the rich Kyushu countryside, including butter, eggs, crayfish, rice, maize and other crops.

The complete harbor works was not finished until 1928, at a cost of $2,000,000, when the Government benevolently made it a port of entry, establishing customs and quarantine stations. Then the Mitsuis hung up the three-bar shingle and went to work garnering the trade of Kyushu.

Today the harbor works employ 1,843 men, only one of whom speaks English. He was born in Vancouver, and spends odd moments wondering why he is stuck away in Omuta, where he never gets a chance to use idiomatic English. Not even when the British steamers coal there does he practise his English, for the officers, with customary British doggedness, address all Japanese in the dockside Chinese picked up from their own crews.

For the higher-ups in the Mitsui organization who occasionally go to Omuta on an inspection tour, the mining company maintains two clubs. They are large, foreign-style residences, one in the center of town and the other on a hill out nearer the mines. Baron Dan was an occasional visitor to Omuta, even after he became famous as Chief Managing Director of all the Mitsui interests. Lesser officials had come, too, but no one at Omuta recalled that any of the Mitsui family had ever visited their holdings there.

The crews of all the Mitsui liners come from Omuta and vicinity on Shimabara Bay. They come from traditionally seafaring families, who manned the boats of coastal trade even in the centuries when Japan was closed to the outside world. Many of the young seamen on the modern Mitsui freight-and-passenger liners plying between New York and Yokohama boast that their grandfathers were Mitsui sailormen. They are interrelated, clannish and proud of their heritage.

Mitsui Line officials, in turn, boast that they have never lost a man by desertion. The line is free with shore-leaves when the ships call at American ports; Mitsui sailors invariably are back on board hours before sailing time. They are higher paid than most Japanese merchant seamen and have the additional benefit of occasional time off with full pay for the duration of a round-trip voyage by their ship.

Baroness Shidzué Ishimoto, one of the few liberals left in Japan and the nation's outstanding advocate of birth control for her country, is an authority who maintains that conditions at Miike were not always as happy as I found them in the current war boom. The Baroness was one of the four hundred persons detained for questioning in the nationwide round-up of Left-Wing suspects in December, 1937. She was held for a few days and then released. She goes about with ostensible freedom now, but when I met her in the Imperial Hotel in Tokyo in the spring of 1938 she was nervous and fearful that she was being watched. I asked her about conditions at Miike as she experienced them before the World War. Her husband was a junior engineer at the Mitsui mines. In answer to my questions she referred me to her book, *Facing Two Ways.* In this she wrote, in 1935: —

It was only recently that Japan adopted prohibitive measures against the employment of women miners and against midnight labor in general for women, both regarded as evils in Western countries long ago.

While I was at the Miike mines, wives and daughters of miners went down in a half-naked condition, mingling with the naked men laborers. They followed the men and carried out the coal as the men loosened it with their picks. It was ridiculous to expect morality in such circumstances. Women who worked in the darkness had a pale complexion like the skin of a silkworm; they spoke and acted shamelessly, the last sign of feminine dignity sloughing off. Often pregnant women, working until the last moment, gave birth to children in the dark pit.

The miners I knew were usually desperate. They saw no hope in the future and sought merely momentary pleasures. Men and their wives quarreled a great deal. Men beat women and children. The quarrels were more frequent on pay days, which came twice a month. Many men literally drank nearly all their pay before they brought any pennies to their families. But it would be rash to blame them! Who would dare preach family obligations to men who got only $20 for a month's work? The average wage for men in those days was about 40 yen, and 24 yen was the maximum pay for women for their monthly labor. Today, this pay has been raised a little. [In 1936, wages in general industry averaged 47 yen a month.]

The low rate of workers' wages was not only due to the low social status of laborers, but must be largely attributed to the lack of efficiency. They could work only 16 days a month on the average, for their physical condition was unequal to greater strain, owing to conditions in the pits and to the low quality of their food and housing. The women usually went down with their husbands, sometimes taking their babies on their backs when there were no nursery provisions. As soon as children were old enough, both boys and girls went to work, competing for wages with adults. But there was no other way for the population to keep alive unless it could manage to control the overflooded market for cheap labor by exercising birth control.

The people were strictly watched and loyalty to their employers was enforced. It was impossible for them to run away; nor could labor organizers get among them, for labor unions were severely banned in the coal field. Even today the miners are unorganized and exhibit only meek feudalistic submission. However, perhaps because of their meekness, the Japanese miners are fortunate enough to be protected as citizens. They have never been attacked with machine-guns as has happened to some so-called civilized countries! *

* From *Facing Two Ways*, by Baroness Shidzué Ishimoto, copyright, 1935, and reprinted by permission of Farrar & Rinehart, Inc., Publishers.

Chapter XV
THE HUMANIZING CAMPAIGN

THE LAST OF THE eminent hired hands to direct the affairs of Mitsui was Seihin Ikeda, graduate of Harvard in the class of 1895. Retired now from the Mitsui organization, and from high Government posts he filled after leaving the Mitsuis, Ikeda is still one of the strong men of Japan's financial world and frequently is consulted by wearied officials attempting to maintain a show of economic equilibrium in the present warfare.

Ikeda rightfully enough has been called a Fascist and has contributed much to the growth of Fascism in Japan — but one tenet of Fascism he has fought tooth and nail since he first became acquainted with its manifestations in Italy in 1929. That is: imposition of a State Socialism in Japan which would level off the holdings of the great financial houses or convert them entirely to State usage.

Perhaps more than any other man of his time Ikeda knew the peculiar structure of Japan's capitalism. Ikeda was just starting with the Mitsuis as a young banker when he saw an older State Socialism averted for Japan, and hand-made into a capitalistic system. It was the new centralized Government of Meiji that took the initiative in developing Japan industrially. That early Meiji Government was an out-and-out corporate stateship. Then, when fledgling industries in private hands became able to stand alone, the Government turned over its economic interests to these firms and gave them the go-ahead signal. It was then that the Mitsuis and a few other wealthy families acquired too many privileges and too much power to permit a re-imposition of State Socialism in later years, when that idea began to emerge as a chief tenet of the Fascist system gaining a foothold in Europe.

Like so many other Mitsui men who reached top rank, Ikeda was a Keio-to-*Jiji*-to-Mitsui product. He was born in 1861, the eldest son of a high official of the Uesugi clan government. In his eighteenth year he was admitted to the private school of the famous liberal educator, Fukuzawa, and when the Fukuzawa School became Keio University, Ikeda was one of its first students. From Fukuzawa, he sometimes would say, he learned his most important lesson in life — to say Yes or No and recognize no fringes. After Keio he went to Harvard to study economics, and on returning to Japan joined the *Jiji* as a reporter. Here he came to the attention of the current chief of staff of Mitsui, Nakamigawa, who was editor of the *Jiji* on the side. Nakamigawa offered Ikeda a minor position in the Mitsui Bank. He was managing director by the time he reached his forty-second year.

As a Mitsui banker, Ikeda is remembered for his unmatched fighting tendencies, pertinacity, and progressive ideas. It was generally agreed that he had no equal among the higher officials of any of the Big Five of Japan's banking families. Privately, he was mild-mannered, urbane and even generous; but to find this Ikeda, one Mitsui engineering friend said, "you have to diamond-drill through a crust of granite." His salary was large, but none knew how his earnings vanished. He was commonly reputed to be the poorest, financially, of all Mitsui executives.

An apprentice in capitalism, a student of capitalism, and a

practitioner of capitalism, Ikeda went to Italy in 1929 for no other reason than to study the effects of European Fascism on private fortunes. When he came back he was not slow to make known the convictions he had reached during his trip, coincident with the start of the world depression. Ikeda boldly criticized the structure of the Mitsui holdings in the light of what had happened to foreign wealthy families. He contended that the Mitsuis should invest more in outside concerns, rather than to try to accumulate too many interests wholly for themselves. He even advocated giving up the Mitsui Bank. Above all, he advised that the family spread out its holdings over a more even surface rather than concentrate on building up its giant combines.

Although Ikeda joined the highly nationalistic *Kokuhonsha* (Society of the Foundations of the State) headed by the present Fascist Premier, Baron Hiranuma, he privately warned the Mitsuis to head into the wind and batten down hatches for the approaching storm of Fascism threatening Japan. Differing vitally from the European type of Fascism, the movement sweeping forward in Japan was directed in no small part against "the greedy capitalists" and the plutocratic families.

Almost immediately after his return from Europe, Ikeda ran into a feud with the ruthless trading head of the Mitsui organization, "Razor" Yasukawa. Yasukawa got his name for his sharpness and lack of ethics in driving hard bargains. He was head of the *Mitsui Bussan*, a born trader who had grown up with the firm as a protégé of the great Masuda.

Ikeda and Yasukawa clashed on a strange issue in the House of Mitsui: Should the Mitsuis keep on piling up tremendous profits by smothering small businesses and at the expense of the little consumer, or level off and start giving away some of their fortune? For the first time in the history of the firm someone in authority had dared raise that question. Perhaps none but Seihin Ikeda could have done it, for he commanded the utmost confidence in the Mitsui family. Throughout his career he had served the Mitsuis with complete self-abnegation and with an almost religious devotion to doctrines handed down by Mitsui ancestors. No other Mitsui firm member outside the actual family was so loyal to the Mitsuis as a dynasty.

But some members of the family and the firm were equally impressed with the service of Yasukawa, who knew only one idea, to make money, which also was in line with Mitsui policies. For all practical purposes, Ikeda and Yasukawa started their contest on equal footing.

While Yasukawa was in power, one contemporary writer observed: —

As merchants and bankers, through their subsidiaries and through the agents of those subsidiaries, they [the Mitsuis] finance, organize and control the greater part of Japan's domestic industry and small-scale factory industry. A large part of their profits, accordingly, is derived from financing the small commodity producers of town and village. . . . The writer can cite the fact that in a part of the Ichinomiya district near Nagoya, Mitsui had seven men traveling, selling woolen yarn to the "manufacturers" on sixty days' credit, on the security of land, houses or government stock. The agent of Mitsui with whom I visited the district told me that when a small manufacturer fails, as happens very frequently, he is not sold up by his creditor but is kept on working on a charge system which is continually being extended.

To eliminate just these policies in his efforts to "humanize" the Mitsuis, Ikeda centered his fight on Yasukawa.

*   *   *

Popular indignation rose against the Mitsuis in 1932, when some newspapers published the report that *Mitsui Bussan* was selling barbed wire to the famous Nineteenth Route Army of China, then standing off Japan's attempt to capture Shanghai. There were also reports that the Mitsuis had been selling munitions to Marshal Chiang Hsueh-liang to be used against Japan's forces in Manchuria. In the midst of these rumors came the assassination of Baron Dan, and Ikeda became Chief Managing Director of the Mitsui enterprises.

Ikeda himself narrowly missed assassination at the time. Eiji Furuichi, former primary school teacher, one of fourteen members of the Blood Brotherhood responsible for the assassination of Junnosuke Inouye and Baron Dan, testified at the trial of the Brotherhood a year later: —

"We decided to murder twenty politicians, financiers and those of the privileged class. Each member of the brotherhood was assigned to at least one victim."

"Whom were you assigned to dispatch?" asked the judge.

"Mr. Seihin Ikeda, managing director of the Mitsui Bank."

He told how he had rented a room in the neighborhood of Mr. Ikeda's residence to watch for a chance to carry out his assignment. He even went to an out-of-town villa owned by the banker but did not even catch a glimpse of his intended victim for several days before and during the reign of terror.

In control now as Dan's successor, Ikeda put aside for the moment his fight with Yasukawa and started effectuating his own ideas for popularizing the Mitsuis. The Mitsubishis, also thoroughly scared, were quick to follow Ikeda's lead.

Within a month Mitsuis and Mitsubishis decided to put up 10,000,000 yen each to aid the new Manchurian state of Manchukuo which had come into being about the time Baron Dan was assassinated. The new régime had asked the Japanese Government for a loan of 20,000,000 yen, but the Government was slow to respond. Tokyo had not yet formally

recognized Manchukuo, and feared that the immediate donation of 20,000,000 yen would invite suspicion abroad. Addi-
tionally, the Government's finances were strained and the
authorities did not know where to look for such a large amount
on such short notice.

It was just such an opportunity that the Mitsuis wanted
in order to demonstrate their new attitude toward public affairs. The Mitsuis planked down the money. The
press immediately applauded. Said the *Jiji:* "The Mitsuis
are to be admired for the loan to the Manchurian Government. Their motive is not desire for profit but a desire
to help the new state develop favorably. It is an international
event worthy of praise and it opens the way for others like
it."

Said the *Miyako:* "The generous offer of Mitsui and Mitsubishi will go a long way toward correcting the general impression that the capitalists do not care much for the well-being
of the masses. The attitude of wealthy people is to blame in no
small measure for the prevailing unrest among the people. If
Japanese capitalists had more public spirit there would be a
decrease in the movement of extremists."

Said the *Asahi:* "It is to the credit of the houses of Mitsui
and Mitsubishi that they have attached no conditions to their
financial assistance of the new state. There would be more
public indignation with serious consequences should there be
any cause to suspect that two or three financial houses are going to monopolize the fruit of Government efforts toward developing favorably conditions in Manchuria. We sincerely
hope that other financial and industrial interests will emulate
Mitsui and Mitsubishi in co-operating with the Government
in Manchuria."

*   *   *

The assassination of Premier Inukai on May 15 spurred the Mitsuis to still greater efforts to appease public opinion.

The Mitsui family on June 8 announced a contribution of 3,000,000 yen to be used for unemployment relief to mark the three hundredth anniversary of the founding of the Mitsui business organization.

"We have been planning to do something for the community at large," said Takakimi Mitsui, son of the head of the House. "We have considered many plans and finally decided on an outright gift to the Government, which is in a position to see that the fund will be used where it will do the most good."

Baron Tatsuo Yamamoto,* Minseito Home Minister, was voluble in his expression of gratitude and praise of the Mitsuis. "The Government has been doing its utmost for relief," he said, "but has been hampered by financial difficulties and our efforts have not been sufficient by any means. Fortunately, just at this time, the Mitsui family has made 3,000,000 yen available for relief measures. I immediately accepted the offer. There is a great need for increase in the number of free lodging houses for laborers and we also face the problem of supplying of the unemployed with food. The Mitsui money will be used for this purpose. The action of the Mitsui family is significant. It will not only relieve the profound suffering of the people but will have a good influence on society as a whole."

Ikeda, however, lost no opportunity of exploiting these undertakings with emphatic announcements that they were

* No relation to Jotaro Yamamoto, generally regarded as a representative of the Mitsui interests in the Seiyukai. Baron Tatsuo Yamamoto, on the contrary, had had a long business career with Mitsubishi.

being undertaken for public benefit alone, insisting that the Mitsui wealth was being scattered for the public weal.

And so the Mitsui philanthropies continued, to an unheard-of degree.

In November, 1933, the Mitsui family set up a 30,000,000 yen fund "for the welfare of the Japanese people." The fund established the greatest foundation of its kind in the history of the nation.

The objectives of the Foundation, or the *Mitsui Ho-onkai*,* were fourfold: (1) Scientific research and industrial experiments for cultural enterprises which are of immediate necessity. (2) Social enterprises and other public establishments in cities and towns. (3) Public institutions and facilities of various kinds for the development of agricultural and fishery villages. (4) Support to public welfare organizations now existing or to be established in the future.

"Although Japan's industries have made great progress in the last few years, so much so that they now compare favorably with those of all other countries of the world," said Ikeda, in announcing the establishment of the Foundation, "not a few enterprises having important bearing on national development still lack management because of the difficulty of promoting them without someone incurring a great sacrifice.

"The Mitsui family has instructed the *Mitsui Gomei Kaisha* to select adequate causes from among the enterprises of such nature and concentrate on them, thereby making some contribution to the country.

"As for the purely public enterprises of our country, we can

* *Mitsui Ho-onkai*: literally, "Mitsui Society for Return of Gratitude."

by no means consider that they are fully developed at present. The Mitsui family in the past has devoted attention to that subject, assisting to some extent various enterprises of the kind, and even establishing some facilities itself, but now it has decided to establish a foundation which will be devoted directly to welfare work.

"The present step was decided by the Family Council on the basis of the traditional spirit of the Mitsui family and is intended to contribute a bit of what the family owes to the country."

In order to carry on the work of the Foundation on a sufficiently large scale the trustees were empowered to dispose of the principal as well as the income and it was provided further that the principal might be increased in the future if warranted. Up to the end of 1936, the Foundation had distributed to various charitable and educational purposes nearly 5,000,000 yen. The list of contributions is too lengthy to be mentioned here, but among the more noteworthy was the gift to the Japan Cancer Institute to purchase 1,000,000 yen worth of radium, a slightly smaller contribution for the establishment of leper homes and tuberculosis hospitals, and the free distribution of 5,000 head of sheep among the farms in northeastern Japan. In 1934 another 3,000,000 yen was donated by the Mitsuis personally, not through the *Ho-onkai*, for the relief of distressed areas in northeast Japan where a serious crop failure had occurred.

The donation was used in part to run soup kitchens for the hungry and to set up common workshops in villages and small towns.

*   *   *

Ikeda then turned his attention to the pressing need of ridding the Mitsuis of "Razor" Yasukawa. Yasukawa's carelessness about methods in piling up profits helped prove his own undoing.

It had been Yasukawa with his incredible audacity in trade ventures that had started Japan toward so many conquests in the world markets, beating older economic empires at their own game. Yasukawa engineered Mitsui control of the vast South Sea rubber plantations, leading to Mitsui's domination for many years of world rubber markets. He made Japan practically self-sufficient in aluminum. It is reported on good authority that he had aerial scouts flying over Canada's forest lands looking to the establishment of pulp mills. In Brazil, Manchuria, New York, South China and Europe, Yasukawa expanded Mitsui interests.

One of the direct causes of his defeat at the hands of Ikeda was the Toyo (Oriental) Rayon Scandal.

Toyo Rayon was one of Yasukawa's pet projects. Backed by Mitsui money it entered the field when rayon was still an infant industry in Japan. Yasukawa sent agents to Germany and Italy to learn the secrets of technique, and buy the necessary equipment. The Toyo Rayon Company was formed in 1926 with a capital of 10,000,000 yen, later increased to 25,-000,000 yen. Yasukawa himself became managing director and all the shares were held by *Mitsui Bussan*.

When Ikeda in his drive to "humanize" the Mitsuis persuaded them to offer their industrial shares to the public, Yasukawa protested bitterly. He had had a long struggle with Toyo in a highly competitive field, and for the first time the company was beginning to show the necessary lucrative returns to delight Yasukawa. But Toyo Rayon was forced to join the plan. It was then that Yasukawa was accused of dividing the stipulated quota of shares to be offered to the public among friends and relatives. Some 150,000 shares valued at 12.50 yen each were disposed of at 19.50 yen each to a syndicate of insurance companies reportedly selected by Yasukawa. In answer to criticism, Yasukawa contended there were 400,-000 shares in the company and he had to take "precautions" against failure to sell the rest, a thin argument in view of the growing importance of the rayon industry. When the sale was announced, 70-yen "old shares" jumped to 80 yen, and Yasukawa was accused of disposing of a number of these 70-yen shares at 40.50 yen each to a quickly organized group of brokers calling themselves some such name as the "Security Syndicate."

A number of Yasukawa's friends were permitted to buy these at bargain prices, but when he extended his favors to second-flight executives in *Mitsui Bussan*, blocking off those he disliked from purchase, intra-company discontent arose and his position was greatly weakened. In this respect Yasukawa played into Ikeda's hands, and the cold, calculating Ikeda struck boldly.

Backed by a family decision, Ikeda sent an emissary to Yasukawa's palatial home in Koishikawa Ward, Tokyo, in December, 1933, and informed him that he was to be ousted. Yasukawa still fought back, but this time he lacked support from higher-ups in Mitsui personnel. Yasukawa was removed the following January. This was the signal for a wide shake-up throughout the *Mitsui Bussan*. Yasukawa had staffed the trading company branches throughout the world with men imbued with the same ruthless policies and ideas that he had fostered. The Ikeda forces contended it was impossible to change these men's methods overnight and the best plan was to remove them altogether. From Bombay to New York, elderly Mitsui men began packing their bags to return to Tokyo, some of them to find places with Yasukawa in a new venture.

The installation of Kaneo Nanjo as head of *Mitsui Bussan* was indicative of the general shake-up sweeping the whole structure. Nanjo was one of four managing directors of the *Bussan*. He was known for his eminent respectability, and as a model gentleman of the British squire type, and incidentally was quite pro-British until Japan and Britain entered their period of strained relations in 1937. The contrast between the two was marked. An opportunist and trade adventurer, Yasukawa had made huge profits and sometimes huge losses for Mitsui. But Nanjo was no gambler; he had never incurred heavy losses nor made spectacular profits. He was of the reliable type desired by Ikeda — and when Ikeda himself retired he was succeeded as Chief Managing Director by Nanjo, who now holds that post.

Personnel shifts in the key posts throughout *Mitsui Bussan* were paralleled by some changes in business policy. Some of the new Mitsui executives began to talk about "business ethics," and a good many of them joined the new Rotary Club in Tokyo. The company's attitude towards small independent businessmen began to be characterized by a hitherto unknown diffidence. Some lines of business actually were dropped, or turned over to friendly competitors.

Ikeda had won his fight. At last, to his own satisfaction, he had "humanized" the Mitsuis. He has been called, not incorrectly, "the Ivy Lee of Japan." It is true that he did not fool all of the spectators. Pertinent observers of the transformation were quick to speak of camouflage and forced penitence, but with the public his methods were generally successful. There have been no more outbreaks or demonstrations against the Mitsuis.

In 1936 Ikeda himself willingly consented to be a victim of the retirement system he had set up in the Mitsui structure. He chose April 30 as the day for retirement because he had begun his business career with Mitsui forty-one years before on that day. On that morning he rose from a sickbed where he had been confined with a painful gallstone ailment and attended two meetings, one before Mitsui business executives in the morning and the other before the Family Council in the afternoon. On both occasions he announced he was forced to retire because of ill health.

To an interviewer, after the second meeting, he said: "I hope to improve my health by quietly spending the rest of my life walking and reading. I can't say anything about the future of the Mitsuis."

But, said an article translated from *The Economist:* —

Will Mr. Ikeda desert the Mitsuis wholly and forever? He will not. He will remain an ever imposing influence in the background of the firm, though his name will be stricken off the active list permanently. Mr. Nanjo and the others he left in key posts will continue to be faithful to him. He will never cease to play the role of highest adviser to the Mitsui plutocracy because the line-up of new directors reflects his personal influence, because there is no leader who is so capable as he and because he holds the highest confidence of Baron Takakimi Mitsui, practical ruler over the entire business activities of Mitsui.

The effect of Ikeda's policies with the Mitsuis brought varied reactions from the public.

Mr. Kanichiro Kamei, a labor member of the Diet, rose in the Lower House of the Diet and jubilantly exclaimed: "When they [the Mitsuis] decided to make the 30,000,000 yen donation for the public they decided at the same time that in the future they would not give a copper penny to any of the existing political parties. That means the Seiyukai will no longer obtain work from their old allies, the Mitsuis. This, I believe, is to account for the trouble within the Seiyukai which we have been hearing so much about lately."

It was true that the Mitsuis not only had broken with the Seiyukai but had decided no longer to wield a heavy financial hand in party politics. It was obviously too costly and risky.

Ko Tanaka, a writer on economic subjects, was skeptical. He thought the Mitsuis were "stricken with terror in their hearts. They will recede to the background, simply because they do not know where to turn or proceed. In that mood they will linger for some years to come. Ikeda's resources practically were exhausted when he thought upon the idea of the 30,000,000 yen donation."

Tanzan Ishihashi, chief editor of the *Oriental Economist Magazine*, was most pessimistic. He wrote in 1934: "What are we to do? That is the question not only with Mitsui but with all of us. We don't know. Nobody knows. What are the Mitsuis going to do with their business? Have they shaped their policy in conformity with the trend of the times? If the Mitsuis can solve this question by a gift of 30,000,000 yen, they will have solved the question for all the Japanese people. In that sense they would do a great service to our country."

Most penetrating of all was the analysis of Mr. Hidekichi Wada. Mr. Wada is chief editorial writer of the Tokyo daily *Chugai Shogyo*, owned by the House of Mitsui. The *Chugai Shogyo* is anything but a house organ for the Mitsuis. Never is there any attempt on the part of the family to control its editorial policy or news content. There is no direct wire between the Mitsui sanctums and the modest building in another part of the city that houses the *Chugai*. ("We wish," Mr. Wada told this writer, in 1938, "that the Mitsuis would help us a little more. They have never been known to favor us in advertising. In fact, we often come out second best with Mitsui advertising contracts in favor of papers with greater circulations. The Mitsuis regard the *Chugai* just as they do any of their other properties. It's got to pull its own weight in the boat or go overboard.")

Of the purpose behind the 30,000,000 yen fund set up by the Mitsuis in 1934, Mr. Wada was unconvinced. First, because he learned about the proposed contribution not from the Mitsuis but from a member of the Japanese Army clique. He argues that even if the contribution was not the outcome of military pressure, it undoubtedly was the result of an "understanding" with the Fascist elements rather than a genuinely voluntary contribution. He believes that the *Ho-onkai* was interpreted generally by the public as a breakwater against the Fascist tide. Even in the army some of the younger elements were unsympathetic to the extent of calling the contribution a confession of guilt and of the depth to which the Mitsuis had been exploiting the public.

In June, 1936, Mr. Wada discussed the Ikeda humanization movement in a very candid article entitled "How Big Capitalists Camouflage Themselves to Show Their Penitence." Mr. Wada's article appeared in the *Nippon Hyoron*.

The two biggest plutocrats of Japan — Mitsui and Mitsubishi — have long acted in concert in their social policy [he wrote]. If the former made a donation of 1,000,000 yen to a certain cause, then the latter was always willing to contribute an equal sum. This tradition has been done away with in recent years, especially since the Manchurian Incident of 1931 and the May 15 Incident of 1932, for Mitsui has become more eager to show signs of penitence and reform than has Mitsubishi. Public resentment has centered around Mitsui and has overshadowed the rest of the big capitalists. Because of this, the late Baron Takuma Dan, a dominant factor in the Mitsui Kingdom, was made the victim of a radical assassin, and then his successor, Mr. Seihin Ikeda, had to bear the brunt of the hatred against capitalists as a whole, while no such concentrated attack has been directed upon any specific Mitsubishi personage. Mitsui has had to take upon itself the whole venom of anti-capitalism on behalf not only of Mitsubishi but also of Sumitomo, Okura and all others.

The reason is not far to seek. Mitsui controls a capitalist kingdom larger than does any other, and its business principle has been one of aggressive commercialism sweeping over all lucrative fields, no matter how small might be their annual trade, at the expense of the bulk of small-scale industrialists and traders. Typical of this principle is the *Mitsui Bussan Kaisha*, the trading machinery of the plutocracy. It is capitalized at 100,000,000 yen and controls a large number of subsidiaries and affiliated corporations.

The Mitsubishi Trading Company, however, is smaller in capitalization and less aggressive in business principles. It employs an authorized capital of 30,000,000 yen, less than one-third that of the *Mitsubishi Bussan Kaisha*; does not enter into any line which injures the interests of small-scale firms, and embraces only a few subsidiaries under its direct control. Both in the employment of capital and in scope of activity Mitsubishi is not a match for the *Mitsui Bussan Kaisha*.

The Mitsubishi Trading Company restricts its activity within the fields which it deems proper, or at least natural, for a trading and industrial capitalist, but the *Mitsui Bussan Kaisha* goes beyond these limits and trespasses upon minor fields, even such as milk, apples and fodder for domestic fowls, all of which bear directly upon poor merchants and the general consuming public. Besides, Mitsui was assailed as having speculated in dollar exchange, smuggled debentures out of the country, entered into unmoral transactions with the Chinese, and for having committed other "sins." The greater the public accusation, the more pronounced the signs of penitence the accused must make. Because of this, Mitsui made a donation of 30,000,000 yen to finance the Mitsui Requital Foundation [Ho-onkai], this step being taken without previous intimation to its rival plutocrat.

Mitsubishi is not at the mercy of its employed directors, contrary to the Mitsui method. The head of the Iwasaki family, owner of the Mitsubishi interests, has held personal sway over its interests ever since its inception. This accounts for the fact that it lacks as many able executive leaders as the Mitsui.

Baron Koyata Iwasaki is the practical leader over the vast Mitsubishi interests, but he does not know the world, nor know how to cope with the present tide running against all capitalists.

Nevertheless something had to be done to evade the Fascist attack and to make Mitsubishi appear smaller than it is, in view of the many camouflage schemes devised by Mitsui. Consequently Mitsubishi decided to embark upon certain measures in 1934 that are largely in line with those of Mitsui.

These measures, though acclaimed as signs of penitence and exaggerated as sweeping reforms by the press, are nothing more than an attempt to find shelter from unfavorable circumstances by sacrificing a small fraction of stupendous earnings gained at the expense of the economic interests of the nation at large.

Today, it is a well-nigh impossible task to compute even in general figures the total amount of wealth still owned or controlled by the Mitsuis.

The *Mitsui Gomei Kaisha* (Mitsui Partnership Company)

is the central holding company, the general headquarters and the nerve center in which the administration of all the Mitsui interests, direct and subsidiary, is concentrated. The *Mitsui Gomei* originally was formed with a capital of 50,000,000 yen. Today it is capitalized at 300,000,000 yen, but that is only a superficial figure. The companies, direct and indirect, which *Mitsui Gomei* control have a total paid-in capital, according to Mitsui figures of 1938, of 654,774,000 yen. (These figures incidentally are at considerable variance with those listed by the *Japan Year Book* as of 1935. But Mitsui officials point out that the firm had disposed of a great deal of its holdings since 1935.)

The actual value of all these companies is much greater than the paid-in capital amounts. In addition to the family fortunes, the huge real estate holdings and multifold business investments, another billion-and-a-half yen of deposits in the Mitsui Bank, the Mitsui Trust Co., and the Mitsui Life Insurance Co., are at the disposal of the Mitsui interests.

The total amount invested in the nominal 300,000,000 yen *Mitsui Gomei Kaisha* comes from the eleven Mitsui families. Baron Takakimi Mitsui is president of the holding company, Baron Takakiyo Mitsui and Morinosuke Mitsui are the "auditors." These officers, chosen by and from the eleven Family Heads, are assisted by a board of directors. Although persons outside the family manage the company, not one of them owns any interest in *Mitsui Gomei Kaisha*. They are merely hired hands.

Each partner in *Mitsui Gomei* — that is, each Family Head — assumes an unlimited liability. The partners and their investments in *Mitsui Gomei* are listed as follows: —

Name	Investment	Percentage of Total
Takakimi	Yen 69,000,000	23 per cent
Takahisa	34,500,000	11.5 per cent
Takanaru	34,500,000	11.5 per cent
Takakiyo	34,500,000	11.5 per cent
Takaharu	34,500,000	11.5 per cent
Takanaga	34,500,000	11.5 per cent
Takamoto	11,700,000	3.9 per cent
Morinosuke	11,700,000	3.9 per cent
Takaakira	11,700,000	3.9 per cent
Benzo	11,700,000	3.9 per cent
Takateru	11,700,000	3.9 per cent

The *Gomei Kaisha* directly controls six principal Mitsui companies with a total paid-in capitalization of 312,000,000 yen. These six companies, and their paid-up capitalizations, are: the Mitsui Bank Ltd., 60,000,000 yen; *Mitsui Bussan*, 150,000,000 yen; Mitsui Mining Co. Ltd., 81,500,000 yen; Toshin Warehouse Co., Ltd., 12,500,000 yen; Mitsui Trust Co., Ltd. 7,500,000 yen; and the Mitsui Life Insurance Co., Ltd., 500,000 yen.

The *Mitsui Bussan* directly controls twenty-seven companies with a total paid-in capitalization of 215,730,500 yen.

In addition, Mitsui has control, directly or indirectly, over many subsidiaries of these companies, which in turn have their own branches and ramifications. Besides the influence which the Mitsuis wield directly, through the power of their money, they have a great deal of influence in many companies not directly associated with the Mitsui organizations, but with the principal employees of Mitsui concerns. Most of these higher-ups are wealthy men and their total private investments run into big figures.

Typical of these is Ginjiro Fujihara, president of the powerful Oji Paper Company, life member of the House of Peers, collector of art objects and devotee of *Cha-no-yu*, the Japanese tea ceremony.

Fujihara became the newsprint king of Japan when, through the good offices of Seihin Ikeda, he engineered a merger of the Oji Paper Company with the Karafuto Industrial Company. Ostensibly, the object was to eliminate wasteful competition; in doing so it gave Fujihara control of 85 per cent of the nation's paper output.

He is essentially a "Mitsui man," although he is left much to himself now. In 1936, Oji Paper doubled its capitalization to 224,990,000 yen, making it one of the largest industrial corporations in the country. At the same time the Mitsuis sold 100,000 of their shares in the firm to the public as a measure to appease public feeling. This "decentralization" left Mitsui with 215,000 shares, however.

Mr. Fujihara was one of those bright young newspapermen picked up by the Mitsuis before the turn of the century. After graduating from Keio University, the alma mater of most Mitsui leaders, he joined the staff of a provincial paper. In addition to editorial work, he was given charge of the business end. After four years of that job he was discovered by Hikojiro Nakamigawa, managing director and talent scout for Mitsui.

His first job under the Mitsuis was in their bank. From that post he was shifted to one of the Mitsui silk mills, where he was manager, and then to Formosa as manager of a branch of the Mitsui Trading Company. In each successive position he made money for the firm, a feat that was rewarded in 1911 by transfer to the struggling Oji Paper Company, first as managing director, then as president. He was expected to reorganize it and put it on a profitable basis.

When he went in, the company was capitalized at 6,000,000 yen and had paid no dividends for years. After the recent merger, the capital totaled 225,000,000 yen and dividends steadily have been ten per cent. It operates thirty mills in all parts of the empire, from Saghalien to Korea.

A few years ago Fujihara maneuvered half a dozen important Tokyo newspapers into a fantastic competition that more than trebled their consumption of his newsprint. It was a typical Mitsui high-pressure deal.

The bigger Tokyo papers have complex backgrounds and affiliations which apparently played a part in this incident. The Mitsuis own the *Chugai Shogyo* in entirety and, through the Oji Paper Company, hold a five per cent interest in the Osaka *Mainichi*, which in turn publishes the Tokyo *Nichi Nichi*, one of the two leading dailies in the capital. Tokyo editors are strong for innovations, but they rubbed their eyes one morning over the announcement that the *Nichi Nichi* was going to publish several "neighborhood editions."

The Shitamachi edition was to be for downtown readers, the Joto edition for those in the eastern end of the city, the Johoku edition for residents of the northern suburbs and the Yamanote edition for the central residential district. The *Jiji* came out with a "Central *Jiji*" for the downtown man. The *Kokumin* announced a section called "The Charm of Tokyo," and the *Yomiuri* was not far behind in the stunt. Only the liberal *Asahi* hesitated.

This wave of new editions was the result of the terrific competition in the capital. All the papers were putting out regular city and mail editions, many designed for particular regional readers. The situation was comparable to having the New York papers issue a Manhattan edition, a Brooklyn edition, a Bronx edition and a Queens edition.

The business manager of the *Asahi*, hoping to avoid this new competition, called a meeting of representatives of the *Nichi Nichi* and *Hochi*, proposing to abandon the obviously useless "Tokyo editions." The *Hochi* agreed to desist, but the *Nichi Nichi* held out until the *Yomiuri* announced its plans. The conference moved to the office of the publisher of that sprightly, Hearstian paper. Shoriki reserved his answer.

Shoriki was known to have close business connections with Fujihara. According to the *Chuo Koron*, which exposed the conspiracy, Shoriki called on Fujihara and explained the situation ("as if Fujihara were not already acquainted with it," the magazine said). He added that if all the papers published local editions, something like 1,200,000 additional copies would have to be printed each month and Oji Paper would increase its profit about 1,000,000 yen.

The magnate smiled at this fortunate circumstance and intimated that, if the *Yomiuri* entered the competition, the paper would be reimbursed for any expenses it might incur as the result [the *Chuo Koron* went on]. A few days later, Mr. Shoriki told the *Asahi* that it could not justify abandoning the Tokyo editions, particularly as it needed the increased circulation. The cooperation failed and the *Asahi* was compelled to bring out its own local editions. The fantastic competition among the leading Tokyo dailies resulted.

These editions are none too ably edited, being devoted to sordid and often incredible stories, wastefully written. They are an insult to the intelligence of the readers. The papers had previously been circulating in the regular editions all the news available in the capital. Publication of these new sections as Tokyo editions is ridiculous. It is not too much to say that the practice is forcing on the public worthless, unsatisfactory stories, when it is already suffering from a flood of unreliable news. At the same time, the competition is putting a heavy burden on the publishers through the increased use of newsprint.

It was notable that the Mitsui-owned paper, the *Chugai*, remained serenely out of this competition, while Fujihara rolled up profits for the Oji Company.

Fujihara himself is a distinguished-looking gentleman, now well along in years. He lives in a large, but not ostentatious, home in the best residential section of Tokyo. He delights in showing visitors his famous art treasures. In one corner of the dining room is the "invincible armor" of the renowned General Sengoku, who never knew defeat while wearing it.

Fujihara has traveled extensively in Europe and America, where he has many friends. His connections made him a logical choice as president of the 1940 Exposition in Japan. The event was intended to parallel the Olympic Games, but the whole plan was indefinitely postponed when the China campaign started. One of the unsolved problems was the disposition of money received in the advance sale of tickets. At the time of writing it is still on the books, presumably for a World's Fair in the distant future.

Officials of the *Gomei Kaisha*, in preparing a list of Mitsui holdings, pointed out that some economists were inclined to magnify the ramifications of the Mitsui enterprises, labeling any firm however remotely connected with the Mitsuis as Mitsui "subsidiaries." Others regard as subsidiary, companies with which the Mitsuis have severed connections.

"There are some companies which, if not giving themselves

out as Mitsui subsidiaries, even invite themselves to be so regarded," one official complained.

Some of the more important subsidiaries, however, may be noted. The Shibaura Engineering Works, Ltd., with a paid-up capital of 15,000,000 yen, is a joint enterprise of the Mitsuis and the International General Electric Company of New York. The plant at Shibaura near Tokyo was almost completely razed in the earthquake and fire of 1923, but has been rebuilt at Tsurumi, Yokohama, on a 1,200-acre tract. It turns out a wide range of electrical machines and appliances.

The Japan Steel Works, Ltd., with a paid-up capital of 15,000,000 yen, is a joint enterprise of the Mitsuis and the British Armstrong and Vickers. Practically every item of military ordnance needed by Japan, as well as aircraft engines, steel and iron castings and industrial machinery, is manufactured by the company at its three plants at Muroran, Yokohama and Hiroshima.

The Hokkaido Colliery and Steamship Company, Ltd., with a paid-up capital of 53,800,000 yen, has 98,800 acres of mining concessions in the Hokkaido and turns out about 3,200,000 tons of coal a year.

The Tropical Produce Company, Ltd., 5,525,000 yen capitalization, owns and operates a 6,100-acre rubber estate in the Malay Peninsula and another large tract in Sumatra.

The Sanshin Building Company, Ltd., 1,000,000 yen capitalization, owns one of the best situated office buildings in Tokyo, an eight-story building overlooking Hibiya Park and the grounds of the Imperial Palace. The top floor of the building is given over to a foreign-style restaurant well patronized by Tokyo businessmen, and the Sanyu Club, a social club maintained for the exclusive use of all Mitsui employees of any rank.

The club is one of the best equipped in Tokyo, featuring golf-driving ranges, billiards, bowling, a large library, reception rooms, game rooms, a bar that serves the lowest priced well-made cocktails in the capital, and a room devoted to *ussai* or Japanese choral singing, an art historically fostered by the Mitsuis. The club, while a gift to the employees, is actually used by them and is a favorite rendezvous where all lines are let down and relaxation of many kinds is obtainable.

The *Mitsui Gomei* has two other clubs in Tokyo, one on spacious grounds with a large modernistic building at Hamadayama, for the use of all Mitsui employees and their families. The other is the extremely exclusive Mitsui Club in Kogai-cho, Tokyo, used only by members of the family in entertaining and by a few high officials of the *Gomei*. It is a large, Japanese-style house, staffed by Mitsui servants and furnished with Mitsui silver bearing the old Sasaki family crest.

The Nitto Development, Agriculture and Forestry Company, capitalized at 9,450,000 yen, has charge of three enterprises for *Gomei*. One is afforestation in Korea, where 200,000 acres of foothill and valley land which had become completely denuded have been planted with trees. Nitto Black Tea, bearing the familiar three-bar Mitsui crest, finds its way to many tables abroad from the Mitsui plantation in Formosa. The third enterprise is reclamation of waste lands in Korea. Altogether the *Gomei Kaisha* owns about 250,000 acres of forest land, rice fields, reclaimed land and tea fields in Formosa, Korea, Hokkaido and Japan Proper.

The big profit maker of Mitsui for years was the *Bussan*, ("trading company") whose operations have been discussed elsewhere in this book. The business of the company is divided into eleven general lines: raw silk and silk goods; coal and oil; machinery; iron, steel and other metals; cereals and fertilizers; sugar, timber, general merchandise, shipping, insurance, and wharves.

The silk department handles about one-fourth of Japan's total raw silk exports, trades in Chinese and Italian raw silks in the principal markets of the world and exports silk and rayon goods. The coal and oil department handles more than one-third of the entire Japanese output and is a large importer of foreign coals. Fuel and Diesel oils also are imported in large quantities and stored in Mitsui tanks throughout Japan.

The machinery department, besides selling and distributing machines and tools made in Japan, co-operates with the following companies in the manufacture in Japan of specialties under domestic and foreign patents: Toyo Babcock Company, boilers; Toyo Otis Elevator Co., elevators and escalators; Toyo Carrier Engineering Co., Ltd., air-conditioning equipment; Sanki Engineering Co., building equipment; and the High Speed Engineering Co., Ltd., automobiles and parts.

The metal department acts as sales agent for the Nippon *Seitetsu Kaisha* (Japan Steel Corporation, Ltd.) and has close business connections with many other steel and metal manufacturers. The cereals and fertilizers department deals in rice, wheat, flour, beans, seeds, vegetables, feed grains, bean cake and animal and mineral fertilizers. Manchurian soy beans are one of the many discoveries of the company which has been the leading exporter of this staple since 1907. The Japan Flour Milling Company, Ltd., is one of the largest concerns of its kind in Japan and its subsidiary, the Oriental Flour Milling Company, is a leading industry in Manchukuo.

Other articles handled by the company include cotton piece goods, flax, hemp, jute, Portland cement, paper, pulp, raw wool, woolen and worsted goods, salt, tinned and bottled goods, fresh and preserved provisions, coffee, cocoa beans, nuts, tobacco, matches, beets, camphor, ginseng, soap, drugs, chemicals and dyestuffs. The timber department owns 100,-000 acres of forest in northern Japan, exclusive of lands owned by *Gomei Kaisha*, imports most of Japan's American timber, has a subsidiary at Davao in the Philippines and serves the forestry bureaus of the Korean and Formosan Governments-General as sales agent.

The shipping department owns a fleet of sixteen motor-ships, eighteen steamers and two motor tankers. It operates eight regular lines of cargo and passenger service: Straits-Philippines-Japan-New York; Japan-Madras; Japan-Bombay; Japan-Iranian Gulf; Japan-Bangkok; Japan-Philippines; Japan-Dairen; and Moji-Tokyo. In addition, it frequently charters tramp steamers of all nationalities.

The Tama Shipbuilding Co., Ltd., recently was formed with a capital of 5,000,000 yen to take over the business of the shipbuilding department of the *Bussan*. The company's ship-building yard at Tama on the Inland Sea occupies 293 acres. It turned out the first ocean-going cargo motorship ever built in Japan. During the World War it built two steamers for the American Government. Altogether, since 1917, it has launched ninety-five vessels of a total of 290,000 tons, of which forty-three are motorships. The company also manu-factures various kinds of machinery. It is the sole licensee in Japan of Burmeister and Wain's Diesel marine and stationary engines and locomotives, and other foreign makes for which it shares in patents.

The Oriental Cotton Company, Ltd., paid-up capital of 25,000,000 yen, was formed in 1921 to handle the business of the cotton department of *Mitsui Bussan*. It is the largest firm of its kind in Japan, handling from twenty to twenty-five per cent of the total imports of raw cotton and from fifteen to twenty per cent of the total exports of cotton goods.

Warehousing has been a major business in Japan since the beginnings of foreign commerce. Mitsui was the first to erect warehouses at Kobe for overseas trade. The business was conducted for many years by the Mitsui Bank, but in 1909 it was given to the subsidiary, Toshin Warehouse Company, Ltd., capitalized now at 12,500,000 yen. The company has eight reinforced concrete and brick warehouses with a total storage area of about eighty acres in Japan's principal cities. Merchandise stored in these buildings represents on the average a value of about 125,000,000 yen, or nearly one-fifth of the total balance of goods regularly stored in Japanese warehouses.

The Mitsui Trust Company, Ltd., was the first Japanese trust company established under the Trust and Trust Companies Acts of 1922, permitting trust business to be carried on only by joint-stock companies with a capital of not less than 1,000,000 yen. The Mitsui firm has an authorized capital of 30,000,000 yen, of which 7,500,000 yen is paid-up.

The Mitsuis entered the life insurance field in 1926 by acquiring control of a small company with only 2,900 policies. Ten years later it had 81,409 policies for a total insurance of 524,374,723 yen. Now the company has fourteen large branch offices in the principal cities of the Empire, 181 local offices and 1,978 agencies. The company maintains a department for giving medical advice and operates traveling clinics for its insured living in the rural areas.

Chapter *XVI*

THE JUGGERNAUT ROLLS ON

TODAY, WITH THE SINO-
Japanese war going into its third year, it is apparent that the
Mitsuis have ridden too far with the military clique. The
juggernaut they helped to set up has them on the wheel, roll-
ing on to a State Socialism of industries which would nation-
alize the great Mitsui holdings.

Ironically, it was the "humanization" of the Mitsuis under
Ikeda that led them into that Fascist pitfall.

When Ikeda swerved the Mitsuis from dollar-grubbing in
foreign and domestic trade he set them more purposefully
in the field of heavy industry. The growing influence of the
military-Fascist group was producing basic changes in Japanese economy, beginning with the creation of Manchukuo
and the huge preparations for the present drive in China. The
need for armaments to carry out the new aggression opened
a new lucrative field for the Mitsuis and others in heavy industry. In 1931 metallic, machine-tool and chemical industries accounted for only 33.7 per cent of Japan's total industrial production while textiles, for instance, provided 37.2 per
cent. By 1935, the trend was being substantially reversed,
heavy industries having risen to 47.2 per cent while textiles
dropped to 30.9 per cent.

As Japan's foreign trade fell off, it was clear that Mitsui's
chief profits more and more were going to be bound up in
war preparations and plans for aggressive expansion on the
Continent.

The Mitsuis, together with several of the other leading financial combines, already held a monopolistic position in the manufacture of major munitions. In addition, they shared with Mitsubishi large holdings in most of the so-called national policy firms set up by the military to further Japan's war preparations.

Of the nation's total coal output, Mitsui was handling 25.1 per cent and Mitsubishi 14.9. The Mitsui Mining Company, offering a large number of chemicals, explosives and dye stuffs, was a monopolizing producer of chemical munitions.

Bullets are made out of lead and Mitsui was producing 78.8 per cent of Japan's lead supply. Mitsui also had a monopoly on zinc production, while Mitsubishi took care of the tin industry. In gold mining Mitsui was offering 13.9 per cent of the national total and Mitsubishi 10.8.

The *Economic Year Book* of Japan estimates that, during the five years from 1932 to 1936, dividends from Mitsui's munitions industries totaled 115,000,000 yen, while Mitsubishi's dividends were put at 59,000,000 yen.

If the Mitsuis had any lingering doubts about the wisdom of tying up with the military group, these must have disappeared after reforms following the bloody military coup in Tokyo on February 26, 1936. Six days before, there had been a general election which had returned a large majority for the Minseito, the more liberal rivals of the nationalistic Seiyukai. The Social Mass Party, the small voice of the proletarian movement, made a surprising showing, increasing their membership in the Lower House from eight to eighteen. Clearly, the Japanese voter was voicing his disapproval of the army's war preparations. Military extremists decided it was time to teach the nation a lesson.

The *coup* that followed was abortive in a sense, but it ushered in a period of new gains for the Fascist movement. Four high Government officials were assassinated, but this time the Mitsuis were untouched. Members of the family and leading personalities of the firm remained secreted and guarded in their homes on the day of the *coup* and for days afterward. The assassination of Baron Dan in 1932 and the 1936 outbreak clearly left the Mitsuis in no mood for a further collision with the army.

But the clumsiness and general senselessness of the coup brought new leadership in the army clique. Generals Terauchi and Sugiyama took the reins. The Mitsui and Terauchi families had always been friendly. The new leaders had little difficulty in forcing much larger "defense" appropriations on the Diet, and in gaining pledges of a stronger foreign policy, heavy tax increases and "administrative reform" from the Hirota Cabinet.

The new army leadership, utilizing its growing power, kept to the essential aims of the general military-Fascist program but worked more circumspectly. It held out the rosy prospects of profits for the heavy industries and at the same time let fall a warning now and then to the Mitsuis and Mitsubishis that any failure to co-operate might bring something worse than a repetition of the February 26 coup.

Thereafter, amid a series of Cabinet changes, Japan moved rapidly toward a totalitarian régime. In the fall of 1936 the budgetary proposals reached the unprecedented total of 3,041,000,000 yen with military-naval estimates amounting to nearly half. New taxes were introduced for the first time in several years, some of them bearing directly on the financial community but most, including a national sales tax and reduction of the income-tax exemption limit, hitting the masses.

The budget deficit stood at 806,000,000 yen in spite of the tax increases and soon there were other reactions to the war budget. Prices rose sharply, the yen showed signs of weakness, and a flight of capital ensued.

On November 25, 1936, Japan signed the anti-Comintern pact with Germany openly lining up with the Fascist bloc in world politics.

The war budget came in for sharp attacks when the Diet convened in January and the Hirota Cabinet was overthrown, but Terauchi and Sugiyama retained the upper hand. The new Cabinet was headed by a general, and no portfolio went to any party member.

The Ikeda-Mitsui policies now began to bear even more fruit. The new Finance Minister, Toyotaro Yuki, named Ikeda as Governor of the Bank of Japan.

"The practical abilities of these two men [Yuki and Ikeda]," wrote one commentator, "were reassuring to the more conservative capitalist groups. They were uniquely fitted to harmonize capitalist interests and unite them behind the army program, and thus summed up in themselves the new political course which Japanese industry and finance were charting."

In the general elections that spring, Ikeda ("once a Mitsui man, always a Mitsui man") campaigned for "repletion of the national defense" and establishment of a "semi-wartime economy." And General Sugiyama stated the objective: "The myriad affairs of the State must be made to harmonize with the keynote of full armament."

The war started in July, 1937, and Japan went completely totalitarian by enacting a "General Mobilization Law" whereby constitutional checks on executive action could be set aside by the simple process of invoking an ordinance to apply its terms.

The new law, however, was not applied until May, 1938, following the serious defeat of Japanese forces at Taierhchuang, China, which brought about a ministerial crisis. Then the main provisions of the act were put into effect and three weeks later the Cabinet was reshuffled.

In this reorganization Ikeda was brought in as Minister of Finance and Minister of Commerce and Industry, two separate portfolios. Thus the Mitsui exponent of "productive expansion" evidenced the close working co-operation between big business and the military group pushing the war in China. Ikeda's appointment was widely hailed as marking an advent of "common-sense financing." Under Ikeda, Government bonds issued to support the costs of the war were absorbed at the rate of 300,000,000 yen a month. A nationwide savings campaign put on by Ikeda increased individual savings accounts in a year to more than 3,000,000,000 yen.

The Mitsui survey of business profits in Japan covering the first six months of 1938 showed that enormous profits had been raked in by munitions and heavy industry companies. The combined profits for the period, of such industries as machinery, shipbuilding, mining, chemical and metal, amounted to 281,400,000, or a gain of 38 per cent over the corresponding period of 1937, according to figures of the Industrial Bank of Japan.

During the last six months of 1938 the Mitsui Mining Company reported a net profit of 9,614,000 yen, of which 5,852,000 was distributed as dividends at the annual rate of 12 per cent. The Oji Paper Company netted a profit of 18,-455,000 yen and paid out 11,249,000 of this in dividends.

Of 1,470 companies investigated, — a fourth of them

Mitsui-owned or subsidiaries in some form, — the Industrial Bank of Japan found that 1,420 earned profits amounting to 756,544,000 yen in six months, equivalent to an annual 13.1 per cent on paid-up capital.

The prosperity of the munitions industry was more than enough to counterbalance the depression suffered by peacetime industries, the Bank pointed out.

But while the "humanized" Mitsuis rolled in the profits, as did other heavy industry concerns, numerous disquieting factors began to enter the economic picture. The public debt had risen to 13,021,000,000 yen by April, 1938, due to Government bond issues. This was almost equal to Japan's total national income. Taxpayers shouldered a 40 per cent increase within a year. The foreign trade balance became even more adverse and by July Japan had shipped $84,300,000 in gold to the United States to cover adverse balances. After the Government reduced the statutory gold reserve of the Bank of Japan by 300,000,000 yen, it made strenuous efforts to stimulate the Empire's gold production, and even appealed to the people to donate precious metals to the Government. The ever-patriotic Mitsuis themselves lined up an imposing array of gold and silver plate bearing the family crest, and "donated" it to the Government.

As the war costs mounted, it became apparent that the burden would have to be spread to the upper levels. That was where the worm turned, and Seihin Ikeda became alarmed at the prospects of complete State Socialism. Friction developed behind the scenes between Ikeda and the military leaders over the tempo at which economic mobilization for the war could be invoked. The clash came into the open late in 1938, over the application of the famous Article XI, the Fascist teeth of the Mobilization Law.

Article XI reads: —

When it is deemed necessary under the National General Mobilization in time of war, the Government may restrict or prohibit establishment of companies, capital increases, amalgamations, changes in purposes of business, flotation of debentures or the second or subsequent assessments on subscribed capital, or may issue necessary orders regarding the disposal of profits, writing off of assets or accounting and management of corporations, or may issue necessary orders against banks, trust companies, insurance companies and other persons who may be designated by Imperial Ordinance, regarding the operation of their funds.

Ikeda, the Mitsui protagonist, saw in that article something more than an attempt merely to cope with a wartime emergency. He saw the outlines of a permanent new order in which the basis of economic activity was to be changed from the acquisition of private profit to the furtherance of Japan's "national destiny" at home and abroad — the avowed aim of the Fascists. Standing out boldly in the Article was that power given to the Government to limit dividends and issue orders regarding the disposal of corporate surpluses.

The Japanese businessman who objects to the principle of State interference in economic life is placed in an equivocal position [summarized the *Far Eastern Survey*]. He is generally quite willing, and in any case he can hardly refuse to accept, such restrictions on the conduct of his business as may be necessary to win the war. But he fears that in so doing he is putting his head in the lion's mouth. Hence he argues for voluntary controls enforced by businessmen themselves, and opposes, so far as he can, any measures that give promise of becoming permanent fixtures. In particular he objects to control measures that seem to be directed toward broader objectives than merely winning a military victory. In this complicated situation it is quite impossible without the aid of second sight to draw any hard and fast line between emergency measures and those which have a more lasting significance. But the opinion may be ventured that intensification rather than relaxation of the present control system is to be expected until Japan's imperialist venture has been crowned either with complete success or dissolved in abject failure.

Ikeda took a bold stand against the application of Article XI. He told the military-Fascist leaders outright that he regarded invocation of the Article as a drastic attack on private property rights. Fears for his personal safety were expressed as he battled the Fascists and military to keep the Mitsuis and other big industries out of the clutches of Article XI.

In the end, Ikeda could not forestall adoption of the Article, but he succeeded in modifying its effects. While companies now paying dividends of more than ten per cent must have Government permission for any increase, it is noted that there is no provision for compulsory decrease. Special commemorative dividends of a non-recurring character are exempted, and possibly many other loopholes which may be discerned by Mitsui accountants and legal advisers.

After he had done what he could to prevent Fascism's assault on "the last citadel of economic liberalism," Ikeda expressed a desire to resign from the Cabinet. His chief, Premier Prince Konoye, descendant of the Fujiwaras, as are the Mitsuis, went out with him. Early in 1939 Baron Hiranuma, acknowledged head of the civilian Fascists of Japan, was installed as Premier. An obscure bureaucrat went in as Finance Minister to succeed Ikeda. His first contributions to Japan's wartime economy were typical. The new Minister announced he would ride to work in a streetcar, wear sharkskin shoes and have his clothes, when worn-out on one side, remade inside-out.

Ikeda retired to his modest Tokyo home.

Today the Mitsuis are between two fires. They are being milked by the military for capital to go into development enterprises in Manchukuo and the newly conquered areas of China. They are cut in for huge blocks of industrial enterprises which show little prospect of early profit, if any. They cannot protest too audibly. There is little choice about it. A Japanese economist in the *Central Review* observes: —

Apart from the invocation of Article XI, financial circles have been compelled to lend large-scale capital to various companies since the national emergency confronted this country. For example, Mitsui and other financial groups subscribed for Manchukuo loans amounting to 30,000,000 yen. Of late Japan's plutocrats and banking circles have subscribed, or rather have been more or less compelled to subscribe, for shares in the large national policy companies on the continent, such as the North China Development Company and the Imperial Fuel Development Company. Investments of a similar nature will be made in the future in other national companies.

The liberty of handling profits is the only bit of incentive to activity left to the economic world. The loss of this liberty will therefore impair the very objective of Article XI, namely the expansion of productive power. As regards the giving of orders to banking circles to lend funds to the munitions industry and other companies, when necessary, it is fraught with the danger of dislocating the credit machinery which is the basis of the banking business.

The regulation of dividends and the lending of capital under compulsion are doubtless a menace to the capitalists, but the greater menace still is the "what next?" sort of uneasiness arising from the fact that the entire economic structure is subjected to State orders.

The Japanese Fascists have long been working to destroy the power of "greedy capitalists." The chief weapon in their hands now is the National Mobilization Law. But what is confusing is that the struggle to convert Japan's capitalism into a totalitarian economy is going on in the midst of an actual war.

Devoted as they are to the principles of *laissez faire*, the Mitsuis are willing to come under a measure of State regulation of economic life while the China war is on, with the assumption that such regulations will be removed when the war is over. But that is no safe assumption in Japan today. Whatever the outcome, the pace is accelerating, and the Mitsuis are caught in it.